THE LEGENDARY GROGAN

BY THE SAME AUTHOR

Eleven and a Half (1967)
The Daughter of the Sun (1969)
Fables from Kenya (1971)
Tippu Tip and the East African Slave Trade (1975)

THE LEGENDARY GROGAN

The Only Man to Trek from Cape to Cairo
Kenya's Controversial Pioneer

by

Leda Farrant

HAMISH HAMILTON
LONDON

To the memory of Robert and Florence

First published in Great Britain 1981
by Hamish Hamilton Ltd
Garden House, 57-59 Long Acre, London WC2E 9JZ

British Library Cataloguing in Publication Data

Farrant, Leda
The legendary Grogan.
1. Grogan, Ewart Scott
2. Explorers – Africa – Biography
I. Title
916'.04 DT11

ISBN 0-241-10592-7

Printed in Great Britain by Bristol Typesetting Co. Ltd,
Barton Manor, St Philips, Bristol.

CONTENTS

ILLUSTRATIONS

between pages 180 and 181

ACKNOWLEDGEMENTS

Without my husband's help in researching for this book and his encouragement I could have never written it. Therefore, my most sincere thanks must go to him first and foremost.

So many other people and institutions have helped me, to a greater or lesser extent, that I can only thank them in alphabetical order and acknowledge their contributions in the Notes and Sources.

These are:

Alex Abell, Dr Anderson, Taj Ahmed, Reggie Alexander, Michael Aronson.

Arnold Benjamin, Nicoletta Baldensperger, Joanna Babault, Sir Michael Blundell, Doria Block, Graham Boswell, Esmond Bradley Martin, The British Museum, British Library of Political and Economic Science, Mrs Brittain of Jesus College, Cambridge, Marchesa Antonella di Bugnano, Sheila Barker, Sunny Bumpus, The Bodleian Library, Oxford.

Rose Cartwright, Cynthia Crawford (E. S. Grogan's daughter), Peter Colmore, David Coward, Gertrude Chapman (E. S. Grogan's niece), Jean Crawford (E. S. Grogan's grand-daughter), W. E. Crosskill, Mr Criticos, Cambridge University Library.

Lord Delamere, Zia ud Deen, Roy Dunstan, Ministry of Defence (U.K.).

Jane Elliot (E. S. Grogan's daughter), Lady Erskine, *East African Standard*.

Gary Farrant, James Foster, *The Financial Times*, Ann Frontera, Foreign and Commonwealth Office Library and Records' Office.

Dr Gregory, Ezekiel Gombe, Terence Gavaghan, Michael Grogan (E. S. Grogan's nephew), Christopher Grogan (E. S. Grogan's nephew), Harold Grogan (E. S. Grogan's nephew).

Dorothy Hughes and her mother, Lady Claude Hamilton, Elspeth Huxley, Mrs G. Harrison (E. S. Grogan's niece), Sir Wilfred Havelock, Mr and Mrs Gordon Hunter, Alan Hunter (E. S. Grogan's nephew), Husseinbhai Hebatullah.

Stephen Joelson, Mary Johnson.

Kenya National Archives (Dr Kagombe and Oliver Mwalagho).

Mr and Mrs A. M. Lowis, Heini Lustman, Betty and Jock Leslie Melville, Mr and Mrs T. Latham, Mr and Mrs A. Landra, London School of Economics Library.

Miss Muggeridge, Sir Charles Markham, Jack Mason, Colin Kyle Milward (E. S. Grogan's great-grandson), Micki Migdol, Mr A. T. Matson, Mr Eliud W. Mathu, Mr and Mrs Joseph Murumbi.

The Hon. Charles Njonjo, Mr Gerald Nevill, Natural History Museum, London.

Mr L. O. Oates, Thomas Ofcansky, Ministry of Overseas Development, London.

John Phillipson, The Duke of Portland, W. K. Purdy, Public Record Office Kew.

Edward Rodwell, Dr M. G. Redley, John Riddoch, Eddie Ruben, Ruth Rabb, Royal Geographical Society, London, Rhodes House Library, Oxford (Mr F. E. Leese), Royal Commonwealth Society (Mr D. Simpson), Mr S. Rao.

David Slater (E. S. Grogan's grandson), Mrs Marian Szlapak (E. S. Grogan's grand-daughter), Sir Humphrey Slade, Dorothy Slater (E. S. Grogan's daughter), June Sutherland, J. L. Sim, Mrs Teresa Searight, The Savage Club (Mrs Alan Wykes), Sir Malin Sorsbie, G. de Souza.

Mrs Lilly Torr, Errol Trzebinski, Ann Thurston, Mrs K. G. Taylor, *The Times* Archivist (Gordon Phillips), Mrs Mary Thorold.

Sir Ernest Vasey, Donald Vincent.

Mrs Dorothy Ward, Peter Wilson, Norman Wymer, Joan Waddington, Mr Michael Wood, Winchester College (the Archivist).

Brian Yonge.

I would also like to express my special thanks to my editor, Miss Caroline Tonson Rye.

They tell the tale of Empire, do these winds;
Wild calling to wild, and the urge and surge
of blood which must carry our people willy nilly
into the last attainable confines of a finite earth,
there to persist, absorb, dictate, boss and
impose our Will.

Ewart S. Grogan

FOREWORD

by

Sir Michael Blundell

Leda Farrant has once more drawn aside the curtains of Africa's little known past and allowed us fascinating glimpses of its history as she did in her *Tippu Tip and the East African Slave Trade.*

Ewart Grogan—Ewart to his intimate friends and Grogs to the general European public which was often spellbound by his oratory—was sometimes almost a hero to his contemporaries in Africa, and is now fast becoming a legend to those who did not know him.

Gifted with a brilliant brain—especially in the field of finance—a marvellously tough and sinewy physique, as a young man he came to fame through his walk from Cape to Cairo which he undertook to win the hand of his future wife. Despite the hardships of that journey and the horrors which he experienced, he returned to Africa and there spent the rest of his life. There was no field in which he did not excel. He had an uncanny sense of future values and was able to see how a deserted coral creek in Mombasa would one day be part of a great modern port; how vast uninhabited areas of forest in Kenya would eventually create a timber industry; and how a despised unhealthy swamp would one day become the centre of the city of Nairobi. He had an irresistible urge to control any water within his reach with which to fructify the dried earth. His great domain at Taveta was a marvel of planning, agricultural experiments and irrigation. Here was the land he understood. Here, after a lifetime spent in developing the economy of Kenya, interspersed with turbulent periods in politics, he found peace surrounded by the Africa he loved, the limitless harsh brown-grey bush and the African people to whom he had grown accustomed, and with whom, in the end, he sympathised in their ardent wish for political advance.

Though more than thirty years separated us, (he was ninety-two when he died), and though his political thinking was utterly different from my own, he accorded to me his special friendship and understanding. Perhaps because Africa with its harshness, its rawness and vitality had captured my heart as it had his.

In *The Legendary Grogan* we see how in a single man's lifetime the people of this Continent have been catapulted from the age of tribal clashes and despotic, almost inhuman rule to the age of technology.

'Ewart' was the product of an historical period when, in Africa, individuals could still create great enterprises. He played his part in laying the foundations of modern Kenya and its economy and Ewart deserves the tribute which this book gives to his memory.

Sir Michael Blundell was a Member of the Legislative Council during the colonial period and a Minister after Kenya's Independence. He wrote *So Rough a Wind*, a very successful book on Kenya.

Chapter 1

THE PREMISE

On 30 April 1900, the Lecture Hall of the Royal Geographical Society in London was filled to capacity. The first man to walk the length of Africa from the Cape to Cairo was to address an audience of experienced explorers, geographers, historians, professors and the King of Sweden. His name was Ewart Scott Grogan and he was one of the youngest men who had ever spoken there. To speak at the Royal Geographical Society was an honour. To be invited to speak at the age of twenty-six was exceptional.

Neither the distinguished public nor the place disconcerted Grogan. Public speaking would always be one of his favourite occupations.

He started his speech by telling the audience that there was a saying in Africa that any man who had set foot on its soil would always return. Despite the hardships, and sometimes 'the abominable discomforts', a man who had seen Africa once would always hanker after the freedom of its wide open spaces. He went on to say that 'anything more ridiculous' than the possibility of his return to Africa after the hardships of the Matabele war in 1896 and nearly dying of dysentery and black water fever, never occurred to him as he shook his fist at Beira from his homeward-bound steamer, and he was happy at the thought that he would never again set foot on 'those accursed sands'.[1]

Thirteen months later he was standing on those very sands

again, ready to undertake a two year walk through unknown and uncharted lands to win the hand of a New Zealand girl.

Throughout his life Grogan remained fearless, impulsive, a lover of women and ever ready for any adventure. The greater the challenge, the stronger his determination to win through. He was also a rebel and at least one of his Irish ancestors lost more than Ewart ever did in pursuing rebellion.

The Grogan clan, or *sept*, can be traced back in existing records to the thirteenth century, and Ewart Grogan's branch of the family has been traced, in a direct line, to John Grogan of Antrim in Northern Ireland, born circa 1570.

His great-grandson, also John (1653–1720), obtained Johnstown Castle near Wexford by marriage; he also acquired another vast estate in Wexford, and his great-grandson Cornelius' head ended up on a pike on Wexford Bridge. Cornelius (1738–1798) was not satisfied with being High Sheriff of Wexford and a member of Parliament. In the Irish rebellion of 1798 he joined the rebels and was Commissary General of their army. When the Royalists captured Wexford, Cornelius was court-martialled and sentenced to death. He was beheaded on Wexford Bridge, his head mounted on a pike and his body thrown into the river. His followers recovered and secretly buried it. His brother Thomas fared no better on the side of the Royalists. He was killed in battle. Johnstown Castle was confiscated by the Crown but was later returned to the family after payment of a very heavy fine.

After this some of the Grogans thought they might do better to pursue more peaceful occupations. In fact, Ewart's great-grandfather Nathaniel is believed to have moved to England and his son Nicholas (1784–1848) became a prosperous wine merchant in London.[2]

Grogan's family feel that Ewart's rebellious nature might have been inherited from Cornelius, but his father William was not exactly a man to submit gracefully to royalist commands either.

William Grogan (1825–1891) was a rich estate agent in London with powerful friends and clients. Benjamin Disraeli was one and William Ewart Gladstone another. William Grogan so admired Gladstone for his support of the Irish Home Rule Bill that he named his first son by his second wife Ewart.

Another powerful client was Queen Victoria. William Grogan was the Surveyor-General of Houses and Buildings to Queen

Victoria's Duchy of Lancaster, but, as far as William was concerned, this appointment did not mean that he was at the beck and call of his despotic monarch.

Soon after Ewart's birth, William was enjoying a Scottish holiday with his second wife Jane when he received a summons from Queen Victoria to 'wait upon her' at Osborne House in the Isle of Wight. William did not consider his Queen's order to travel to the Isle of Wight to discuss estate affairs important enough to interrupt his holiday with young Jane and he sent a message to the effect that a later appointment, when Queen Victoria was at Buckingham Palace, would suit him better. Nobody, not even her favourite William Grogan, could so ignore that Queen and within a few months he was discharged, although given a canteen of silver cutlery appropriately inscribed with the Queen's gratitude for services rendered.

Before marrying Jane, the widow of a drunkard by the name of Sams, William was married to Mercy Mary Adams who gave him thirteen children before she died at the age of forty-four. Ewart, born on 12 December 1874, was his fourteenth child, but he was so in love with Jane who was twenty years his junior, that one more child merely delighted him. How delighted he was after seven more children, nobody knows, except that with a family of twenty-one children he was always rather mixed up about who was who. When his last daughter Hilda was born in 1888, his first son, William, was already forty years old.

Ewart Scott Grogan was christened, with the Queen's permission, at the Chapel Royal, Savoy. This was also known as the Chapel of the Royal Victoria Order and it was the Queen's private chapel 'in right of her Duchy of Lancaster'. Originally it was part of the ancient Palace which was erected in the Manor granted to Peter of Savoy in 1246. It was bombed during the Second World War and a lot of records were destroyed, but it was rebuilt and the long panelled chapel with the huge organ above the royal seats still retains its simple dignified beauty.

William Ewart Gladstone was Ewart Scott Grogan's godfather and the name Scott was his mother's family home. Grogan was never very fond of his godfather whom he considered a useless individual.[3] Gladstone gave the baby a silver christening mug which is now the property of Michael Grogan, his nephew.

William Grogan's bank account did not seem to be greatly affected by the size of his family or the loss of his most troublesome client, Queen Victoria. The Grogan family always lived very well, in large comfortable houses. Ewart was born at No. 61 Eaton Square in London, but when his brother Philip was born in 1876, that house seemed somewhat cramped and William purchased two houses in Queen's Gate and knocked them into one, which gave them forty-two rooms, not counting servants' rooms, kitchens, stores, laundries and bathrooms. The ten indoor and the two outdoor servants did not have much time on their hands as the family grew in size, and ten to fifteen children of all ages ran up and down the three-storeyed house.

The house had a good garden for London but so many small children needed a bigger outlet for their energies, and William bought a house at Hove for the holidays. The packing alone for those holidays must have been like an army manoeuvre, but young Jane was the kind of Victorian mother who ran her family like a well disciplined army. One hour of every day was given to deportment. Carrying books balanced on his head and lying down on the floor to straighten his back were not Ewart's favourite pastimes, but he was very fond of his mother and tried to please her. On the other hand, being her favourite, he got away with a lot more than the other children. Jane was not a particularly warm person, but Ewart was the recipient of a great deal of the love she was capable of giving. She encouraged his musical talents and he learned to play the banjo at a very young age. He had a good singing voice and could whistle well, despite his mother's disapproval. Nevertheless, he whistled classical and popular music for the rest of his life, to the irritation of the people who had to listen to him.

At the age of six Ewart was sent to Dr Priddens' private school, Boxgrove, near Guildford and there he distinguished himself by swallowing a sausage whole to win a bet, and as he gave every sign of choking a doctor was sent for and a stomach pump restored his health and popularity.[4]

From Boxgrove he won an Exhibition into Winchester College, which is the nearest thing to a full scholarship and meant that his father would have to pay for only part of his fees. Winchester prides itself on a very high academic standard and boys wishing to enter it have to take the school's exam and not the general Common Entrance as for other public schools. To win an Exhibition you had to be very good academically. As in Ewart's day, there is still a saying at Winchester that if you got a scholarship at Eton you would probably find it difficult to get into Winchester.[5]

Ewart entered Winchester in September 1888, three months before his thirteenth birthday and he was quickly promoted from one 'book' to another.[6] Promotions were according to merit, not age, and Ewart was always one of the youngest to be so promoted. 'He had a very respectable academic record,' the school wrote about him. In his last year he was a Commoner Prefect but he never joined the army class.[7] He was not the army type. Although sports were never very important to him he did win his cricket and football colours. His ambition in the sporting field lay a long way from Winchester. He was already thinking of hunting in Africa, avidly reading all the explorers' accounts and dreaming of hunting elephant, rhino and lion. To this ambition he added seeing Lake Tanganyika. Livingstone's writings about that lake fascinated him and he was determined to see it one day, *and* shoot an elephant, a rhino and a lion.

His dreams were suddenly shattered when he received news that his father had died. At the age of sixty-six, in June 1891, William Grogan was found dead in his bed, and Jane with her large young family was forced to sell the Queen's Gate house and move to a smaller one in Sevenoaks. Ewart was not yet seventeen but he showed extraordinary maturity and in that period he gave his mother the practical and moral support she refused from her step-children the eldest of whom was two years older than herself. Ewart helped her with the sale of the Queen's Gate house, the purchase of the house at Sevenoaks and the removal, and then suggested a holiday in Switzerland.

Zermatt was the ideal spot as far as Ewart was concerned. Mountain climbing was another of his ambitions but he didn't tell his mother this, merely suggesting that the change would do them all good.

Hilda was only three years old so she was left with Nanny Redwood, but the rest of the family went to Zermatt and Ewart immediately embarked on arrangements to climb the Weisshorn with an experienced guide. After a short period of training the guide took young Ewart up the Weisshorn and this book would never have been written if the ropes that tied Ewart to the guide had not held as the guide fell into a crevasse and Ewart was dragged after him. They were badly bruised but in one piece. The only problem was that they were trapped and remained so for hours until another party of climbers heard their shouts and they were rescued.

The fall and the worry of being trapped indefinitely in the crevasse were as nothing compared to the dressing down Ewart received from his mother who had been in an agony of worry since she had heard there had been an accident on the mountain. He was too old to get a spanking, but he would have preferred that to the lashing her tongue gave him. He was irresponsible and selfish, she said among other things. It surprised him to hear that she had regarded him as the man of the family, but now her trust was shattered. He was obviously unworthy of her regard. He suffered the scolding in silence, all the while wondering how he was going to arrange for more climbing. The experience, far from discouraging, had stimulated him; therefore, despite her pleas and threats, he was soon climbing every peak around Zermatt. His purpose was to be accepted into the select Alpine Club.

For four seasons he went back to Switzerland to climb with famous guides such as Perren, Summermatter and E. L. Strutt who was the second in command of the Everest Expedition in 1922. With these guides he climbed every important peak from the Matterhorn to Mont Blanc, and finally at the end of the fourth season he was elected a member of the Alpine Club.

Life was not all climbing and dreaming of hunting in Africa. As the time for entering university approached he worked harder at Winchester and, as he told a friend much later in life,[8] he carefully studied the complete *Oxford English Dictionary* because he liked to make the task of his examiners that much more difficult when marking his papers. Shades of later speeches in the Kenya Parliament and at public meetings when some of the language he used was above most people's heads. His knowledge of the English language was always exceptional.

He passed into Jesus College, Cambridge, in October 1893 to read Law. By the number of Ewart's escapades in the two and a half years he was at Cambridge, one would think he was left with very little time to study Law or anything else. In fact, he was interested in much more than the Law. He attended classes in medicine and mathematics, showing great aptitude for the first and a brilliant grasp of the second. He had mastered French during his Alpine exploits and always remained proficient in that language.

He 'kept' rooms in Chapel Court, consisting of a 'keeping

room' (study), and a bedroom, and he shared the 'gyp room' (kitchen) with another student, with whom he also shared the 'gyp' or man servant.[9] As he did for the rest of his life, he kept his rooms simple but filled with books.

By this time Ewart Grogan had grown into a handsome youth with brown wavy hair, large brilliant blue eyes, a straight Roman nose, a strong mouth and a determined jaw line. He was six feet tall, and held himself rod-straight (perhaps his mother's training paid dividends), thus appearing taller. He was strongly built with wide shoulders and narrow hips. A perfect specimen of a sportsman, but he only pursued sports for fun rather than to win. He was gregarious and the conviviality of a team suited his character, therefore he rowed and played rugby at neither of which was he outstanding. The college magazine *Chanticlere* remarked that in the 1st rugger football team Grogan's 'collaring was really good, but he has not learnt to shove. He ought to be good when he knows the game better.' He certainly learnt to 'shove' in later life.

Apart from sports, studies and pranks, Grogan also pursued intellectual activities, and he was treasurer of the Halliwell Shakespeare Society, although this was not very well attended. Not as well attended as the Fabian Society which he was invited to join. His answer was not greatly appreciated. Straight speaking was the quality which got him into trouble for the next seventy years. He told the Fabians that they were 'a very unwholesome gang of chinless men and bosomless women', and he didn't think he qualified.[10]

Some of the friends he made at Cambridge remained so for most of his life, and one of them, Eddie Watt, became his brother-in-law. One of his constant companions, especially when pranks were being organised, was the future Lord Justice Luxmore.

Charles Luxmore and Grogan both detested a student by the name of Senior who also lived in Chapel Court and they decided to do some telling damage to his room. They climbed on the roof carrying two buckets of water and, having calculated which was the victim's chimney, they poured the water down one of the dozen chimneys. They climbed down the roof and, laughing, rushed to Grogan's study to celebrate, only to be greeted by soggy soot all over the floor. Frustrated by their failure they decided to nail their victim's door so that he could not get out of his room. They performed that task so well that a carpenter had to be called to release the unhappy Senior.

A don, Arthur Gray, was next on the list. On Guy Fawkes' night Grogan piled a lot of wood in front of his door and lit it with fireworks. The Fire Brigade was called, and the Dean, 'Red' Morgan was not amused at this latest breach of discipline. He engaged a detective to catch the culprit. Having been told about this by Eddie Watt, Grogan, Luxmore, Watt and a few others surrounded the bushes where the detective was hiding and caught him. They marched him in front of the embarrassed Dean saying they suspected the man of being a thief. The Dean thanked them and assured them that he would deal with the situation. The detective was not seen again.

Then came one of the saddest blows of his life. Unknown to him or the other children his mother had been suffering from heart disease for some time and one morning she died suddenly in her bathroom in March 1895 when she was only forty-nine. The news was unbelievable to Grogan when he first heard it. His mother was the most important person in his life, but realising he was now truly the head of the young family, he quickly rallied and when he consulted his step-brothers it was decided that a legal guardian was needed for the younger children. His step-brother Walter Grogan (1854–1924) was elected and he moved three of the children into his house at Wonersh near Guildford. By then Philip had joined Ewart at Jesus College, Norman had died of measles when he was three years old, Quentin and Archibald were at boarding school and that left Margaret, Dorothy and Hilda to be cared for. When her mother died Hilda was only seven years old.

Having found a guardian did not mean that Ewart washed his hands of his brothers and sisters. On the contrary, he shared the responsibility with his step-brother and became as strict as an over-possessive father with the girls, making sure they were always chaperoned and behaved as 'young ladies should'. Faithful Nanny Redwood stayed with the younger children and this gave them some of the security and the love they lost when their mother died. Ewart was also a strict disciplinarian as far as money was concerned. William Grogan had left his children well provided for and Jane had been a careful manager, so money was not a problem; but Ewart insisted that his brothers and sisters should account for every penny of their meagre allowance.

He was always a generous man with others but never a spendthrift himself, therefore he expected people to respect money. He had definitely inherited his father's business ability.[11]

A 21-year-old Victorian university undergraduate could not allow emotion to show, and having received the condolences of his friends with the dignity expected of him, he threw himself into all college activities as before—or even more so. In fact, his wild escapades became wilder and the last one cost him his degree.

At the beginning of the Lent term of 1896, after a game of rugger which his team had won and while they were in particularly high spirits drinking at the Red Lion, Grogan decided he should show a taste of his sense of humour to one of the masters who had left the College for the night. Somehow he procured a billy goat and locked it in the master's study. Unfortunately for the goat and the master's possessions, the don stayed away for longer than expected and the goat had satisfied its appetite on papers and books and in final frustration it had butted all the stuffing out of the furniture. When the master returned he was not very happy with what he saw and smelled. Nor was the goat by that time.[12]

'Red' Morgan, the Dean, decided that Ewart Scott Grogan had gone too far this time, and he was sent down. But H. A. Morgan seems to have forgotten the trials and tribulations he had suffered at the hands of Grogan when he wrote a glowing letter about the young man's qualities after Grogan's return from his famous walk from Cape to Cairo. He wrote: 'I consider Mr Ewart S. Grogan, formerly a student of this College, possesses remarkably robust and vigorous mental powers, unflinching energy and perseverance, a calm and sound judgment and that perfect nerve and readiness of resource so necessary when difficulties have to be faced and successfully met . . . A highly capable and cultivated gentleman . . .'[13]

Chapter 2

ART OR AFRICA

Grogan was not the type of man who wasted his time or regretted past mistakes. What was past was past and the future was all that mattered, but he needed time to think and he always thought best with a pencil in his hand. He drew well but had never pursued the talent seriously. This interim period gave him the opportunity to see just how well he could draw and he enrolled at the Slade School of Art.

It was immediately evident to the teachers at the school that Grogan had talent, especially in drawing animals, as can be seen from the drawings in his book *From the Cape to Cairo*, but there were a few problems in becoming an artist. The main one was the years it would take to become competent, let alone to earn money. The other was the type of people who were surrounding him now at the Slade and would most likely surround him for the rest of his life. He positively did not share the Bohemian love for long hair and dirty personal habits. He referred to them as 'long haired lizards' and apart from their love of art, he shared nothing else with them. A decision had to be made and he discussed the possibilities with his teacher.

Grogan always liked to shock people and his sense of humour was often cynical. He liked to see people's reactions to his more outrageous statements and he was amused at his teacher's irritation when he stated that he wasn't sure whether he wanted to be an artist or a policeman. The teacher argued that the two professions were hardly comparable and if Grogan was considering being a policeman he had better make up his mind quickly and not go on wasting the school's time.

'All right. I'll decide now,' Grogan said taking a penny out of his pocket. 'Heads, I become an artist; tails a policeman.'[1]

It came down tails and Grogan did not hesitate. He thanked his teacher and without even picking up his drawings walked out of the Slade, not to become a policeman but to enlist as an ordinary trooper to fight against the Matabele in what became Rhodesia and is now Zimbabwe.

The Matabele were a tribe of Zulu origin who had moved north and settled in 1838 in the region where Bulawayo stands today. Matabeleland was rich in minerals. An irresistible attraction for Cecil John Rhodes.

When Cecil Rhodes, the son of a clergyman, went to South Africa in 1870 at the age of sixteen, he had no imperial expansionist dreams. He was sent there to recover his health. He joined his brother Herbert in Natal and farmed, but that same year diamonds were discovered at Kimberley and with his brother he became a digger. By nineteen he was healthy again and financially independent. Diamonds were attractive but digging for them was not, so he invested his money on other people to go on digging and make him richer and travelled alone by ox wagon through Transvaal and Bechuanaland. These countries did not fail to impress him. They were empty and fertile and he immediately saw the possibilities. His dreams began there: Africa British from the Cape to Cairo. British settlement extending further and further north. But before that he wanted his degree from Oxford and in 1873 he returned there to resume his studies. Not for long. His heart and lungs were affected again and he was given six months to live. Africa was recommended again and again he recovered his health. He certainly did not look a delicate man. He was very tall and broad with an unusually large head and fair curly hair and an oddly high pitched voice for such a big man.

Like Grogan, who resembled him in many ways, he was not a man to give up anything easily, therefore he returned to Oxford once again and obtained his degree. But he had too much invested in Africa to forget about it and in 1881 he amalgamated his Kimberley mines which became the De Beers Mining Company with a capital of £200,000. Making money to Rhodes was as important as his political ideals. Again like Grogan, he had simple personal tastes but he needed money to further his ideas.

At this time he was given a permanent seat in the Cape Assembly and he advocated self-government for South Africa with Dutch and British participation. This made him very popular with the Dutch population, but in 1885 he was fighting President Kruger for British supremacy in Bechuanaland.

North of Bechuanaland was Matabeleland under chief Lobengula and soon Rhodes realised that the Germans and the Dutch were manipulating Lobengula to allow them mineral rights. Rhodes moved fast. He obtained a charter to establish the British South African Company to trade and mine there as far as the Zambezi and the southern end of Lake Tanganyika under British protection, hoping to create, with Nyasaland, a British chain of possessions. His dream was of course defeated in 1890 by the British/German agreement to allow the Germans into Tanganyika. Meanwhile, in October 1888, he had come to an agreement with Lobengula to give his company all mineral rights in Matabeleland, an area covering more than 75,000 square miles, for a payment of £100 per month, a thousand rifles, ammunition, and a gunboat on the Zambezi. Lobengula never got the gunboat.

The move shocked a number of liberals in England and even Queen Victoria wrote to Lobengula, a fat and somewhat primitive monarch who wore a kilt of monkey skins and a naval cap (he obviously wanted the gunboat to go with it). In her letter she wrote: 'It is not wise to put too much power into the hands of men who come first, and to exclude other deserving men. A king gives a stranger an ox, not his whole herd of cattle, otherwise what would other strangers have to eat?' She was probably thinking of her son-in-law, the Kaiser, as being excluded from the share of the loot.

All was not peaceful in Matabeleland and in 1893 Rhodes' company was involved in frontier incidents over cattle between the Matabele and the Mashona, their neighbours to the north who had meanwhile also granted Rhodes' company mining rights. The march to Mashonaland was led by the celebrated professional hunter, Frederick Courtney Selous, and on the 13th September 1890 the Union Jack was hoisted at what is now Salisbury. After the defeat of his troops, Lobengula retreated with his followers to the hills beyond Bulawayo (which means place of slaughter) and there next year he died of smallpox. Before dying he is supposed to have told his people to hand over the gold to the white man because 'the white man will never cease following us while we have gold in our possession, for gold is what the white men prize above all things. Give them the gold and tell them I want peace.'

Peace lasted only a short time because in 1896, six years after Rhodes had been made Prime Minister of the Cape with the support of the Dutch population, the British miners in the Transvaal revolted against the Boer Government and Dr Leander Starr Jameson led a force of 500 over the border in what is known as the 'Jameson Raid'. Rhodes gave money, arms and the weight of his great influence to the rebellion but he didn't take part in the abortive raid. Nevertheless, his participation cost him his Premiership and thereafter he dedicated himself to the development of the country which was to bear his name: Rhodesia.

Many years later Grogan wrote of Cecil Rhodes: '[He] bewitched a strange medley of Jews, aristocrats, roughnecks, statesmen and tribal savages as his following in a then seemingly hopeless attempt to develop Darkest Africa.'[2]

The Matabele chose this difficult period to rise again. This second rebellion was no mere quarrel over a few head of cattle but a full scale affair involving killing, burning and looting. The white settlers were enraged at having their women and children killed and their cattle slaughtered, but there was little they could do. As a consequence of the Jameson Raid, the Europeans in Matabeleland were disorganised and defenceless. Some of them organised volunteer units but against the hordes of Matabele they were not very effective. Imperial troops had to be sent out from England, among them Ewart Grogan as 'a mere bloody trooper,' he later wrote. 'The felicitous term applied to those who for five bob a day, a cupful of mouldy rice, and a blown tin of bully beef, swore and sweated in the (as it transpires) ridiculous task of painting the map red.'[3]

He wasn't given much time to enjoy the natural beauty and home comforts of Cape Town. With the other troops destined for the Matabele war he boarded a train to Mafeking, 'which meant four dismal days and three yet more dismal nights in a most dismal train, whose engine occasionally went off on its own account to get a drink, and nine awful days and nine reckless nights in a Gladstone bag on wheels, labelled coach,' he wrote in 1900 in his book *From the Cape to Cairo*.

On arrival at Mafeking he was immediately told that his first job was to take a mule wagon convoy of ammunition up to Bulawayo 600 miles away. Oxen could not be used because of rinderpest in the region and Grogan found the drivers as frustrating as the obstinate mules. He was warned before leaving that the drivers of the wagons would try to desert, so he decided that the best spot from which to control the situation was the roof of the leading wagon whence he could watch the drivers and the country through which they passed for possible attacks. His precautions were all in vain. At the first stop where he decided they would camp for the night half the drivers deserted. There was nothing else to do but tie the wagons together in a chain. A rope from the end of the leading wagon was tied to the mules of the second and so on.

By the time he reached Bulawayo he collapsed with exhaustion under a tree where he promptly fell asleep only to wake up hours later with a strong feeling of nausea. Hanging from the tree above him were two dead bodies in an advanced state of putrefaction.

This was his first welcome to the war and what he subsequently saw did not endear the Matabele to him. He saw women who had been raped and murdered, and men who had been left to die in the scorching sun with their hands and feet pegged to the ground; but the sight that affected him most and which he never forgot were the children who had been tortured and whose limbs had been torn from their bodies. He loved children to the end of his life, but not all children as we will see.

He was promoted as a Number 4 on a muzzle-loading seven-pounder in the thick of the fighting and, despite the danger, the discomforts and the lack of food, he much preferred this to the horror of seeing women and children massacred. There were no tents and very little food and in later life, to see people's expression of disgust, he was fond of telling the story of how he had shot a vulture which had been feeding on a dead Matabele, cooked it and enjoyed the feast. He claimed it wasn't as bad as the 'blown tins of bully beef'.

One of the highlights of the campaign for Grogan was meeting Cecil Rhodes for the first time. In England he had followed with great interest the reports on Rhodes' career and he was filled with admiration for the man who was the best example of what Imperial England represented.

At that time imperialist expansion was something to be proud of and nothing to apologise about as Grogan wrote many years later. In 1929 he wrote to a friend:[4] 'I am lucky to be able to see many of our dreams now actualities. How times change. Pioneering in those days was regarded as a rather decent sort of job—now most home folk seem to rank it one degree below burglary. But I notice they enjoy the proceeds. Anyhow it has been a great lark, hasn't it?'

For a short time Grogan was part of Cecil Rhodes' escort and like most people who met Rhodes he was greatly affected by the man's personality and strength of character. Later he wrote: '[Cecil Rhodes] was kind to men in the Matabele war . . . He inspired me to explore the route from Cape to Cairo with a view to ultimate rail connection and later[5] asked me to promise to devote my life to the development of British interests in Africa. A positive, pragmatic, and ruthless sentimentalist.'[6] His admiration for the man was not entirely blind.

Despite their superior numbers the Matabele and the Mashona (who had meantime joined the rebellion) were soon forced to retreat under the superior fire-power of the British troops, but the impregnable Matopo Hills gave the Matabele the upper hand again. The British troops and their heavy equipment could not penetrate the forest. They had to content themselves with surrounding it and waiting for the Matabele to surrender. This did not suit Rhodes who wanted to see a quick solution to the war.

He decided to move his tent away from the main body of troops and there waited for six weeks for the Matabele to contact him. His patience was his reward. After six weeks he was invited to attend a council of elders deep in the hills. Unarmed he attended the council with three friends. One of them was F. J. Clarke for whom the Matabele had great respect after chief Lobengula had named him 'Mopani' because he said he was as tall and as straight as the Mopani tree.

The talks were long and full of the African love of tortuous arguments, but Rhodes patiently listened to their grievances and agreed to many changes in the administration of the country and at the end he asked: 'Now, for the future, is it peace or is it war?' The chiefs, laying down their sticks as a symbol of surrendered arms, declared: 'It is peace.' He had staked his life on trust and a deep liking of the Africans and on 13 October 1896, the rebellion ended.

No one was more relieved than Grogan at the end of hostilities. His first taste of Africa was not what he had expected and his observation on that period of his life was typical of his caustic remarks for which he was well known. 'Africa is not polite,' he surmised; but having come this far and not having forgotten his childhood dream of hunting lion, elephant and rhino, he arranged to go on a hunting trip near Beira with three Dutchmen.

The outcome of the expedition was disastrous. The three Dutchmen died of fever and Grogan contracted dysentery, blackwater fever and, as if that was not enough, he had a burst liver abscess. His life was saved by Alfred Lawley, a man whose kindness Grogan never forgot.

Many years later Grogan wrote: 'A very remarkable character that I met in those very early days was Alfred Lawley, the main driving force in the great contracting firm of Pauling and Company. I was first conscious of his existence when I woke up in his house in Beira.

'I had supposedly died of blackwater fever complicated by a burst liver abscess in Fontesvilla, the starting point on the Pungwe River for the construction of the then two-foot gauge Beira Railway. The inhabitants of Fontesvilla (which had an annual death rate of from 50% to 70%) disliked burying people because coffins were hard to come by and had an inconvenient habit during the flood time of the rains of re-emerging and coming to rest on people's verandahs. My carcass was therefore wrapped in a blanket and tossed into an empty truck, and on arrival at Beira was reported to Lawley, who was in charge of the railway construction. As there was no smell of death Lawley opined that I must still be alive and took me to his house, where he nursed me like a mother.

'He was an amazing person, the son of a Sussex farm hand, and as he told me, nourished on beer from the age of six months. He built railways anywhere and everywhere from South Africa to Russia, and when the pace slackened he used to fill a train with food and drink, dash up to rail-head, knock off all work, make everybody, white and black, comatose for a couple of days, and thus recover his standard of "Boys, a mile a day". He was a dear friend of mine for many years, and I am happy in the thought that the day before he died, and contrary to his doctor's orders, I filled him up with roast grouse and the best bottle of burgundy from the cellars of the RAC.'[7]

But in 1896 Grogan, who was still weak from his illness, announced to Lawley that he intended to see the sights of Beira and enjoy a little Portuguese female companionship before returning to England. Alfred Lawley warned him that Portuguese men did not take kindly to strangers approaching their women, but Grogan laughed that off and with a few friends visited a number of bars and finally ended up in a dance hall. It wasn't a very reputable hall, and he danced happily with any girl who would let him take her on the dance floor.

He was enjoying himself with one such girl when, reflected in a cloudy mirror surrounded by gaudy paper flowers, he saw a man lifting a knife behind his back. In one quick movement Grogan turned and punched the man on the jaw. The man fell, hit his head on the corner of a table and died instantly. Grogan was stunned but he had to recover his wits quickly as the dance hall turned into a mass of angry fighting Portuguese. With his friends he managed to fight his way out of the bar, but the Portuguese authorities were not pleased at the incident. They were convinced that the British troops going through Beira on their way from Rhodesia were planning to take over Mozambique and insisted on arresting Grogan and his friends. Only after days of diplomatic discussions with the British Consul were they released and allowed to board their ship.

A friend[8] who many years later heard the story from Grogan asked him if perhaps the Portuguese girl he was dancing with was a girl-friend or even the wife of the man who tried to knife him.

'How could I know that,' Grogan replied. 'I didn't speak Portuguese.'

Grogan's later reputation with women makes it almost certain that he picked the best looking girl in the room, regardless of whom she was with and what the consequences would be.

When Alfred Lawley put him on the steamer on the way back to England, Grogan was happy to see the last of Africa and, as he said at the Geographical Society, he shook his fist at 'those accursed sands' and swore never to set foot on them again.[9]

Chapter 3

THE CHALLENGE AND WALKING THROUGH AFRICA

Lawley had saved his life and Grogan was well enough to travel back to England, but he was far from recovered. The family doctor advised a long rest and good food, as in his opinion Grogan should have died of the burst liver abscess if not from blackwater fever, and how he had survived those two killers, plus dysentery, the doctor could only attribute to Grogan's remarkably strong constitution.

'What would you say about a long sea voyage and a holiday in New Zealand,' Grogan asked the doctor.

Regardless of the doctor's opinion Grogan had already made up his mind that going to New Zealand with Eddie Watt, his friend from Cambridge, was exactly what he needed.

After his return from Beira he had met Eddie in London and told him he was bored with convalescing and Eddie had suggested they should go together to New Zealand where his sister Helen was getting married. Grogan accepted the invitation with enthusiasm, but he had no suitable clothes, he said. There was no time to shop before Eddie's ship sailed, so Eddie lent Grogan clothes and without a second thought, as if New Zealand were only across the Channel, he sailed with Eddie. Anything for the sake of adventure.[1]

The Watt family in New Zealand were direct descendants of James Watt, the Scottish engineer and inventor of the steam engine, and money was never a problem for the Watt children: Edward, Helen, Gertrude and Florence. They were born in Oakland where their father was a rich sheep-rancher but after he died their mother married an equally wealthy merchant from Napier and there they lived the rest of their childhood in a beautiful house perched on a cliff overlooking the sea. Coleman, the step-father, had no control over the money left by Watt to the children, but he controlled everything else. By all accounts, he was a thoroughly unpleasant character and perhaps this is the reason why Mrs Watt decided to send Eddie to school in England and the girls to finishing school in Switzerland.[2]

Gertrude Edith Watt was twenty-one, a year younger than Grogan, when he arrived in Napier. She was not a great beauty, but she had classical features, soft blue eyes, rich thick brown hair and, most attractive of all, a gentle feminine nature which immediately appealed to Grogan. He had often believed he was in love, but never like this. And it was mutual. Within a few days, to Gertrude's surprise, he was talking of marriage but his impulsive nature soon received a blow when he spoke about their intentions to Mr Coleman, Gertrude's step-father.

The first thing Mr Coleman asked Grogan was what he had achieved in his twenty-two years. Except for the Matabele war, Grogan was hard put to list anything else—except perhaps being sent down from Cambridge, a fact of which Mr Coleman was well aware and immediately confronted Grogan with. He was asked how he intended to support his step-daughter, and there again Grogan was evasive, though he was stung by the suggestion that he was perhaps a fortune hunter. Money had never entered Grogan's head. He had no idea that Gertrude would bring him a great deal of it if he married her.

The interview was not going according to plan and Grogan thought fast. Since leaving Beira he had often speculated about Rhodes' scheme to connect the Cape to Cairo with a railway and a telegraph line, but who was surveying the land through which the railway and the telegraph would have to pass? The railway had now reached Bulawayo but Rhodes knew very little of what lay ahead and Grogan suddenly decided that *he* was the man to bring back the information needed.

As Coleman was about to leave the study where the interview had taken place, Grogan impetuously asked if his intention to walk from the Cape to Cairo would change Mr Coleman's mind as to his suitability. Mr Coleman merely laughed and went into a long Philippic about the difficulties Stanley, Livingstone and other explorers had encountered in traversing only portions of Africa, let alone the *length* of it. And for what purpose such a useless enterprise, Coleman asked. Merely to win the hand of a girl? Mainly that, Grogan answered, and also to prove that Cecil Rhodes' plan was not just a dream. Having caught Mr Coleman's attention for a spell, Grogan spoke quickly and knowledgeably of Cecil Rhodes' plans and almost convinced Coleman that it was all worth while. The end of the interview was equivocal as far as Grogan was concerned. Coleman still thought the whole idea a youthful and impractical joke, but, pressed to promise his consent if Grogan completed his walk from the Cape to Cairo, he agreed, convinced that this young fool would never even reach the half way mark of his ambition.

There was no time to lose; he had to get back to England and organise the expedition. Eddie was enthusiastic when he heard of Grogan's intentions, but Gertrude was worried. She had complete trust in Ewart, but what he proposed to do frightened her and despite his loving words of reassurance she could not help worrying then as she worried for the next two years when she didn't know whether he was dead or alive 'somewhere' in Africa. All he wanted from her was a promise that she would wait for his return and then, whether Coleman gave his consent or not, they would be married. Gertrude of course promised and Grogan left with a number of addresses given him by Eddie of people who would help him with financial backing for the expedition.

The first person he contacted in England was Arthur Henry Sharp, Gertrude's uncle, a man in his late forties who was a keen hunter, strong and well built and full of youthful enthusiasm. Grogan did not hesitate to accept when Arthur Sharp proposed that they should undertake the 'walk' together. Grogan always referred to the two-and-a-half years of staggering hardships he suffered, as 'the walk', giving the impression that he merely strolled through Africa for the fun of it.

With Sharp they went to see other relations of the Watt family, the Eyres of Dumbleton Hall in Evesham where Grogan had often stayed with Eddie during his Cambridge days. To his delight the Eyres agreed to finance the expedition after he had lightly explained to them that his plan was to take as little as possible and to live 'off the land' where he passed.

Weeks of feverish activity followed. Tents, sixty-four cases of food, including champagne, whisky and brandy. Guns, ammunition, clothes and medical supplies. A theodolite, fishing rods and even a phonograph were bought and packed. Not forgetting a copy of Shakespeare's works and *Whitaker's Almanack* which always travelled with him. This was Grogan's idea of travelling light and compared to Stanley's mountains of supplies it was. He also took three Union Jacks. He explained to Sharp that he intended to run the expedition as a well organised army, with orderly camps at every stop and the British flag flying wherever they went. One flag he reserved for the Queen. He would present it to her when they came back. He never doubted that they *would* come back.

The next step was to contact the Foreign Office and the War Office. Although, like Mr Coleman, these august bodies doubted that the young man would ever come back, if indeed he would ever begin his trek, they asked him to bring back information on French, German, Belgian and Portuguese boundaries. They wanted intelligence information as to whether these nations were infringing their boundary treaties and news of their military movements. There was also the question of Lake Kivu and Lake Edward which was not yet satisfactorily resolved. The reports brought back by previous explorers were not clear enough, and Grogan assured them he would supply them with the information. The fact that he was not trained for any of these investigations did not trouble him in the least. All he needed was cameras, survey instruments, a compass and a few inadequate maps which he fully intended to complete. At the Foreign Office and the War Office he was warned that war was a possibility in the Sudan and that the Khalifa still had Khartoum in his clutches. Grogan felt sure that by the time he reached Khartoum the British would have resolved that problem.

*

Since his famous crossing of Africa, and because the title of the book he wrote after the walk is *From the Cape to Cairo*, and also because throughout his life he always spoke of his walk being from the *Cape* to Cairo, people who have not read his book attentively have always assumed he *did* start from the Cape. In fact, he spoke of the Cape because he had travelled from Cape Town to Bulawayo during the second Matabele war. In his book

From the Cape to Cairo he clearly states that with Arthur Sharp he travelled from England to *Beira* on the Deutsch Ost Africa Cie., which was a pretty 'badly managed boat' according to him, but a lot of fun.

'On February 28th in the year of our Lord 1898,' he wrote, 'Arthur Henry Sharp and Ewart Scott Grogan, in company of sundry German officers and beer enthusiasts, took part in the usual D.O.A's Liner manoeuvre of violently charging a sandbank in the bay of Beira on a flood-tide, to the ear-smashing accompaniment of the German National Anthem. In the intervals of waiting to be floated, and finding out how many of our loads had been lost, we amused ourselves by catching sharks, which swarmed round the stern of the vessel. Beira, as every one knows, is mainly composed of galvanized iron, sun-baked sand, drinks, and Portuguese ruffians.'

One Portuguese, who was not a ruffian but a doctor and a gentleman on board a corvette where Grogan and Sharp had been invited to dine, helped them clear their luggage through customs. 'And those who know Beira will understand what that means,' he wrote. Grogan described him as 'a most charming specimen of the Portuguese gentlemen (and a Portuguese gentleman is a gentleman)'.

In Beira he was happy to meet 'the evergreen' Mr Lawley, but he was as anxious to leave the port this time as he had been on his previous visit. With Sharp he decided that what they needed most now was a little practice in shooting game, walking a number of miles every day and generally training their bodies for the months ahead. Besides, Grogan still wanted to bag the lion, elephant and rhino he had been thinking of for so long, so they decided 'to have a few months shooting' before going north. Africa was not to be rushed at. Nobody 'did' Africa in two weeks as in today's safaris.

They took a train to Umtali, then hired a wagon and for three days bumped along to Chief Mtambara's kraal near the Sabi river where they heard reports of lion. From there they walked with a few porters collected at the kraal, but the only lion they saw Sharp managed to miss. Shooting lion was somewhat different from partridge. There were plenty of bees though, and their staple diet became honey and rice which they had to eat under a mosquito net.

This was not good enough. Besides, porters were difficult and

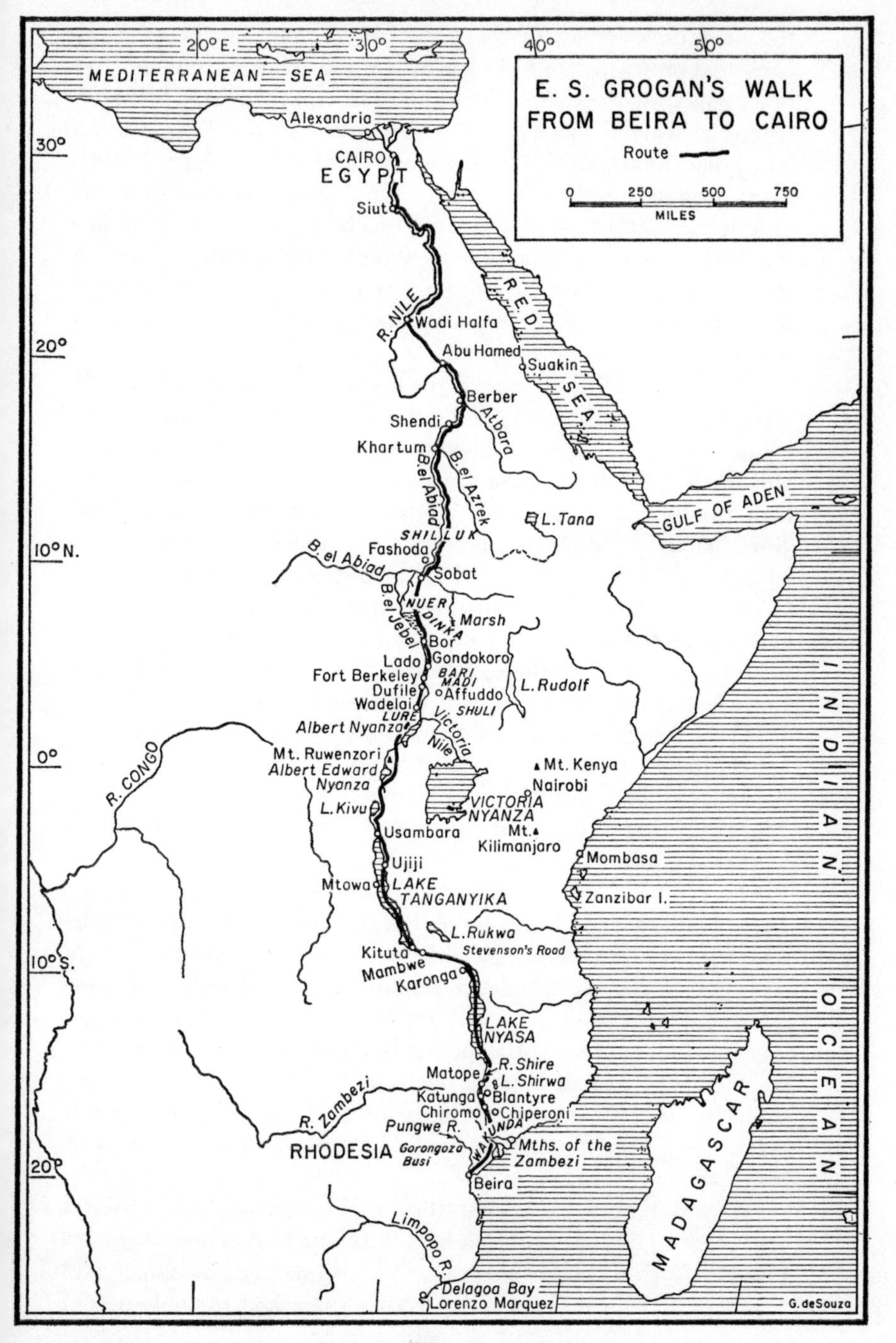
E. S. GROGAN'S WALK
FROM BEIRA TO CAIRO
Route
0
250
500
750
MILES
20° E.
30°
40°
50°
30°
20°
10° N.
0°
10° S.
20°
MEDITERRANEAN SEA
Alexandria
CAIRO
EGYPT
Siut
R. NILE
Wadi Halfa
Abu Hamed
Suakin
RED SEA
Berber
Atbara
Shendi
Khartum
B. el Abiad
B. el Azrek
L. Tana
GULF OF ADEN
SHILLUK
Fashoda
B. el Abiad
Sobat
B. el Jebel
NUER
DINKA
Marsh
Bor
Lado
Gondokoro
Fort Berkeley
BARI
MADI
Dufile
Affuddo
L. Rudolf
Wadelai
SHULI
LURE
Albert Nyanza
Victoria Nile
R. CONGO
Mt. Ruwenzori
Albert Edward Nyanza
Mt. Kenya
Nairobi
VICTORIA NYANZA
L. Kivu
Usambara
Mt. Kilimanjaro
Mombasa
Ujiji
Mtowa
LAKE TANGANYIKA
Zanzibar I.
INDIAN OCEAN
L. Rukwa
Kituta
Stevenson's Road
Mambwe
Karonga
LAKE NYASA
R. Shire
Matope
L. Shirwa
Katunga
Blantyre
R. Zambezi
Chiromo
Chiperoni
Pungwe R.
WAKUNDA
RHODESIA
Gorongoza
Busi
Mths. of the Zambezi
Beira
MADAGASCAR
Limpopo R.
Delagoa Bay
Lorenzo Marquez
G. deSouza

the heat unbearable, so they decided to split up, Sharp to go back to Fontesvilla and Grogan to walk to Umtali, a mere sixty miles which he walked in nineteen hours, and then on to Salisbury where he wanted to visit some old friends. His first bout of fever and a bad foot laid him up for a couple of days. '[Here] I had a great dream,' he wrote in his diary.[3] 'She [Gertrude] came and looked at me and told me to cheer up: so next morning I was all right. This sounds foolish: but on the veldt it is these things that signify: many a man has pulled through for a dream or a chance remark: one settles so quickly into a coma . . .'

Also at Umtali he attended the opening of the latest hotel. 'A typical South African orgy,' he wrote, 'in a long, low, wooden room, plainly furnished with deal tables, packed to overflowing with the most cosmopolitan crowd imaginable, well-bred 'Varsity men rubbing shoulders with animal-faced Boers, leavened with Jews, parasites, bummers, nondescripts, and every type of civilized savage. Faces yellow with fever, faces coppered by the sun, faces roseate with drink, and faces scarred, keen, money-lustful, and stamped with every vice and some of the virtues; a substratum of bluff, business advertisement, pat-in-the-back-kick-you-when-you're-not-looking air permeated everything . . .'

When he joined Sharp at Fontesvilla, Dan Mahony, an acquaintance from his first visit to Beira and an experienced hunter, was invited to join them for their next hunting attempt. Mahony knew the region and all about lions and a lion was first on the list.

On 1 May 1889 they started their march along the Pangwe river, reaching the Urema by night fall, where they camped. The country was not teeming with animals although there were plenty of buffaloes, impala, zebra and eland, but somehow these green hunters didn't get anything for the pot that first evening. The next day was a little better but not much. Grogan got a warthog and a small impala, but a python nearly got him. That was one shot he managed to place perfectly. When Grogan called his porters to carry it back to camp, it took eight men to lift.

He said that the Africans they had as porters and servants were 'quite raw, and rather a trial to the flesh. A request for soap brought forth in succession a bottle of Worcestershire sauce, and a suit of pyjamas'. When the 'cook' was asked to make cocoa for breakfast, he placed two cups filled with water in the fire and served the tin of cocoa. 'If a native is told to do anything,' he wrote, 'and it is within the bounds of his diabolical ingenuity to do it wrong, he will do it wrong; and if he cannot do it wrong, he will not do it right.'

Grogan and Sharp's mode of dressing for their African expedition was unusual even for those days. They both wore Australian slouch hats, boots and socks which were fairly normal attire, but for some unknown reason their trousers only reached just below the knees causing their shins to be continually exposed to thorns, ticks and mosquitoes, let alone porcupine quills.

Lions were heard in the neighbourhood all night and Mahony dropped a beautiful one next day. 'The sight of the old lady's pelt in camp,' Grogan wrote, 'roused me to a frenzy of desire, and for days I haunted that donga and the banks of the Urema, working morning, noon and night, till at last one misty morning I heard the rumbling roar of an old lion, and the sob sob of the chorus. The joy of it! Never had I heard such music; were my wildest dreams of ambition at last to be realised? A lump like cold porridge rose in my throat . . . I hurried forward, and when about a quarter of a mile from the donga sent a boy up a tree to prospect, he soon came down trembling with excitement, and told me that he had seen three skellem [wild beasts] lying under a tree about three hundred yards from where we were. With loving care I loaded the .500 magnum, and crept cautiously in the direction indicated. When I had advanced about one hundred yards, two heads suddenly appeared above the intervening grass, and to my mad joy I dropped them with a right and left; at the same instant I saw a body dash past the scrub on the ant-hill where they had been lying, and popping in another double-barrel, he spun round and came rolling down the slope. A loathsome mangy hyena . . . Then I sat down on that ant-hill and looked at them lying there, my three lionesses in the guise of disgusting grinning hyenas, while the tears coursed slowly down my cheeks . . . and then I swore; rippling, fruity, full-bodied, sonorous . . . till, feeling better I rose and staggered on.'

This was his last disappointment. The area was full of lions as Mahony had predicted and the next day Grogan dropped his first. Although it took more than one shot to bring it down and he had to suffer the jeers of his companions back in camp who had expected him to bring back a cartload by the sound of the shooting, he says: 'Thus ended the unique morning of my life, and my first acquaintance with *Felis Leo*.'

Unfortunately Sharp and Grogan were not satisfied with a few specimens of game. On that trip they killed, not for the pot alone or to collect special trophies but just for the sport of it, and in this age of game preservation, it all sounds shocking.

They moved from area to area and everywhere they found enormous quantities of game. Hyenas seemed to have a particular attraction to Grogan. One night he heard them lapping up the soapy water in his rubber bath and chased them off, but they liked the taste of rubber even better than the soapy water, so they made off with the bath and by the time Grogan recovered it, it was in shreds.

Apart from small game, lions and hippos, they also saw hundreds of buffaloes and for the first time realised that the stories they had heard about buffaloes were not bar-room yarns but very real.

Stalking the herd with Sharp, they both shot at their chosen targets and thought they had been successful, but the buffalo shot by Sharp 'suddenly rose at thirty yards and charged hard, nose in air, foaming with blood, and looking very nasty. I put both barrels in his chest without the slightest effect, and then started for the river, doing level time and shouting to Sharp to do likewise; all the crocodiles in the universe seemed preferable to that incarnation of hell. But Sharp had not yet learnt his buffalo, and waited for him. I heard a shot, and stopped in time to see the beast stagger for a second then come on in irresistible frenzy; but still Sharp stood as though to receive a cavalry charge. Crack rang out the rifle and the great brute came pitching forward on to its nose, and rolled within three yards of Sharp's feet. Now Sharp knows his buffalo and is prepared to do his hundred in 9⅘ seconds.'

The area where they now camped by the Urema watershed was more beautiful than any other they had seen. Park-like and lush, where 'herds and herds of game appeared as though dancing in the mirage, and the whole scene was one to delight the heart of a lover of nature: there indeed one felt one was far from the madding crowd.' There were hundreds of fish and huge crocodiles in the river, leopards and lions and the ubiquitous hyenas who dashed in and out of the camp carrying off all they could, including Grogan's best waterbuck head. Here he bagged his best lion,

9′ 10½″ from tip to tip, and heard the first real lion roar. 'The pukka roar is undescribable,' he wrote. 'It seems to permeate the whole universe, thundering, rumbling, majestic.'

In this area they killed a lioness before they realised she had cubs and there was nothing for it after the shooting but to take the cubs back to camp. 'Five small rolls of fur and ferocity slung on poles. They were great fun in camp, and throve amazingly on cooked liver, of which they devoured huge quantities.' Three of them, one male and two females were sent back to the Regent's Park Zoo in London and for this and later contributions, Grogan was made a Fellow of the Zoological Society.

Charging buffaloes, dead lions who suddenly came to life again and were dropped a few feet away, and a quill shooting porcupine were unusual and frightening, but not as frightening as being caught in a stampede of zebras being rounded up by three lions. With dust that blinded him and terrified zebras whirling around him there was nothing Grogan could do but wait flattened against a tree stump. When eventually the zebras broke and he could make his way back to camp he was greeted by panic there. One of their porters had been bitten by a night adder, one of the most deadly snakes in Africa.

Grogan believed that he could cure everything with permanganate of potash but this time his cure-all did not work. The man was still writhing in agony so Grogan poured a bottle of whisky down his throat, slit his finger and exploded some gunpowder in the cut. To no avail. The next morning the man was still alive, which said something for the gunpowder, but 'his arms, chest and left side swelled to the most appalling proportions.' There was no choice. More whisky was administered, a pot of water and permanganate of potash put on the boil and the man's hand plunged into it. 'His yells were fearful, but the cure was complete, and the following morning, with the exception of the loss of the skin of the hand, he was comparatively well.' To show his gratitude the man made off with all he could conveniently carry. At the end of his book Grogan gives many examples of African ingratitude and he remarks that there is no such thing as gratitude or pity among Africans.

It was time to strike camp and join Sharp who had gone ahead to their original site at Fontesvilla where they had left provisions, trophies and some of their contingent of porters. On arrival Sharp had found that a number of 'Portuguese ruffians' had raided the camp, beaten and imprisoned their porters. When they reported the incident to the British Consul in Beira, he diplomatically told them to make a written report but that, in fact, nothing could be done about it.

The only thing left to do was to pack the remaining trophies for shipment to England and prepare for the real purpose of their trip. 'Though very loath to leave our happy hunting grounds,' he wrote, 'we had to tear ourselves away and made preparations for the long march north.'[4]

Chapter 4

FEVER AND DESERTION

The long march north had to be postponed yet again when they realised that Beira was not the best place to stock up with provisions and buy another .303 'in case of accidents'. Besides they wanted to check their chronometers and the best place for that was Durban's observatory—a mere few weeks away. But at last they were on a boat called the *Peters* destined for Chinde on the Zambezi estuary. All would have gone according to schedule except for the fact that their gear (tents, luggage, food, instruments etc.) had been loaded on a boat at Beira going in the opposite direction to them, Delagoa Bay, 500 miles south of their present position. There was a telegraph line but not many messages came through owing to the white ants eating the posts as fast as they were erected and keeping the line in a state of collapse most of the time.

What to do? Why not hunt and forget the Portuguese and their inefficiency. After all they would be exploring the route they had planned to take to the north, and meanwhile they were assured their loads would be retrieved and sent to them.

The only thing that upset Grogan was a lack of Worcestershire sauce, 'without which,' he said, 'life, or rather native cooking, is intolerable'. They borrowed a tent, bought a few tins of sardines and embarked on a river boat which 'with a minimum of comfort and a maximum of charge' delivered them at Chiromo in Nyasaland where a French company was making whisky from sugar cane, importing labels and bottles from Scotland and employing Scotsmen to supervise the process.

Chiromo was a very primitive place where the day before they landed a lion had carried away an African, but Grogan was very much impressed by the wild beauty of it. The name Chiromo means 'the joining of the streams' which was where the village stood, between two confluents of the Zambezi, the Ruo and the Shire. Years later when he built a house between two streams in Nairobi, he called it 'Chiromo'.

He was also very much impressed by a detachment of Sikhs who had just arrived from India under Lieutenant Godfrey and in his diary Grogan wrote: 'It was splendid to see the contrast between the manners of these magnificent men and those of the locals.'

On the other hand there was always the naive individual who had just arrived to take up some official duty and who wanted to know whether in Chiromo 'it was usual to leave cards on the converted natives and their wives,' Grogan wrote. 'He appeared to be a striking example of the appalling ineptitude of many of the officials chosen for the difficult and serious work they undertake.' The dislike and disapproval he had for the civil servants started then and continued for the rest of his life.

Their loads finally arrived although some equipment was missing. A valuable camera was a particularly heavy loss for them. They were left with one camera to record their journey and discoveries and that was stolen later on. McCormick, who was the illustrator of the book *From the Cape to Cairo*, relied entirely on Grogan's sketches.

They decided to travel by river and lake as far as possible, and the next boat which was to convey them to Blantyre, the *Scott*, was no more than a 'pea in a drum' Grogan said, and when the skipper announced that he could not run the boat because he was ill with fever, Grogan and Sharp took over. There was a Mr Sharpe on board, 'a great shikari', and he advised Grogan on how to shoot an elephant. A lesson he never forgot. According to Mr Sharpe the best way to do it was to let the elephant come to within four yards of himself and then blast in his face. Grogan said the method never missed. In later years he used to say that one of his toes was flat because an elephant had stood on it:[1] the risk of allowing an elephant to come too near before shooting.

The highest navigable point before the rapids was Blantyre,

and here everything had to be carried off the boat and up past the rapids by porters. In the young colony coffee was being cultivated and Grogan said it was obviously going to be 'the greatest industry of British Central Africa, provided that the administration send the right men, and not just any one whom they consider good enough for Africa. No country requires a more delicate adjusted combination of dash, tact and perseverance than Africa,' he wrote.

Blantyre was beginning to flourish and he was amused that 'there was tennis accompanied by a tea-party', but they were anxious to reach Lake Nyasa, so they quickly left the pleasures of the incipient town for the lake which fascinated Grogan because of its 'marsh gas' which was inflammable and a lighted match could produce sheets of flames. Other parts were crystal clear and the coast very beautiful, except for the clouds of kungu flies which the Africans caught and made into cakes. Grogan thought the taste very pleasant. Everywhere they stopped there was evidence of progress in spite of the short time white people had been there. Missionaries were planting pineapples and teaching Africans to operate printing presses and making simple furniture. Some folding chairs Grogan bought from them he carried all the way to Cairo.

It was Christmas 1898 when they arrived at Karonga at the top end of Lake Nyasa and here they would have to engage porters to carry their supplies as far as Lake Tanganyika, and Grogan thought he had better reorganise the loads. The job was not amusing as he found that the firm responsible for the packing in England, 'either as a practical joke or an experiment in the cultivation of fungus, had packed chocolate in paper wrappers and laid them in hay in a leaky wooden box,' he wrote. 'As a practical joke it was weak, but as a venture in fungi-culture a complete success. In fact, unpacking the boxes reminded me of the days when I used to dig for worms in the garden manure-heap.'

Having arranged everything and reduced the loads to a minimum he succumbed to a dose of fever again and spent Christmas day shivering and sweating in turn, and drinking tea on his camp bed.

Porters were now going to be their problem. He visited a number of villages with no success despite his promises of wonderful things to see and experience. He told them they would see Lake Tanganyika, then another great lake, 'mighty mountains that made fire, and then another lake, and still mightier mountains so high that the water became as stones'. He told them that finally they would reach 'water without end' and he would send them back to their homes in steamers as big as villages, and then they could tell their brothers of all the wonderful things they had seen. The villagers were very much impressed. They thought him the best liar they had seen yet. They wanted to know how he knew all these things and he said he had learnt them from books, which didn't impress them in the least, but finally four Watonga agreed to go with him—at least a little way. In fact all four, including a man by the name of Makanjira who claimed to be a chief, stayed with him as far as Cairo and, as promised, he sent them back to Nyasaland by boat, although, much to Grogan's regret one of them, Chacochabo, died on the voyage. The next day, 'a nude dirty little ruffian' who looked like a small boy, and who also reached Cairo with him, presented himself at the camp and demanded to be taken on the wondrous trip, and Grogan wrote: '[He] is now setting up a reputation as a liar on his own account.'

Twelve more recruits enlisted and Grogan handed them over to the local sergeant to be 'drilled', which didn't make much impression on them because they all deserted en masse a few days north of Ujiji.

Before setting out the great chief Mirambo invited him to his camp and Grogan was under the impression that he was an Arab as he wore Arab dress and entertained him 'with true Arab courtesy, and loaded my boys with magnificent pineapples and lemons' when they left. 'It was pitiable to see the poor old man who, a few years ago had commanded thousands, putting on the faded relics of his greatness to do me honour.'[2]

Fever was now to stay with him, on and off, throughout the journey, but unless he collapsed he always continued walking and hunting.

Sharp had gone ahead with some of the loads and although Grogan was still feverish he followed a new type of buck for hours. It had beautiful grey colouring and large eyes and it reminded him of the girl he was doing all this for. He finally shot it and named it 'Thomasina reedbuck (Cervicapra Thomasinae), after a great friend.' Thomasina was his nickname for Gertrude and he always called her that. The buck was later identified as a new species by Dr Slater of the Zoological Society.

At Karonga he was impressed by the men working on the telegraph line to Salisbury. 'Quiet men, rotten with fever. Above their base floated a diminutive Union Jack; no pomp, no fuss, not even a bugle; yet all worked like clockwork.'

It was time to start the 210 mile march to Lake Tanganyika, but fever confined him to bed for several days and he did not start until 24 January 1899. 'To add to the joys of life,' large blood-sucking flies settled on his face and neck without him feeling them and then drove their 'proboscis, like red-hot bodkins, half an inch' into his skin. Heavy rain kept their clothes, their tents and their blankets soaking wet for days, and made it impossible to light a fire. Despite this he kept a watchful eye on the Anglo-German Boundary Commission and wrote reports for the Foreign Office as promised. He reported that contrary to the terms of the agreement the Germans terrorized the Africans who wanted to cross over to British held territory.

The fever which had been with him for the last two months now made him delirious and he had to be carried to a mission station, but as soon as he was able to stand again they marched on. He says he survived on a diet of Worcestershire sauce and limes. They finally arrived at Lake Tanganyika where he had always wanted to go. Everywhere he passed he described the tribes, the land and even the musical instruments, but he grew tired after hours of three-note music. The chief who owned these musicians had had the men blinded to discourage them from going anywhere else. In fact, he observed that mutilation in various forms was widely spread and it was not unusual to see people with their ears, lips and hands cut off. A punishment for women, on the other hand, was the removal of breasts. The people were armed with guns they obtained from the Arabs but their chief industry was 'pombe drinking[3] and the making of bark cloth'. An unusual feature of this tribe, the Awemba, was their use of black cloth for dead relatives. They wrapped a band around their heads whenever one of their relatives died.

Grogan and his porters boarded the *Good News*, a steamer which had been brought to the lake in sections by the first English Mission in 1884 and which was now full of cockroaches as large as mice. Mosquito nets literally collapsed under the weight of these household insects. The captain did not seem to care what happened or even where he was going. He appeared to sleep all the time. One of the porters who had proved particularly inept and was told to go back to his village, was determined to have a free ride on the boat. All went well for him until he decided to throw a crate of chickens overboard to make himself a place to sleep. Grogan did not record what happened to the stowaway.

They were caught in a squall for which Lake Tanganyika is famous and had to put in at a French mission where they were given Algerian wine and an excellent dinner but Grogan remarked how sick the three nuns looked. They also had to put in at M'Towa, on the Congo side of Lake Tanganyika, which was full of Belgians who had fled the rebels west of the lake and were now short of food and arms.

He finally joined up with Sharp after three months. During their trip they often split up in order to cover more territory but when Grogan saw Sharp this time he thought it was the end for his brave companion. At Ujiji Sharp nearly died of fever which like Grogan he had been carrying for months, but again with the help of missionaries he recovered.

Ujiji, Stanley and Livingstone's historical meeting place, was now no more than a few primitive buildings and mango trees. Instead of the rich Arabs who had carried out their profitable slave business there, Greek traders were now prominent and a German station kept the peace. The German commander advised them on the route to take to Kivu and the few remaining Arabs were as hospitable as ever, and when both Grogan and Sharp succumbed to fever again, 'venerable old Arab gentlemen' who had been the masters of the region and were now in very reduced circumstances, sent them fruit, eggs and vegetables. The Germans, on the other hand, plied them with champagne, brandy, beer and vermouth, which did not help with a temperature of a 110°F in the shade and 105°F in the body. The Germans insisted that drink was the best cure for malaria and said that 'no teetotaller had ever left Ujiji for any other part of the world'.

Drink did not work for Grogan who became so ill that he lost control of his hands, but finally with the help of the Germans they collected porters, although they were warned that these were Manyema cannibals, and marched out of Ujiji on 12 April. Of the original sixteen Nyasa contingent two were elected kitchen boys, and four gun bearers and tent-pitchers. Altogether they had 150 men, but Sharp, who had recovered enough to march, could not even carry a gun so painful were his hands from poisoning caused by hundreds of mosquito bites.

They skirted the lake but marching was difficult on the terrain which was muddy in parts and full of shingle in others. Grogan was interested in the local tribe's method of enjoying snuff which they stuffed up their nostrils and kept there by clipping their noses with wooden pegs.

Finally the heat and continual rain, which kept them soaked all the time, made their fevers worse and they were forced to hire two big canoes on which they rigged an awning and placed their two deck chairs on each. In this manner they proceeded for a while down the lake, but at their first stop they discovered that the cook and ten askaris had bolted. Sharp volunteered to take the cook's place but his soup turned out to be a revolting pot of hot water with a blob of fat on top.

Wherever they passed, chiefs dressed in Arab fashion, in long kanzus and white turbans and followed by large retinues, often presented them with pombe, bananas, chickens and sometimes even a goat. Of course, Grogan and Sharp had to give presents of equal value which was determined by the givers, and they always chose cloth and beads. As the Africans did not understand the European love for eggs they often brought them when they already had chicks in them which in their opinion made them a lot more valuable.

Grogan says that while he was ill Sharp became a passable cook under his tuition, but when Sharp was 'reduced to a most pitiable plight' by sun stroke, Grogan had to take over the cooking. In fact, they seemed to take over from each other as nurse and cook continuously as either one or the other was ill all the way to Kivu.

When they arrived at Usambara (the north end of Lake Tanganyika) Grogan was running a temperature of 106.9, but here they were fortunate that there was a well organised German settlement. Even the sick Grogan had to admit that 'Usambara, with characteristic German thoroughness', was flourishing.

The Rusisi river which flows from Lake Kivu to Lake Tanganyika was in front of them. This was now the unknown, 'the first real stage of the task we had set ourselves, and for long it seemed as though I had struggled thus far only to die at the very gate,' Grogan wrote, as he was forced to take to a hammock strung on poles and carried by the twelve extra porters that

Lieutenant von Gravert had found for them at Usambara.

Despite the fever the beauty of the scene fascinated him, 'with its eddying mists and fading hill, redolent of mystery, it seemed a fitting entry to an unknown land.' Fever and desertion seemed to plague them at every step, and now three of the new recruits plus the new cook bolted during the night, taking with them a month's pay and two months' rations which they had been given in advance. They had bought a number of cows at Usambara in order to have fresh milk on their journey but somehow they always had sour milk. The herdsmen insisted that these cows only produced sour milk but when Grogan enquired a little deeper into the mystery, it transpired that the herdsmen drank the fresh milk and procured the sour milk from the villagers.

The caravan did not always march in one long line as the typical pictures of early caravans show, but moved through the land in scattered groups depending on the vagaries of the individual porters, which was a clever ruse to avoid camp duties. The various groups always had good excuses for being late in arriving at camp, but finally Grogan who was against flogging —the usual method of punishment—devised an effective method to discourage future delays. Anybody who arrived late enough to find the tents erected and their food cooked, was made to stand in the middle of the camp, with the loads on their heads until sunset and, as the Africans liked their afternoon naps and visiting the nearby villages 'to show off their clothes to the local beauties', this kind of punishment was enough to discourage them in their tricks for a month at a time, and for an African to remember anything for a month at a time, he said, he must be very impressed.

In turn, he was impressed with the Manyema's ability to 'shoot the rapids like arrows in pursuit of an old billy goat' when the beasts were carried off by the current as they crossed a stream.

At last they entered Ruanda and here a chief by the name Ngenzi presented himself and insisted on accompanying them to Kivu. There was no way of getting rid of him without creating an incident and, as he was followed by one hundred armed warriors, 'not forgetting the inevitable cup-bearer with his gourd of pombe and the regal sucking straw', they agreed to allow the chief to accompany them. Soon they were to regret their decision very bitterly.

Chapter 5

ENCHANTMENT AND CANNIBALS

Suddenly Lake Kivu lay in front of them. 'The mighty sheet of water, dotted with a hundred isles and hemmed in by a thousand imposing hills, was of surpassing beauty,' Grogan wrote.

Speke had heard of it in 1861, and Count von Gotzen had been there on a brief visit in 1894, but nobody had studied it. Now Grogan proposed to fill the many gaps of information Europe wanted about this beautiful lake surrounded by gentle hills, mighty peaks and volcanoes. The hills were covered by miles of banana plantations and vast fields of maize, beans, pumpkins and peas which gave 'a touch of green to the purples, reds and yellows of the luxuriant pastures'. He was so impressed with the prevailing air of prosperity that he thought it was 'a striking indication of the possibilities of native races left to work out their own destinies'. The Arab slavers stayed away from the Ruanda who were considered too fierce to enslave, and now the Belgians maintained only a post manned by the natives with Sudanese officers who relieved the locals of goats, sheep, fowls and anything else they needed for their own use or for trade. When Grogan's caravan arrived the Sudanese immediately sent the Ruanda with goods for barter but they collected the proceeds.

The Ruanda were made up of the proud tall Watusi and their slaves, the small Wahutu who did everything for them. Both excelled at thieving, and Chief Ngenzi and his followers were of the former tribe.

Having been warned by the Manyema of the Ruanda's propensities, Grogan and Sharp placed sentries around their camp that first night and especially around the tent where all their provisions were kept. To no avail. The next morning they discovered that not only valuable supplies had been stolen, but also the sextant, artificial horizon, boiling point thermometers, a bag of 100 sovereigns and even Grogan's tent, whilst he slept under it, together with most of his clothes, books, papers and photographs.

Chief Ngenzi who had followed them for forty miles was summoned and with great dignity he admitted that his people were thieves, but, of course, he knew nothing about the previous night's robbery. If the Europeans' goods had been stolen by his people he would see that they were returned. Within a few minutes, and to prove his willingness to help, he came back with a few socks and shirts saying he had 'found' them. Grogan and Sharp needed no more evidence, they placed the chief in a tent under guard and went off to his village to requisition his cattle which they threatened to turn over to the nearest German post if their property was not returned by midday—which of course it was not.

The Manyema were delighted to see the proud Watusi humiliated. Cattle was everything to a Mtusi but Grogan and Sharp had no intention of travelling more miles to hand over the cattle to the German post, so eventually they had to return the chief and the cattle to his village, and, except for a few books and some trousers, they never saw their belongings again. They did not care so much about the provisions or clothes, but the loss of their scientific gear meant the difference between success and failure—and perhaps, life and death.

Even so, Grogan was full of admiration for the qualities of the Watusi, and especially their understanding of agriculture and animal husbandry. He describes how the Watusi call their cattle by name and are understood, how at milking time they light fires to keep the flies from irritating the cows, and how all their utensils are kept clean by using the cows' urine to disinfect them. He also admired their grace and their looks. 'Tall, slight, nonchalant with delicate features. I noticed many faces that, bleached and set in a white collar, would have been conspicuous for character in a London drawing-room. The legal type was especially pronounced,' he wrote. On the other hand he remarked that the Wahutu were quite the opposite, their character having been stamped out of them. They did all the hard work 'and unquestioning, in abject servility, gave up the proceeds on demand,' despite the fact that there were one hundred Wahutu to one Mtusi. Grogan remarked that the unity of the Watusi, unlike other splintered and warring tribes, was their strength.

Pigmies also brought them food for sale and Grogan thought them 'curious little fellows but immensely powerful'.

It was all fascinating and the exploration of the surrounding mountains and volcanoes very rewarding. He was filling notebooks with valuable information, taking pictures, sketching and drawing maps. Three small mountains at the east of the lake, which he named after his three sisters: Dorothy, Margaret and Hilda, he felt convinced were the true source of the Nile. He named another mountain Mount Sybil, after the daughter of the family who financed him and an inlet of Lake Kivu he named Gertrude Bight. He felt he could have stayed much longer but camp life had become an impossible trial. If the Ruanda did not steal, the Manyema hid loads and then accused the Watusi of stealing and claimed they had been clever enough to retrieve them so they could receive a bonus. The porters soon hooked on to the Ruanda system. They hired porters of their own, and in turn these hired other porters. 'There is nothing new in this world,' Grogan says. But despite the beautiful scenery, 'a lacework of bays, lochs and inlets with endless choppy waves of hills sweeping away to the great purple surf of the distant ranges,' the problems at camp increased.

They received less and less co-operation from the locals who detested the Manyema whose reputation as cannibals had preceded them, and whose ability in stealing almost surpassed that of the Ruanda. 'It would be easier to stop a monkey from scratching than a Manyema from stealing,' Grogan wrote.

Because of the continual complaints from the locals, the culprits were given camp fatigue which did not suit thirty of them and they decided to leave. Tired of all the problems Grogan pursued them with his gun and shot the fez off the ring-leader's head. The thirty were soon back in camp and Makanjira, Grogan's Watonga gun bearer, assured the deserters that Grogan would have killed the ring-leader if he had wanted to. Grogan tried to appeal to their better nature by telling them that it was essential to keep good relations with their hosts in order to buy supplies from them 'and all things that rejoiced the stomachs of men'. This last appeal convulsed them with laughter and all night long Grogan and Sharp could hear the Manyema laughing and joking around the fires. 'From discontent to merry laughter is but a momentary transition with the African,' Grogan learnt early in his dealings with Africans, and he never forgot. Throughout his years in Africa he could always turn a difficult situation into a joke and obtain the co-operation of the African. The Arabs had brought slavery and Swahili to the Congo and other parts of East and Central Africa and Grogan learnt the language during his walk.

The shooting of the fez had settled their internal problems but had not stopped the Ruanda who invariably broke into the camp every night. A particularly persistent thief was finally caught, despite the fact that he had greased himself, and he was handed over to the chief who promptly chopped his head off and placed it on the village path for all to see. This 'definitely settled the thieving question,' Grogan wrote.

Meanwhile they walked hundreds of miles to discover and study the surrounding country and never failed to be dazzled by the 'exquisite scenery', but the day came when they had to move north-west towards the volcanoes where the locals warned them they would find no water. The price they were asked made them decide that the few calabashes they had purchased would have to do and as they climbed higher, they realised they had been made fools of again. There was plenty of water.

As usual they found that mountains and volcanoes had no specific names, or rather dozens of names which differed according to different informers and Grogan decided to name a few more as they explored them. He named an active volcano in the Mfumbiro chain, Mount Sharp. An extinct volcano which reminded him of the Matterhorn and was 13,000 feet high, he named Mount Eyres, after the benefactress who had financed the expedition. One he named Mount Watt after Gertrude Watt and one Mount Chamberlain. But the greatest of the volcanoes he named Mount Götzen after the discoverer of Lake Kivu. It was a populated and well cultivated area but the people were far from friendly. At one point their camp was raided for goats and sheep by the locals and one of their men was wounded; but this did not prevent the chief from coming to trade for salt as if raiding camps was the normal welcome to visitors.

They were warned that to cross the Mfumbiro range, meaning 'the place where there is fire', was certain death and again they were told there was no water and the lava cut people's feet to shreds. They decided that Sharp with the main body of men and provisions should take the longer route around the mountain and Grogan chose six men to explore the volcanoes. He had obtained guides from 'the salt chief' but within hours all but one had disappeared, so Grogan tied the remaining one to himself. There was indeed no water and no one to buy food from. The few pigmies they saw ran away as they approached, and after days of climbing his men were exhausted and hungry. The lava cut through his leather boots and his men's improvised bark sandals. Hunger, thirst and the glare of the sun on the endless lava fields during the day and torrential rain at night, did not produce willing followers despite Grogan's exhortations, and finally he decided to turn back. This did not mean he had given up. Three more times he tried to cross the lava fields and finally succeeded. What greeted him at the other side was not only a pool of water, but a screaming crowd of starved men, women and children who said they were running away from the Bareka, a tribe of cannibals.

He fed the refugees as best he could and then decided to find out the truth for himself. At first he did not believe the refugees but evidence of the unfortunates who had not escaped met him at every step. 'Dried pools of blood, skeletons and grinning skulls.' The scenery was beautiful but he was not to enjoy it for long. Screams of delight in the distance told him that he had been spotted and a 'string of black figures brandishing spears and howling at the expected feast came running down from a neighbouring hill,' Grogan wrote. 'The refugees and the numerous corpses made it obvious that there was something in the wind, but I imagined that it was merely an ordinary case of native fractiousness, some inter-tribal squabble such as occurs every day in these remote corners of the Dark Continent. The diabolical noise made by the onrushing natives decided me that the matter was serious. I questioned my guide as to their intentions, and was scarcely reassured by his naïve remark: "They are coming to eat us".'

The landscape did not offer much protection. He decided to take position behind a clump of grass, and as the Baleka came within comfortable range of his .303 he shot half a dozen of them before they could get over their surprise. This turned the Baleka back and Grogan with his few men went on to the huts from which the cannibals had come. 'A cloud of vultures hovering over the spot gave me an inkling of what I was about to see, but the realization defies description,' he wrote. 'It haunts me in my dreams, at dinner it sits on my leg of mutton, it bubbles in my soup.'

The two Watonga with him, not being cannibals like the Manyema, couldn't eat anything growing in the area for three days, but the Manyema in the party were not choosy. They refrained from eating human flesh in front of Grogan but they enjoyed everything else they found.

'Loathsome, revolting, a hideous nightmare of horrors, and yet I must tell briefly what I saw,' he later wrote. 'A bunch of human entrails drying on a stick. A howling baby. A pot of soup with bright yellow fat. A skeleton with the skin still on lying in the middle of the huts; apparently been dead for about three months. A gnawed thigh-bone with shreds of half-cooked meat attached. A gnawed fore-arm raw. Three packets of small joints, evidently prepared for flight, but forgotten at the last moment. A head with a spoon left sticking in the brain. A hand toasting on a stick. A head, one cheek eaten, the other charred, hair burnt, and scalp cut off at the top of forehead like the peel of an orange; one eye removed, presumably eaten, the other glaring at you. Offal, sewage. A stench that passeth all understanding, and, as a fitting accompaniment, a hovering cloud of crows and scraggy necked vultures.'

As he fled he came across more of the same in burnt out villages. 'Skeletons, skeletons everywhere; and such postures, what tales of horror they told!' He could tell more and worse, he says, and he assures his readers that he has not exaggerated 'one jot, may God be my witness'. He goes on to say that he would not have gone into these revolting details except that he felt the world should know what horrors the people of a peaceful agricultural country had to suffer 'despite stations of the Congo Free State showing on the map but not existing. The whole system of the so-called partition of Africa is bunkum.' He calculated that 3,000 square miles were devastated and depopulated and only two per cent of the population survived the massacre and the ensuing famine.

To escape the cannibals they travelled from sunrise to sunset without stop and at night kept their camp well guarded. Every stream they passed was polluted with rotten carcasses and 'the stench filled the land'. Beautiful land and bloated corpses, 'a terrible combination of heaven and hell. It was a scene that made one wonder if there be a God. Flights of gorgeous butterflies floated here and there, and settled on the gruesome relics.'

He now met a girl and two boys who informed him they were of the Baleka tribe. After much questioning the woman told them where the rest of her party were and suddenly Grogan was 'confronted by half a dozen gentlemen on supper intent'. The unexpected apparition of a white man made them hesitate and Grogan shot one through the heart. He chased the others and found himself in a banana grove where the same ghastly relics faced him, but the rest of the party had escaped.

They kept the Baleka woman and the two boys with them and these informed them that their people were nomads who lived on what and who they found in their path. Grogan says they were mostly naked and he calculated that there were 5,000 in the region he passed through and now he was in a hurry to meet Sharp again and warn him. Everywhere they passed they found terrorised people who could give them only a gourd of water and a few pumpkins. The Baleka were not just satisfied with human flesh, they also destroyed plantations and the people starved.

He was despairing of meeting Sharp again until he met a pigmy: 'A splendid little fellow full of self-confidence' who told him that Sharp together with the rest of the caravan and the animals had gone to camp by the lake. 'These people must have a wonderful code of signs and signals,' he wrote, 'as despite their isolated and nomadic existence they always know exactly what is happening everywhere.' He described the pigmy as being squat, gnarled, proud and easy of carriage. 'The pigmies are splendid examples of the adaptability of nature to her surroundings; the combination of strength and conciseness enabling them to move with astonishing rapidity in the pig-runs that form the only pathways through the impenetrable growth, and endure the fatigue of elephant hunting.'

On re-entering peaceful and rich Bugoie, north of Lake Kivu, he and his men gorged themselves on the first thing they could get which was green bananas, and they were all promptly sick.

It was a wonderful relief to find Sharp in their well organised camp. Despite the difficulties their camps were still neat at this stage. Their two tents stood at the centre with the flag flying proudly from a bamboo pole. Another tent was for valuable stores and the loads were stacked by the tents. The whole camp was ringed by smaller tents for the porters.

Now they felt they had earned the right to enjoy some hunting and, as a great number of elephants were reported in the neighbourhood, they started after them but not with great success. During their hunt they came across a skeleton of a 'gigantic ape' but saw no live ones, although the locals assured them there were plenty in the forest. A group of some thirty men they met puzzled them and they were never able to find out who they were or where they came from. These resembled apes, with hairy bodies, long arms, stooped stance and vacant eyes. They noticed that the locals ordered these ape-men about but their identity was a close secret and after a while they never saw them again.

Chapter 6

ALONE AND MEETING DINKAS

On 26 June 1899 they started their march towards Lake Albert Edward Nyanza, now known simply as Lake Edward. Leaving the relative peace of Lake Kivu was a hard decision to make, but unavoidable. Cairo was still thousands of miles away.

The usual trouble with the thieving Manyema porters plagued them on this leg of the journey as in the past, and to teach one particularly persistent thief a lesson Grogan told him to go back to Ujiji. The man was naturally adamant at the prospect of traversing cannibal and enemy countries, where he would probably be killed. Grogan assured him that if he didn't leave *he* would kill him and to convince him of the seriousness of his intentions he began to shoot over the man's head. Scared out of his wits, the Manyema ran for safety towards the surrounding bush, tripping on tent ropes and loads as he went. Nothing was heard of the frightened Manyema for hours, until next evening when he was seen sneaking back into camp. He never troubled them again.

Elephants were plentiful in the area and as they were running out of fresh meat, Grogan and Sharp decided to hunt, but, except for the three cannibal captives, no one appreciated their efforts. The Manyema said they only ate rhino meat and the locals hippo meat. The Baleka cannibals on the other hand managed to devour ten pounds of elephant meat each and Grogan decided it was time to try what elephant tasted like. His choice of cut was not the best. He boiled part of the trunk for twelve hours and still could not cut through the gristly meat.

In Grogan's opinion the Manyema that night compensated for the lack of meat by eating two of the Baleka captives. The next morning only the blue cloth Grogan had given them to cover their nakedness was found in the bushes. Grogan had given all his porters blue cloth to cover themselves with, but his Watonga were smartly dressed in blue tailored shorts and shirts and red fezes which Grogan had made in Nyasa.

Local fishermen, after receiving presents, informed them that if they continued on the proposed road they were asking for trouble. The neighbouring tribe was raiding everywhere and there was no food to be obtained, so they shot buck and dried the meat over fires whilst Grogan tried to recover his strength after another bout of fever and an infected foot which he treated with the perennial permanganate of potash and 'Elliman's Embrocation'.

He continued with the treatment of his now enormously swollen foot but insisted on walking until they met an armed group of natives who wanted to make blood-brothers. As neither Grogan nor Sharp were keen on the idea, Zowanji, one of the original Watonga who was now a head-man offered to go through the ceremony which entailed holding raw meat in his hands while the natives chanted incantations against all possible enemies. 'May hippo run against him; may leopard tear him by night; may hunger and thirst grip him; may his women be barren; may his children wither; etc., etc.' Two small cuts were then made on each participant by the master of ceremonies and as the blood flowed from the cuts, they smeared the meat they held in their hands with the blood of the other man and ate it. When the ceremony was over the loaded gun between them was fired and Grogan gave them gifts of cloth although he refused to buy the ivory he was offered. He was interested in their new blood-brothers' method of hunting which was done with dogs who chased the game towards the hunters armed with spears.

They now had the kind of fast and faithful friends they did not particularly need or appreciate, but the blood-brothers insisted on following them all round Lake Edward, past burnt out villages and devastated plantations which they said was the work of the cannibals. Grogan's infected foot was now giving him very high temperatures and they decided to cross the upper part of the lake to Katwe by canoe, and at last their newly found friends regretfully said goodbye as they explained that the next tribe were their enemies and they could not go any further.

They were now in Uganda and Grogan was able to carry out a survey which convinced him that the present boundary was a ridiculous conception as the Samliki river would have been the natural boundary and it would not have cut through the possessions of Chief Kaihura, who was now dependent on both the British and the Belgians.

For the first time in many months they slept under a roof at Fort Gerry despite thousands of mosquitoes and armies of rats. They also had the pleasure of tasting fruit again and read English newspapers and books. The porters were equally delighted with the 'civilised' world they had discovered and promptly got drunk on the local pombe, subsequently beating up the Sudanese officers' servants, which in turn elicited a beating for them ordered by the offended Sudanese. Grogan meanwhile, and despite his persistent fever, could not forgo hunting elephant under the Ruwenzori mountains. But to hunt there he had to pay £25 for two elephants which infuriated him because the natives were shooting elephants indiscriminately and without a licence and then, to add insult, he was charged by a herd of elephants who had been stampeded by the local hunters. He shot a small bull and, fortunately for him, the herd turned.

They reached Toro in Uganda and here Sharp finally admitted that he did not have the recuperative powers and stamina of young Grogan. Fever, hardships and lack of proper nourishment had taken their toll on the middle-aged Sharp and, although Grogan felt sad at the loss, he had to let his companion go back to the coast through Kampala taking with him some of the porters and trophies.

Grogan reduced his loads and Sharp promised to send him more supplies to Wadelai. At Toro on 28 August they parted company, Sharp to go back to health and civilisation and Grogan with a few porters and his faithful Watonga to thousands of miles of the unknown.

He skirted the Ruwenzori which he described as a 'mighty bulk, a purple mass, peak piled upon peak, black-streaked with forest, scored by ravines, and ever mounting till her castellated crags shoot their gleaming tips far into the violet heavens. The mists swirl up her thousand gorges, again the storm cloud lowers and broods grumbling round her virgin snows as though jealous of the future, a future of Cook's tours, funicular railways and personally conducted ascents.' He wonders how long before such things will come, how long before 'we shall hear the guttural growl of the Teuton, disputing the guide tariff, and the raucous "'Arry shooting for a tiddley".'

He spent two months studying the Mountains of the Moon, as the Ruwenzori is more popularly known, and eating native kukus (chickens) until he felt that he had a kuku's brain, as a chief brought him his prehistoric gun for 'medical treatment'.

On the Samliki river the locals told him he was mad when he wanted to hire a large canoe for himself and fifteen of his followers. Half way across the seventy yards wide river he realised that the five mile per hour current was not an easy thing to battle against on 'a piece of leaky firewood' in crocodile-infested waters, but he was determined to reach the other side of the river. Here he met the same mixture of people as in Ruanda. 'The sharp, intelligent, almost delicate features of the lithe aristocrats, and the course, squat, ape-like rubble' who totally ignored the most rudimentary coverings for both sexes.

The 'course rubble' meanwhile were busy dismembering an elephant they had chased into the swamp where he was stuck fast in the mud and therefore easily killed. It did not take long for the huge hulk to be reduced to a mere skeleton. The swarm of Balegga, 'stark naked with long greased hair, were inside and outside the carcass, hacking away with knives and spears, yelling, snarling, whooping, wrestling, cursing and munching, covered with blood and entrails; the new arrivals tearing off lumps of meat and swallowing them raw. Great lumps of fat and other delicacies. Old men, young men, prehistoric hags, babies one and all gorging and gorged; pools of blood, strips of hide, vast bones, blocks of meat . . . and in two short hours all was finished. Nothing remained but the gaunt ribs like the skeletons of a shipwreck, and a few disconsolate vultures perched thereon.'

He felt that in two years' time the vast numbers of elephants would be eliminated and he would prefer to see the elephant trained in the Indian way as 'an easy solution to labour problems'. Meanwhile his gun-bearer enjoyed boasting to the locals that his master could kill an elephant with one shot three or four miles away.

To reach Lake Albert they crossed endless miles of ten foot

grass, 'a hopeless tangle of matted whipcord with invisible spines which detach themselves on one's skin and clothes, and set up the most intense irritation', and to add to their frustrations, they kept falling into hidden two-foot holes. Around the lake, elephant, hippo and crocodile were hidden by the bullrushes and were a continual threat. Swarms of mosquitoes 'defied description' even at midday and he ate his meals walking around. At night, despite all precautions to secure the mosquito net, they crawled in by the hundreds, but what distressed Grogan most was the end of his supply of candles. Supplies in general were running low and his boots gave every sign of collapse. He had to hurry on even though chief Katonzi begged him 'with tears in his eyes' to go no further. He said there was no food to be found north of Lake Albert and all the people were dead, and if he died the Belgians would blame him.

As usual Grogan took no notice of warnings but soon discovered that there was indeed trouble west of Lake Albert. The askaris of the Congo Free State were searching for mutineers and rebels and caused panic among the population who fled at their approach. Undeterred, although angry at what was going on in the region, he asked for canoes to cross the lake as he was suffering from fever again and his followers were exhausted.

Suddenly he was greatly excited. He was told a *mzungu* (a European) was coming to bring the canoes. He had his camp made tidy, had the last skinny goat killed and put on a spit and even tried to mend one of his last remaining shirts to receive the visitor. 'Of all the arts and crafts that one is called upon to undertake in Africa,' he wrote, 'such as cooking, shoe-mending, washer womaning, doctoring, butchering, taxiderming, armoury work, carpentering etc., I think perhaps tailoring is the most trying; the cotton will *not* go into the eye of the needle, and the needle will go into one's fingers, and then when you think it is all over, you find you have sewn the back of your shirt to the front, or accomplished something equally unexpected and equally difficult to undo.' Even so, the prospect of meeting a Belgian—he was sure it would be a Belgian in that area—and speaking French again, was so exhilarating that he even brought out a tie to enhance his tattered clothes. The disappointment was great when a small semi-naked man, as black as his brothers, landed on the beach. What gave him the right to be called a *mzungu* was an ancient gun, a Manchester, he carried with great pride.

As in many other areas where Europeans had not been seen before, Grogan was an object of great curiosity, 'especially to the ladies of these communities,' he says, 'who came in large numbers to inspect me (front seats at bath time being in great demand)'. He appreciated the fact that these ladies dressed up for the occasion. They normally only wore a piece of string around their waist, but to visit him they added 'a hopelessly inadequate apron of dried grass.'

When he finally reached Wadelai on 1 October he was delighted to see a white man again. Lieutenant Cape R.A., who had been alone for months, welcomed him, but to Grogan's anxious questions about the provisions Sharp had promised to send there, he replied that nothing had reached Wadelai for months. There was serious drought in the area and even Cape was short of food, but together they did some hunting and replenished their larders. They returned to camp in torrential rain and in time to see their tents and much of their equipment being washed away.

Waiting for his provisions he rested in Cape's camp, but on 22 October he gave up all hope of ever seeing the loads and started down stream with his five Watonga, a small boy from Ujiji and two Warunda. The rest of the Manyema he sent back through Kampala.

With the strong current they made good progress except when an infuriated bull hippo chased them half a mile; or when enormous islands of weeds, driftwood and papyrus brought them to a halt. At Fort Berkeley near the Congo Free State border with Uganda he met more British and Belgian officers and hunted with A. R. Dugmore who later wrote *Camera Adventures in the African Wilds* describing his hunting career.

After months of malaria Grogan was now having trouble with his liver and could not stand up straight but thought activity was the best cure, so he accepted an invitation from Inspector Chaltin to ride on a 'whale-boat' going down the river to look for a steamer carrying Dr Milne, Captain Gage and Commandant Henri who had disappeared four months before. He was glad to leave Fort Berkeley which he described as a 'paradise of malaria, misery and mosquitoes,' and where the askaris in the service of the Belgians ate the local people. He claimed that the askaris who were Manyema, in many cases were 'so vice-sodden from the association with Arabs of the Tippoo Tip fraternity, that it is impossible to make any impression on them.'

When they finally met the survivors of the steamer they were a pitiful sight. For four months they had been bogged down in the sudd. In vain they had tried to cut a channel or drag the steamer over the thick matted vegetation and stinking bogs, all the time sleeping and eating their meagre supplies in the water with crocodiles all about them. They would have died if not rescued then. Dr Milne and Commandant Henri later in Kenya and in the Congo became two of his best friends.

During this time one of his Ruanda men died and the once large caravan was reduced to a miserable seven. He was fortunately able to engage five Sierra Leone men who were in the service of the whale-boat captain and he decided to spend Christmas with his new friends. However, on 30 December he started a 300 mile walk which proved to be the most trying of all. Again he did not believe the reports of what was in front of him. The only precautions he took were to lighten his loads again, disposing of his camp bed and other 'luxuries', but he was angry when he discovered that one of his men, whom he described as a lunatic, disappeared with one of his two remaining shirts. In front of him there were swamps, waterless desert and famine and suddenly an enormous depression fell on him and he wished himself 'quit of Africa and all its abominations'.

He had no choice but to continue, and although he had seen Dinkas in the distance from the whale-boat, 'grey spectres' covered in wood-ash to prevent mosquitoes settling on them, he was not prepared for the giants he now met at close quarters. The majority averaged 6′ 5″ in height and were of the most unfriendly nature. He asked them for a guide but as he had no trade cloth left, they refused and asked him to shoot an elephant for them. This was easier said than done through swamps full of holes and slime. Finally he induced one man to show him the road to the next village by giving him a Victoria Jubilee medal and some beads. The last of the Ruanda died before they reached the next village and Grogan camped where mosquitoes 'defied description and I was literally sucked dry', he says. He piled his possessions around the mosquito net, burnt green wood and smoked native tobacco in an effort to discourage the mosquitoes, but mostly he prayed for morning. 'I used to turn out in the morning feeling perfectly dazed from the amount of poison that had been injected during the night,' he wrote, but he did not feel he could follow the local custom of smearing everything in cow dung and himself with ash and cow's urine.

The only thing was to move as quickly as possible but they had just broken camp when they were faced by an elephant. Boxes, pots and pans were dropped all around him and his porters disappeared leaving him to face the elephant with only soft bullets in his .303. Luckily the elephant turned at the first shot, because most of his ammunition was by then eaten through with rust.

At the next stop life did not appear to be any easier. They were faced by a horde of Dinkas brandishing spears and yelling words he could not understand, so he took the only action he could. Smiling and slapping the huge Dinkas on the back he kept repeating 'Aram', which was the only word he knew in their language, and with much 'grunting and clucking' he finally calmed them and even obtained some fish and milk from them. He says they were magnificent specimens, completely naked except for ivory bracelets and marabout feathers in their hair. To him they looked like water birds who walked like herons 'picking their feet very high and thrusting them well forward. The adaptability of a race to its surrounding is wonderful. The favourite pose of a Dinka is in reality the favourite pose of a water bird,' he wrote.

Having made friends, the Dinkas now followed him around everywhere and although he was flattered by their attention, their continual chanting under the merciless sun 'hardly acted as a sedative' on his fever. Even during the night they chanted outside his camp and some old hags 'danced a wild fandango uttering the shrillest cries conceivable, their loose breasts flapping about wildly'.

The land was flat sun-baked clay, thorn and palm scrub and most of the people in that region found him 'a great joke, but on the whole, not such a bad sort of fool', although not fool enough to distribute his few remaining possessions among them, which they quite expected him to do. One of the tallest men in the group wanted his last pair of trousers and when Grogan refused he screamed like a child and rushed into the tent brandishing a club over Grogan's head. There was nothing much on that naked body he could lay hands on, but somehow he took him by the scruff of the neck and 'the seat where he wished my trousers to be' and ran him out of camp. The others took it as a huge joke and the following day the offended party followed the small caravan in the most friendly fashion.

The plains in front of them shimmered in the heat, bare and without the relief of the smallest bush, the only possible camping site they offered being a small channel which he named the Gertrude Nile.

Grogan wrote a story for children then, but very adult children, which was meant to be the first of a series. Whether he actually wrote any others is not certain as 'The Marabout Stork on the Gertrude Nile' is the only one remaining in the possession of his daughters. He sub-titled it, 'The clownish inquisitive philosopher of the marsh' and, as he says in the introduction, it was written 'during many months of lonely wandering in the vast African wilderness, where I have lived in close touch with the denizens of the forest and the swamp. Day after day, when the morning's work was done, I have crept off alone into bush or reeds to seek respite from the chatter of my carriers. The elephant has come and waved his great ears at me and heeded me not, the marabout has stalked round me in grotesque caricature of some deep thinking don . . . So I turned from my dusky comrades and my heart went out to the great silent elephant, the stately giraffe, the peaceful hippo, the foul-feeding marabout, the sad grand lion, the dyspeptic rhino and all the million forms of African life. I contrasted the staid well ordered sequence of their lives with the wild turmoil of this distorted life of ours. I felt and thought with them; I yearned to draw inspiration from their grand philosophy and climb to the thoughts of beasts . . . I know the brutes do feel, because we, without ceaseless jabber, are unable to express our little weak sensations is no argument that brutes have none.'

Like many a keen hunter before and after him, the killing eventually troubled his conscience, and he says: 'Many beasts have I slain for necessary food or excitement of the chase, yet more often have I stayed my hand.'

In the style of Aesop's fables, 'The Marabout Stork' is a talking animal and a very wise one, who understands his fellow animals and the secret of survival against so many odds, enemies and competitors, one of which, the vulture, he has to outwit for every morsel. Through the eyes and words of the stork Grogan describes the clever manoeuvres he employs to get his share of a hippo which has been killed by men. Mr Marabout's simple explanation for his success are his patience and self-assurance, because he never panics like the vulture, or other foolish animals.

It cannot be said to be a charming story, but then there is nothing charming about death in the wilds, but it is certainly clever and full of understanding for the harsh realities of survival.

Sitting by the banks of the Gertrude Nile, writing his animal story, he had no conception of how near death he would be within the next few days.

Chapter 7

FIGHTING FOR SURVIVAL AND THE END OF THE WALK

The plain north of Bor seemed empty at first sight but suddenly Grogan realised that there were thousands of Dinkas on the horizon marching in single file and that he was being observed by lookouts who stood perfectly still on one leg with the other foot resting on the opposite knee. He thought the best thing would be to stop and camp and let the Dinkas satisfy their curiosity—if that was all their interest in him amounted to.

It was obviously not entirely curiosity. Over a thousand occupied his camp the first day and fingered everything as if to determine what was worth taking. The next day they returned with reinforcements and started helping themselves to the loads, at which point Grogan decided to give a few 'some rough treatment'. He hit one and cut his hand on his teeth. When another Dinka attacked one of his men with a spear, Grogan broke the spear and hit him with his hippo-hide whip. At this they became very excited but two older men who seemed to be in charge pacified the young warriors and led them out of the camp, except for a hundred or so who were the worst trouble makers. Grogan kept his hand on his revolver but this only seemed to amuse them, so he shot a marabout to show them what the weapon could do and they raced off.

He thought he had better move as fast as possible but he received the same treatment at the next village and when he moved from there, he knew there was no avoiding trouble. One hundred odd Dinkas followed them and gradually a group of twenty surrounded him, and the others cut his men off from each other.

His men were panic stricken and throwing their loads down they ran to him shouting, 'We are all lost.' One of them was immediately speared through the heart and two more had their skulls cracked. Grogan did not hesitate any longer. He shot the Dinka who appeared to be in charge and two more by his side and just in time he dodged a spear hurled at him. Surrounded as he was by over a hundred Dinkas it was difficult to avoid all blows and he caught a shattering one on his arm as he tried to protect his head from a heavy club. In turn he thrust his now empty gun in his assailant's stomach. Only in Beau Geste-type films has the hero a loaded gun in his hands all the time, but in real life Grogan could only defend himself using his gun as a club. Fortunately for him the Dinkas must have been surprised at the sudden death of their leaders and they retreated to an ant hill. Africans who had never seen the effect of a gun before always expected the person who was hit to come back to life if the wound did not appear to be a fatal one as from a good thrust of a spear.[1] This gave Grogan a chance to reload his gun and as the Dinkas moved towards him again he shot another. At this they scattered in all directions.

'It was all over in a shorter time than it takes to tell the tale,' Grogan wrote. 'But while it lasted it was fairly warm. I never expected to see my home again, nor did I feel much happier when I had time to look round. I was alone. At my feet lay my Congo askari in the last spasmodic shudder of death; a few yards away lay three more of my men, streams of blood slowly trickling from gaping wounds in their heads. The distorted figures of the three Dinkas, shot at close quarters, were the only other breaks in the dismal monotony of the marsh.'

He shouted and slowly his men appeared from patches of reed and bog-holes. The wounded men came to 'and were quite mad for days after'. He patched them up as best he could and threw away more loads, but they hurried on for fear the Dinkas would come back. News of the gun spread like wildfire and as they approached other villages they were left alone, but he could get no food anyhere, except occasionally urine tasting milk. They survived on muddy fish caught in the marsh and a strange tasting cheese of his own manufacture. The revolting diet produced hours of violent vomiting, the arm which had been hit in the fight throbbed and the mosquitoes never let up. Oddly enough Grogan never suffered from dysentery which plagued all white men in the early days, at least he never mentions it, but his cook now suffered from it. The wounded were delirious under the merciless sun and another had an infected foot, but they struck out through the dusty plains, away from the marshes, to avoid meeting more Dinkas. They had no wood to cook the little food left and no drinking water. 'Our sufferings were intolerable,' Grogan wrote. They had been drinking brackish marsh water for days, but even this was now finished. Half his men collapsed and refused to go any further and Grogan knew that if he did not find water soon, they were lost.

He was beginning to despair of saving the men when climbing up an ant hill he saw a flight of birds, and after an hour's sharp walk, he arrived at a shallow pool of water which was less salty than he had tasted for many a day.

They could march again but left one of the last remaining loads and finally Dinka country was behind them.

In the Nuer the people were of similar features and physique as their neighbours. Very tall, fine featured, naked and wearing strings of cowrie shell around their high bushy hair, but fortunately not of a bellicose nature—or so they appeared—although one of his last remaining Congolese disappeared one night when they were camped near a Nuer village. They looked for him for hours but never saw him again.

There were thousands of birds everywhere and they were now even glad of an old marabout in their diet. There was no other choice. Too exhausted to even try to shoot birds, Grogan listened to a lion who passed through their small camp at night and treated him 'to a farewell roar'.

He did not know then that it was a farewell roar, but the next day his troubles were over. As they wearily plodded along, Grogan wondering if they could reach Sobat which he estimated to be four days march ahead, he suddenly saw in the far distance a curved pole swaying in the wind. For some time it puzzled him, and then he realised that it must be the mast of a boat, but dared not believe it, though certain that no palm tree could swing at that angle. He rushed ahead of his worn out men and saw figures in uniform moving about. Then he was spotted and a Sudanese soldier came towards him inserting a cartridge in his rifle as he approached. Throwing his own gun on his left shoulder, Grogan moved towards the man with a smile and an outstretched hand. The relief was enormous as the Sudanese unloaded his gun and 'with a 3′ 6″ grin shook the proffered hand with vigour'. He learned that Captain Dunn, Royal Army Medical Corps was away shooting but was expected back in camp in a few minutes.

'I could scarcely believe that it was all over, that my troubles were ended!' he wrote. 'Those four days, that I imagined still remained, had been a nightmare to me. All my men were sick; the majority of them had to be pushed along at the point of a spear, to prevent them from lying down and giving up the struggle. There were no more hippo and very little game: all our grain had long been exhausted. Only two pipefuls of sour tobacco remained. And then, at a sudden bend in the river, all this nightmare was dispelled. It was over! From being so long without vegetables, my hands had begun to turn black, and the continual anxiety of the last month, day and night, had told its tale on my nerves.' The relief of sitting down waiting for Captain Dunn 'would be impossible to describe'.

He did not have long to wait. A few minutes later Captain Dunn emerged from the bush and a Stanley-Livingstone-type meeting ensued. Grogan says that the British phlegm immediately asserted itself and he relates the meeting as follows.

Captain Dunn: 'How do you do?'

Grogan: 'Oh, very fit, thanks. How are you? Had any sport?'

Dunn: 'Oh, pretty fair, but there is nothing much here. Have a drink. You must be hungry; I'll hurry on lunch. Had any shooting? Seen any elephants?'

They then washed, lunched, discussed world affairs, and eventually Dunn asked where the devil he had come from. 'All this six hundred miles from anywhere, in the uttermost end of the earth—the Nile swamps. Verily we are strange people,' Grogan surmised.

With Dunn he proceeded down stream from Sobat in a small sailing boat, and he writes: 'In the course of a chequered career I have seen unwholesome spots; but for a God-forsaken, dry-sucked, fly blown wilderness, commend me to the Upper Nile; a desolation of desolations, an infernal region, a howling waste of weed, mosquitoes, flies, and fever, backed by a groaning waste of thorn and stones—waterless and waterlogged. I have passed through it, and have no fear for the hereafter.'

Waking up in the small sailing boat the next morning, he still could not believe his luck. He expected reality to fade like a dream and to find himself still plodding through swamps. 'The transition from ceaseless anxiety and hungry misery,' he says, 'to full-bellied content and tobacco-soothed repose had been so sudden; I was as a man who, after a long time staggering in the dark, is suddenly thrust into the full glare of sunlight, and could hardly grasp that it was at last all over. Nothing to do but sit and be carried along towards clean shirts, collars, friends, all that makes life a thing of joy. How many people realize what all these things mean? How many people have ever caught the exquisite flavour of bread and butter? the restful luxury of clean linen? the hiss of Schweppes? One must munch hippo meat alone, save one's sole shirt from contact with water as from a pestilence lest it fall to pieces, and drink brackish mud for days, to realise all this.'

They reached Fashoda on the west bank of the Nile, which had been secured for the Egyptian Government by General Kitchener only the year before despite Colonel Marchand's efforts on behalf of the French Government to bring it within their sphere of influence. When Grogan arrived he was introduced to the Governor, Captain William Hayes-Sadler, who was in command of the gunboat cutting the sudd.

At Fashoda he was able to mail letters again. The last time he had sent letters to Gertrude and his brothers and sisters, was through Sharp when they parted at Toro, but he had heard nothing from anybody for eighteen months. Now he found a package of letters waiting for him and he was happy once again to know that Gertrude was still waiting for him.

Captain Dunn had brought him up to date with world news including the outbreak of war in South Africa, and now in the letters from home he read of the death of many friends in that war, but one in particular upset him more than all the others. He learned that his best Winchester friend, Jack Taylor, with whom he had spent many happy holidays in his house at Torquay, had been killed.

Captain Hayes-Sadler offered to take him to Khartoum and he gratefully accepted. To reach Khartoum they passed by sudd which was thirty feet thick in places and sufficiently solid for elephants to walk over it. It was cut in blocks to allow it to float away and wherever it was cut fish swarmed. They met the steamer carrying Captain Gage, Dr Milne and Commandant Henri, who were still clearing the river between Khartoum and Uganda, and at Omdurman he was given a dinner where all the British and Egyptian officers were invited to meet the 'tourist' from the south.

Khartoum had been re-occupied by General Kitchener in September 1898 after he defeated the dervishes and killed the khalifa Abdullah, and Grogan was very impressed by the 'great Kitchener' when he was introduced to him. When he arrived the whole army was in a state of panic, he says,[2] as a visit by the Duke of Connaught was expected and Kitchener had refused to pass any expenditure for decorations. Pressed to give permission for such an expenditure, he asked: 'Have we any Greeks in jail?' The reply being in the affirmative, he sent for them all and asked: 'Do you want to be hanged? No? Then decorate Khartoum.'

Grogan went by railway to Wadi Halfa, then by steamer to Assuan and again by railway to 'the roar of multitudes at the station in Cairo'. It was February 1900. When they first saw a train from a distance his Watonga thought it was a huge snake and were frightened by it.

He still felt somewhat 'bedraggled' when he was sent for by Lord Cromer, the British Consul General in Egypt. Lord Cromer asked him to comment on the feasibility of a vast scheme, 'which had been designed *in vacuo*, for the control of the great swamp which is about the same size and shape as England and through which I had just wended my way. I pointed out that it would cost a lot of money, as it involved building a dam on a swamp area of unknown and certainly great depth at least twenty miles long and one hundred miles away from the nearest pebble. The prospect lapsed,' Grogan wrote in 1957[2], 'but its purpose has now been revived by a scheme, which (without recognition) is based on the principle that I suggested on page 331 of my book *From the Cape to Cairo*, published in 1900.'

'And now it was all over,' he wrote.[3] 'A few dangers avoided, a few difficulties overcome, many disappointments, many discomforts, and those glorious days of my life are already dim in the haze of the past. Here I stand, in the prosaic land of certainty and respectability.'

Despite all he had gone through, there is a note of regret in the thought that life would never be as adventurous as he had experienced for the past two years.

In the last chapters of his book *From the Cape to Cairo* he lists his recommendations for the telegraph line and the railway line which, in his opinion, were the only hope for the development of the backward countries he had passed through.

He gives a whole chapter to the 'Native Question' and on page 360 he talks about compulsory labour, which has been quoted and misquoted out of context by almost every writer who has ever mentioned Grogan, and used by his detractors as Grogan's opinion of the Africans *throughout* his life with complete disregard for the fact that what he wrote in 1900 applied to the most backward countries in a time when civilisation was a meaningless word in Africa. The fact that he was to become one of the fairest employers Africa has ever known, carried no weight with the anti-Grogan faction.

The following is the controversial piece of writing from his book: 'A good sound system of compulsory labour would do more to raise the nigger in five years than all the millions that have been sunk in missionary efforts for the last fifty; but at the very sound of "compulsory labour", the whole of the stay-at-home England stops its ears, and yells "slavery"! and not knowing what "slavery" is, yells "slavery" again, nor ever looks at home nor realizes that we are all slaves. Have we not compulsory education, taxes, poor-rates, compulsory this and compulsory that, with "jail" as the alternative? nor are we paid by the State for being educated. Then let the native be compelled to work so many months in the year at a fixed and reasonable rate, and call it compulsory education, as we call our weekly bonnet parades church. Under such a title, surely the most delicate British conscience may be at rest. Thereby the native will be morally and physically improved; he will acquire tastes and wants which will increase the trade of the country; he will learn to know the white man and his ways, and will, by providing a plentiful and cheap supply of labour, counterbalance the physical disadvantages under which the greater part of Africa labours, and thus ensure the future prosperity of the land, whereby, with the attendant security of tenure and of the rights of the individual, he will have that chance of progressive evolution which centuries of strife and bloodshed have denied him. Inducements might be offered to chiefs to make plantations of wheat, rice, coffee, and other suitable products, by exempting a number of their men, proportionate to the area cultivated, from the annual educational course.'

He goes on to say that the Administration should be made the sole labour agent so that 'the rate of pay can be fixed and maintained at a rational level. Undesirable people can be prevented from obtaining labour, and the native is protected against the employer, and guaranteed proper treatment by knowing that he has a court of appeal where he can obtain information and air his grievances.'

He also advocated 'to rule through the chiefs, and refrain from injuring their prestige'. But only the traditional and rightful chiefs, and he goes as far as saying that 'their prestige should be maintained in every way possible, such as exempting them from hut-tax, allowing them a small armed escort etc.'

Finally, he maintains that 'by strict justice, the inculcation of competition, and above all by work, he [the African] can undoubtedly be assisted to progress, but the means to be employed are not those of the missionary.' He had obviously no great opinion of the missionaries.

In Cairo he showed his Watonga the sights and then as promised he made arrangements for them to sail back to Nyasaland. He says that his men believed him to be some sort of magician for making what he told them two years before in Nyasaland come true. The mountains, the lakes, volcanoes, snow and ice and now Cairo, but they simply explained it as a wizard's trick to make these things appear before their eyes. 'You have put them there,' they said.

It was now truly the end of his adventure and, suddenly alone, he felt strange regrets and sadness, but Gertrude was waiting in London, and, after an exchange of telegrams assuring each other of their unchanged feelings, he quickly booked his passage and once again thought he would never see Africa again.

Chapter 8

MARRIAGE AND THE AMERICAS

Gertrude had been waiting for his return at her aunt, Mrs Eyres' large house near Marble Arch overlooking the park, then a most fashionable part of London, and now she was completely happy to be in Ewart's arms again. Her step-father, Mr Coleman, had continued fighting the marriage right up to the last minute, but although Gertrude was of a sweet and obedient nature, she was also very determined, and nothing her step-father could say had any bearing on her decision to marry Ewart. She must have had her mother's support in the matter or she would have not been allowed to leave New Zealand alone in those Victorian days to wait for Grogan in London.

Grogan introduced her to his family and friends and from the first moment they loved her. For the rest of her life Gertrude had that special quality which aroused love in anybody who came into contact with her. She carried herself well and had a pleasant voice, but most of all she had the kind of gentle expression, grace and charm which attracted people immediately. Gertrude radiated warmth, although she was basically a shy person, and Grogan loved her qualities.[1]

Soon word of his achievement spread around London's society and he found himself lionised by hostesses he had never heard of before. This was something he did not enjoy, but he did enjoy being invited to speak at his old school, Boxgrove in Guildford, and at meetings especially organised to hear him talk of his experiences. The most important one was, of course, the speech he gave at the Royal Geographical Society,[2] which was attended by the King of Sweden and presided over by Sir Clements Markham, the man who had inspired Captain Scott to explore the South Pole.[3]

That year's issue of the Encyclopaedia Britannica, under 'Africa—Expeditions' gave his achievement five lines and it has not changed since. He is still listed as the only man who walked the length of Africa.

All this was very exciting, and Gertrude's love all enveloping, but the most important thing for him now was to write a book from the many notes he and Sharp (now safely back in England) had kept during the walk, besides drawing maps and making his reports for the Foreign Office. The degree of accuracy and detail surprised the civil servants, but as for his recommendations for improvements and developments, 'they ended up where all civil servants' memoranda go. Into files—files which only silver fish refer to,' he said.[4]

His book was going well, despite the many interruptions, but he was in a great hurry to finish it. He had decided that the South African War was too important to ignore while he stayed at home writing books, giving lectures and getting married. The British in South Africa needed men of experience like him to defeat the Boers and he was determined to join up again. Having delivered his manuscript to his publishers, Hurst and Blackett Ltd., at 13, Great Marlborough Street in London, with the hundreds of photographs, maps and his own drawings from which A. D. McCormick made the illustrations, he received news from the War Office that his application had been accepted. On 27 April 1900 he received his commission as captain in the 4th Battalion of the Royal Munster Fusiliers, a Militia unit stationed at Gosport in Hampshire where it was being trained and waiting to embark for South Africa.[5]

This did not prevent Grogan giving his lecture at the Royal Geographical Society on 30 April, nor meeting the great explorer Henry Morton Stanley, whose writings he had admired so much in his early youth, and who had been such a great inspiration during his own explorations. Now the great man invited the young explorer to go and visit him, and the disappointment was considerable. 'He was a pathetic-looking little figure like a wizened parrot, and a tear trickled down his cheek as he told me how he had failed to persuade Britain to take over the Congo,' Grogan wrote many years later.[6] Stanley was only fifty-nine then and he died four years later at sixty-three. African exploration killed them young in those days—except for Grogan.

Another important meeting was with Queen Victoria, a few months before her death. The old Queen asked many questions about the countries he had passed through, but she did not seem to connect Ewart Scott Grogan with his father William Grogan who had been her Surveyor General and with whom she had a little misunderstanding when Ewart was born. Her memory was probably not very good in the last months of her life. Grogan told her he had carried a flag throughout the walk hoping she would accept it when he came back, and he asked her permission to present it to her. She said she would be happy to have it and when she received it, her secretary wrote to him from Balmoral Castle by hand: 'The Queen desires me to thank you for your kind thought in presenting to Her the Union Jack which you carried on your remarkable journey from the Cape to Cairo. Her Majesty is glad to possess so interesting a memento of your famous journey; a journey which, the Queen understands, no other traveller has hitherto succeeded in accomplishing.

'I am desired to forward for your acceptance the accompanying signed photograph of the Queen as a present from Her Majesty.

'I am Sir, Yours very truly, F. M. Ponsonby.'[7]

It is said that Grogan then sent the Queen one of his own signed photographs, but although this is rather typical of Grogan's lack of humility, it is not confirmed and an acknowledgment from the Queen does not exist.[8]

More important for Grogan than meeting the Queen was his second meeting with Cecil Rhodes, the man whose vision of a British Africa from the Cape to Cairo, had inspired him. 'Lord Grey, who was in the Chartered Company's office,' Grogan wrote many years later,[9] 'told me that "the Old Man" would like to have one of the flags which I had, in accordance with the custom of those days, carried through Africa. A luncheon ceremony, to be presided over by the Duke of Abercorn as chairman of the Chartered Company, with sundry other V.I.Ps., was arranged for the passing of the flag. I was asked to come early, as Rhodes wanted to have a talk with me. On arrival I found Lord Grey in a state of fluster because Rhodes had started lunch on his own. Grey took me in and said: "Here's Grogan with his flag"—which was wrapped in a brown paper parcel. Rhodes was munching cold meat. He turned and said in his high falsetto: "Thanks; very pleased to have this flag," stuffed the parcel in a voluminous tail pocket of his gamekeeper's coat, got up, and bolted down the stairs. I followed, leaving Grey gaping. History has not recorded what happened to the luncheon party. Later (he) asked me to promise to devote my life to the development of British interests in Africa.'

Rhodes hated crowds and social functions, but now alone with Grogan, he relaxed and they spoke at length of the future of Africa, the telegraph and the railway line.

Throughout his life Grogan spoke of his meeting with Rhodes many times. 'Give yourself to Africa, you will never regret it,' Rhodes said to him. 'But for Rhodes I would have been one of those aimless young men who walk up and down Piccadilly, worrying about their ties,' Grogan wrote. 'Give yourself to Africa' was the advice he passed on to every would-be settler, and which he followed to the full himself.[10]

Later Rhodes wrote a very long hand-written letter which became the introduction to Grogan's book when it was published in September 1900. Rhodes wrote that 'literary composition' was not one of his gifts as his correspondence was carried on by telegram. But to Grogan he wrote: 'I must say I envy you, for you have done that which has been for centuries the ambition of every explorer, namely, to walk through Africa from South to North. The amusement of the whole thing is that a youth from Cambridge during his vacation[11] should have succeeded in doing that which the ponderous explorers of the world have failed to accomplish. There is a distinct humour in the whole thing. It makes me the more certain that we shall complete the telegraph and the railway, for surely I am not going to be beaten by the legs of a Cambridge undergraduate.

'Your success the more confirms one's belief. The schemes described by Sir William Harcourt as "wild cat" you have proved are capable of being completed, even in that excellent gentleman's lifetime.

'As to the commercial aspect, every one supposes that the railway is being built with the only object that a human being may be able to get in at Cairo and get out at Cape Town.

'This is, of course, ridiculous. The object is to cut Africa through the centre, and the railway will pick up trade all along the route. The junctions to the East and West coasts, which will occur in the future, will be outlets for the traffic obtained along the route of the line as it passes through the centre of Africa. At any rate, up to Bulawayo, where I am now, it has been a payable undertaking, and I still think it will continue to be so as we advance into the far interior. We propose now to go and cross the Zambezi just below the Victoria Falls. I should like to have the spray of the water over the carriages.

'I can but finish by again congratulating you, and by saying that your success has given me great encouragement in the work that I have still to accomplish.'[12]

Unhappily for Africa, Rhodes' railway was never completed and the telegraph line stopped at Ujiji in 1911 for lack of funds. With Rhodes' untimely death in 1902 at the age of forty-nine, the impulse behind these schemes died with him despite the fact that he left his fortune to public service and founded scholarships at Oxford for the value of £300 a year for each colonial or American student who won the scholarship.

Grogan was supposed to be in the army but as his fame spread he was always in demand and among others *The Times* asked him to write his opinion on big game in Africa for them.

'With regard to the difficulties to be overcome at the conference for the protection of the big game of Africa now being held at the Foreign Office,' he wrote,[13] 'I consider that an insuperable difficulty lies in the fact that the Latin races and latinized races have no conception of the "sporting idea" so dear to the average Briton.' He quotes an instance when in the Congo Free State he was introduced to an elephant hunter who boasted of having shot fourteen elephants. On further inquiry Grogan discovered that they were fourteen small cow elephants which he had killed in one morning with the aid of sixty soldiers. Another man, 'brimming over with the milk of human kindness,' invited him to shoot and assured him that in one morning they would bag at least twenty hippos. 'I myself saw natives provided with guns and sent out to slaughter game, and, as a result, many antelope with young were brought into the station.' In the article he strongly advocates that every hunter should 'give an honourable record of slain and wounded', but he says it would be impossible to limit the shooting to a certain number 'owing to the exigencies of African travel. Had I been limited during my late journey I should have starved.'

He followed this up with a letter to *The Times* on 7 May suggesting that there should be a hunting season in Africa as in Europe to protect the animals.

For the first contribution he received the rich sum of £10 from *The Times*, which in those days was quite sizeable.[14]

At a dinner in his honour in London he met again a German he greatly admired, Herman von Wissman. They had first met on the Northern Rhodesian border during Grogan's walk and Grogan considered him 'a prime mover in the establishment of German East Africa.' Now Wissman was in London as the German representative at a game preservation conference and he said to Grogan: 'I cannot understand your people. You have a virtual monopoly of the big game specialists of the world and yet you send as your representative a young gentleman who has *once* been on a diplomatic mission to Zanzibar. His contribution to the debate is that we should concentrate on the protection of hyenas because they pull down the old males and thus help in the improvement of the breed.'

'Many and varied are the functions of bureacracy,' Grogan replied. He always enjoyed a story against government ineptitude and bureaucracy.[15]

If the government disappointed him, the army did not seem to come up to expectations either. It was now almost six months since he had enlisted and his battalion was still waiting for orders to embark for South Africa. This was enough for Grogan. He submitted his resignation and his army career officially ended on 18 October. Meanwhile, his younger brother Philip had gone and come back from South Africa. He was in the South Wales Borderers, and like so many others, he contracted enteric fever and was invalided home.[16]

At least one person must have been relieved about Grogan's decision to resign from the army. Gertrude had patiently waited to fix a date for their wedding and meanwhile prepared the large trousseau which was customary in those days, and on 11 October 1900 they were finally married at Christchurch, Lancaster Gate in London. His best man was Captain William Hayes-Sadler, who had taken him from Fashoda to Khartoum after his walk. Apparently it was a 'big' wedding with hundreds of guests but unfortunately no records or photographs of it remain.[17]

Their honeymoon started in Paris and continued for over a year through North and South America and even to Hawaii, New Zealand and Australia.

In Ismailia, at the end of his walk, Grogan had met an American woman, Mrs Strong, who was reputed to be a prominent New York hostess. In the American tradition, Mrs Strong had issued an invitation to Grogan to visit her if ever he came to New York. Now he availed himself of the invitation and the lady immediately organised parties for them and a meeting with Woodrow Wilson.

'Sonny,' she said to Grogan,[18] 'I'm going to take you to meet a great man, who some day will be President of the United States of America.' Whereupon he was taken to Princeton and presented to its Principal—Thomas Woodrow Wilson.

'To my surprise, without prelude, I was treated to a lecture on my duty as a citizen,' Grogan wrote.

As they left he said to Mrs Strong: 'Is that really going to be President of the United States?'

'Sure thing, sonny,' she replied.

'Then God help the USA,' was Grogan's candid reaction.

Years later, after the First World War, he met Mrs Strong in Piccadilly. She threw her arms around his neck and said: 'Sonny, God did not help the USA.'

Grogan's reputation as a good orator had preceded him to America. He was already an impressive speaker and, as Lord Cranworth wrote a few years later,[19] 'He had a presence in full keeping with his reputation. Well read and with a gifted pen, he possessed the power of oratory unequalled in Kenya, and unexcelled in my experience elsewhere. As an instance of this power he once made an after dinner speech which lasted no less than two hours. Not only was he not killed, which must surely seem in itself remarkable, but he had his audience spellbound till the end, and they would have had him go on.'

He had a good speaking voice, wit, good looks and natural charm and wherever he went in America, travelling from one coast to the other, he was acclaimed and feasted.

One of the first lectures he gave was to the Geographical Society in Washington presided over by Alexander Graham Bell, the inventor of the telephone. The next day he attended a civic lunch where Mark Twain did the honours and made 'a most humorous speech'. But William Randolph Hearst had a novel surprise in store at the next dinner. To record Grogan's impressions of his walk from the Cape to Cairo he placed a reporter under the table and then proceeded to bombard Grogan with questions. Grogan says that being young he talked a lot of nonsense, but if this had been so William Randolph Hearst would not have bothered to have the interview printed within hours in all the Hearst papers. Grogan was very impressed with American efficiency if somewhat surprised at the method.[20]

Everywhere they went he considered the possibilities of a future in that country. In Argentina, where Gertrude had a great friend, he seriously thought of settling down and buying land to ranch.[21]

In Hawaii he thought Pearl Harbor a very good investment long before the Americans established a naval base there. His hunger for land had started and as Gertrude brought a considerable dowry, reputed to be in the region of £200,000, projects and possibilities must have gone through his very good financial brain. He always knew, ahead of anybody else, what the value of investments in land would be, even though it meant holding on to seemingly useless land for years.

The year 1901 was drawing to a close. They had been away from England for over a year and when Gertrude announced that she was pregnant they returned to London in November.

Chapter 9

KENYA AND THE UGANDA RAILWAY

On arrival in London their first concern was to find a house to rent and prepare for the birth of their first child. It was due in May and although not ideal in every sense of the word, they took a large house in Gloucester Road.

Gertrude was all absorbed with settling in the new house and preparing for the great event, but Grogan was absorbed by other thoughts and he did not feel at all settled.

One of the first people he saw in London in January 1902 was Cecil Rhodes who took up the old refrain: 'Give yourself to Africa. You will never regret it.' And as he listened for long hours to Rhodes' plans for the development of a British empire in Africa, Grogan became more and more convinced that indeed Africa was where his future lay. Rhodes died two months later, on 26 March, but by then Grogan was fully convinced that what the giant with the high falsetto voice advised him to do with his future was exactly right for him.

There was obviously nothing he could do about Africa until the baby was born, or even for a few months after the birth. He did not want to upset Gertrude who was quite happy to believe that London was their future home. Grogan's book and his tales about Africa had done nothing to make it the appealing land her husband now seemed to think it was.

Meanwhile Grogan occupied himself by writing for *The*

Times, the *Financial Times* and the *Express*. Several people[1] have said that at this time he joined the staff of the *Financial Times* as a junior editor but there are no records of this at the newspaper.[2] My research proved that he wrote a number of articles but staff records do not go back that far, so it is very difficult to state with any certainty whether he wrote as a paid member of the staff or merely as a free-lance contributor. One thing is certain: his knowledge of financial matters was then, as it continued to be for the rest of his life, outstanding.

For the *Financial Times* his writings were on economics and financial matters, but for the other newspapers they varied from tribal customs to leprosy. On this last subject he maintained that his observations during the walk from the Cape to Cairo proved that the tribes who lived near rivers and lakes, and therefore lived on a fish diet, did not suffer from leprosy, whereas in other areas where there was no fish he continually came across people who suffered from leprosy and goitre.[3]

Like all Victorian gentlemen of that class and period he had to belong to a number of clubs and during his absence on honeymoon, in January 1901, he was proposed by his friend Mostyn Piggot and seconded by two other friends Richard Lee and John Radcliffe for membership at the Savage Club in Berkeley Square. He was elected on 21 February and after his return he used the club constantly whenever he was in England, until he resigned in 1923.[4] He also belonged to the Junior Carlton and the New Oxford and Cambridge Club at 68 Pall Mall.

A daughter, Dorothy, was born to Gertrude and Ewart on 2 May 1902 and *The Times* reported the event, but Grogan could not wait for the baby to be old enough to embark on his next adventure. Finally, in November 1902, when Dorothy was six months old, they sailed for South Africa.

It seemed to Grogan that the organisation for such a journey was more complicated than for his crossing of Africa. It was not just Gertrude, Ewart, baby Dorothy and a complete household that had to be moved, but also his sister Margaret, Nanny Redwood, Edith the parlour maid and Martin who acted as cook/housekeeper. Quite a contingent to be moved.[5]

Gertrude must have felt great concern and a few doubts as they sailed away from England. It could not have been easy to move seven people, including a baby, their personal possessions and household necessities without knowing what was awaiting them at the end of the voyage. Grogan could not tell her either, but he had absolute faith—as always—in his own judgement. He was an optimist and the future never held any fears for him.

Having gone into the possibilities of settling down in Cape Town when they arrived there, he decided that Johannesburg was probably the better bet, being a town in the process of development.

The Boer War had been over since the end of May, and, although a great number of Boers were in the process of moving from the Transvaal and there were signs of economic depression, Grogan believed that this was the best time to invest in land around Johannesburg. Not that he went into this new venture blindly, he had read everything there was to read about South Africa and listened to many experienced men, besides Rhodes. Throughout his life he never specialised in anything but often knew more about most subjects than the experts, and if he did not know, his forceful personality achieved what he wanted to achieve. He was hard working and very energetic but he could never have held a 9.00 to 5.00 job. 'He always saw things clear and clean and without emotion.'[6]

Johannesburg had changed since he had been there in 1896 during the Matabele rebellion, but it was still mostly made up of shacks—a frontier town, which did not disappoint Grogan but must have chilled poor Gertrude.

He had no sooner decided to purchase a farm near Johannesburg than the State's Governor, Lord Milner, a friend of Rhodes and a staunch admirer of Grogan's achievements as an explorer, invited him to join the Johannesburg Town Council as his own representative.[7] The Johannesburg Town Council was affectionately known as 'Milner's Kindergarden'. Milner was greatly admired for his part in the surrender terms which he had drafted and for which he was made a viscount. In June 1902 he had published 'Letters Patent' establishing the system for a crown colony government in the Transvaal and the Orange River states. The ravages of war had been enormous and now Milner devoted his efforts to land settlement by British colonists, education, justice and the development of the railways, among other things. He had been offered the post of Secretary of State for the Colonies in England but had refused it in order to dedicate his time to the development of South Africa, and men like Grogan were the type of colonist he wanted.

Grogan's farming venture and seat on the Town Council did not last for long. Apart from recurring bouts of malaria, the walk through Africa left him another legacy. His whole system had suffered through hardships and inadequate diet since his Matabele days, and particularly his liver. Now this organ produced another abscess and a very serious operation was performed on him in Johannesburg.

For a few days his life was in the balance and one can imagine Gertrude's anxiety, but no sooner had Grogan been declared out of danger than he began to plan the next stage of his life. A friend from the days he was in Beira, a Canadian by the name of Edward Lingham, whom he had met again in Johannesburg, visited him in hospital and Lingham seemed to know all about a new and wonderful British possession, Kenya.

Sir Charles Eliot, the Commissioner of this new British Protectorate, like Milner in South Africa, was anxious to attract the *right* sort of colonists to take up land in Kenya in order to make the expensive railway that had just been completed between Mombasa and Lake Victoria a paying proposition. Settlement had to be encouraged by Government to generate traffic on the railway. To this end in August 1902 Eliot sent a representative, Marsden, his chief of customs to South Africa to publicise Kenya and to offer every assistance to prospective settlers.

Unlike other British possessions, the administration and the railway arrived in Kenya before the settlers. But why were the British in Kenya at all? The story goes back to the days when Zanzibar was the centre of the slave trade, from where Arab caravans of the type led by Tippu Tip, the greatest slaver of them all, penetrated East Africa right into the Congo, and the Sultans of Zanzibar claimed those lands as their dominions.

The British were spending £100,000 a year to maintain a naval squadron in the Indian Ocean in an effort to stop the trade, but each successive Sultan and slave trader found a way of transporting the inland slaves to the island of Zanzibar and from there selling them and transporting them by dhows to Saudi Arabia, the countries of the Persian Gulf, and even as far as Turkey.

In 1877 Sir William Mackinnon, the chairman of the British India Steam Navigation Company, was offered by the then Sultan Barghash, a lease of 70 years for the whole of his dominions. The Foreign Office was not interested in supporting the venture and the offer was declined. But when the German Emperor in 1885 gave his explorers a charter of protection, naming it the Society for German Colonization, and this society began to obtain treaties from African rulers, with the full hearted approval of the Sultan after Bismarck blockaded his island with a few German cruisers, the British sat up and took notice and an agreement was signed with Germany defining the 'spheres of influence' those two countries should have over the Sultan's dominions. There was nothing Barghash could do at this point. He had tried for years to place his dominions under British protection and now the Delimitation Commission in Berlin took all the decisions. He was lucky to be left with Zanzibar, Pemba, Lamu and Mafia and a ten mile wide strip along the East African coast. Germany claimed the territory known as Tanganyika and British influence was acknowledged in today's Kenya and Uganda.

In 1888 Sir William Mackinnon received the blessing of the British government and a Royal Charter to create the Imperial British East Africa Company with a capital of £240,000 to administer part of the territories long ago offered by the Sultan. Carl Peters, the originator of the German interest in East Africa was not satisfied with his 'planting flags' all over Tanganyika. He wanted Uganda as well, but finally through an Anglo-German agreement in 1890, Uganda definitely came within the British sphere of influence.

The I.B.E.A. Company, with its inadequate capital and huge territory to administer (it cost £250 to deliver one ton of goods to Uganda by porters), with a small staff of which sixty per cent were lost to malaria, dysentery and other tropical diseases, could no longer support the expense, and finally the British government assumed responsibility for the administration of Kenya and Uganda on 30 June 1895.

In 1890 Britain had signed an agreement in Brussels to do all in its power to suppress the slave trade once and for all. In 1885 Mackinnon had already suggested a railway line from Mombasa to Lake Victoria to help stamp out slavery, but except for ivory there were no exports along the proposed line to support the cost of building and maintaining a railway. Slaves, the only export, could hardly be used to pay for it. But unless a railway were built, slavery would never be put down, the country could not be administered, and development would be impossible.

Besides, the Germans had started building a railway from Tanga to the lake, and a countermeasure had to be taken. The seed was sown and the 'most courageous railway in the world' was about to become a fact.

The British Parliament began discussions about the feasibility and cost of such a railway, but many were the opponents of this 'lunatic' proposal. The most fanatical was Henry Labouchere who published a poem in his magazine *Truth*.

> What it will cost no words can express
> What is its object no brain can suppose
> Where it will start from no one can guess
> Where it is going to nobody knows
> What is the use of it none can conjure
> What is its object there's none can define
> And in spite of George Curzon's superior lecture
> It clearly is nought but a lunatic line.

Fortunately for the railway, which was referred to as the Uganda Railway, on 21 June 1895 the Liberal government, which was against the undertaking, was replaced by a Tory government headed by Lord Salisbury who was in favour of it. When Lord Curzon, the new Under-Secretary of State for Foreign Affairs, supported Salisbury and stressed the strategic importance to the British of the head-waters of the Nile, the bill was passed by 255 votes to 75. This did not appease Labouchere and his radical supporters who ridiculed the estimated cost of £3.6 million and a four year period for the construction. He maintained that it would cost more like £5 million and would take up to five years. As it turned out his estimates were very accurate.

George Whitehouse, an experienced railway construction engineer who had built railways all over the world, was given the unenviable task of constructing 580 miles of railway from Mombasa to Lake Victoria through the most difficult country any railway had ever passed. He arrived in Mombasa on 11 December 1895 and soon realised what he was up against. Indian coolies were going to be used for the building as no local labour could be obtained—the Africans were not interested in labour of any sort—and the first contingent of 350 were due in January 1896, and destined to swell to a staggering 31,983 men.

There was no accommodation for them, Mombasa being a shanty town with a few Arab houses and African huts, and not enough water to satisfy the local population. He had to start from scratch beginning with buying land and building a causeway to join the mainland to the island of Mombasa. He had to build labour lines, sidings, turntables, machine shops, sheds, warehouses and most important of all: water catchments. It is not surprising therefore if a year after he had arrived he had only built twenty-three miles of railway line. At that speed the completion of the line would not take just five years, as Labouchere had predicted, but twenty-five.

Whitehouse and his brave staff were not men to be defeated easily. Immediately facing them were endless miles of waterless scrub—the Taru desert—which had defeated many a caravan and claimed thousands of lives. Heat and water shortage alternated with torrential rains which destroyed miles of track that had taken weeks to lay, washed away culverts and bridges and drenched the workers in their flimsy tent encampments. Tsetse flies killed oxen and mules necessary for haulage of building materials and rolling stock. Malaria and dysentery killed hundreds of men and ulcers crippled them. The men believed that malaria was caused by the freshly turned soil and would not believe that cleanliness would save them from festering ulcers. All the food had to come from India and Australia as there was none to buy in the area the line passed through. The telegraph line being laid along the tracks did not fare much better. If giraffes did not get entangled in it, the locals cut it up for ornaments as fast as it was replaced and termites consumed the wooden poles at an incredible speed. Finally, the lines had to be strung on bushes until a satisfactory solution was found. Meanwhile Sclater and Smith were building a dirt road from Kibwezi to the lake, which was later known as Sclater Road, but Sclater himself never saw the end of it. He died of blackwater fever in 1897.

In 1898 Nyarobi (as Nairobi was called until 1899), let alone Lake Victoria, was still miles away, and now the famous man-eaters of Tsavo began to take their toll of men every night. Twenty-five coolies in all were eaten by lions at Tsavo until Colonel Patterson, after weeks of frustrated efforts, shot two mangy old lions which had been the cause of the disaster and complete disruption of morale for as long as they terrorised the men working on the line.

This did not end the tragedy. In March 1899 a Mr O'Hara, an engineer, was in camp with his wife and two children, about twelve miles from Voi. During the night a lion entered their tent and seized O'Hara by the head killing him instantly. The lion then dragged the body outside the tent without waking his wife or children. When she finally woke up she found her dead husband lying outside the tent and the lion standing within two feet of her. Her screams brought the guards on duty at the camp to her tent and the lion was frightened away by rifle shots, but again a lion had tasted human blood and people lived in terror of their lives every night. Coolies again started to sleep on trees, improvised platforms on top of telegraph poles and even inside water pipes only large enough to admit a man but not a lion. One poor Indian who found such a refuge spent a whole night shrinking away from the searching paws of the lion. The roaring of the beast deafened him for the rest of his life but at least he was alive.

Despite the difficulties ahead which Captain Macdonald had stressed in his survey, such as the impossible Kikuyu escarpment, crossing Masai country and more escarpments, it was a great relief to finally rest in the 'place of cold water' which is what Nairobi means in Masai—a swampy, mosquito ridden plain. In 1890 Lugard, the first European to pass through Nairobi on his way to establish an I.B.E.A. Company administration centre at Ngong, described Nairobi as a 'mere wasteland' and it had not improved by May 1899 when the railway reached it and Whitehouse decided to move his Headquarters from Mombasa. He built himself the first brick house behind the railway club with 200,000 bricks fired at Kibwezi by the Scottish Mission and occupied it on Christmas Day 1899.

Nairobi was only used by the Masai to graze their cattle on their way from Ngong to Kiambu, where they took the cattle for the salt they needed, or to Loresho, meaning 'the place on the river where cattle drink'; therefore there was no constant population until the railway arrived and even that was not meant to settle. Nairobi was only going to be a convenient stop before the escarpment. The flatness of the land and water lent themselves to housing, sheds, shops, workshops and marshalling yards.

It soon became obvious that it would become more than a mere railhead, albeit by accident. The railway administration began to put up essential buildings in wood and corrugated iron whilst staff and coolies lived under tents. Then the tents were replaced by more wood and iron constructions for labour and staff, although the senior staff lived up on what became known as the Hill and juniors were housed lower down.

These were not the first white men in the region.

An illiterate sailmaker from Malta, Antonio Martini, later known as James Martin, is reputed to have been Nairobi's first white citizen.[8] Martin held many jobs in his colourful life. He had been Joseph Thomson's second-in-command when he crossed Masai country in 1884. He later joined the I.B.E.A. Company, and when Whitehouse landed in Mombasa he joined the railway staff. He ended up as a District Commissioner in the administration despite the fact that he could not read nor write. All his correspondence was dealt with by a Goanese clerk.

Eric Smith had built a fort in 1891 for the I.B.E.A. Company at Kabete, just outside Nairobi on the caravan route, and as he only had one arm, he was of course known by the Kikuyu as 'one arm'. He built the first brick house which still exists. His fort, later taken over by Francis Hall, became the centre for the handful of traders and settlers who started to arrive before the railway. The first was Stewart Watt who later started fruit cultivation in Machakos which is still flourishing today. Then the McQueens arrived in 1896. James McQueen had been a blacksmith in Scotland, but he was of an independent and adventurous nature, and the subservience he owed his laird in Scotland did not suit him and he took his wife for a walk from Mombasa to Fort Smith in 1896. She was the first white woman to arrive and her son, born soon after their arrival, was the first white child to be born in the Nairobi area.

Nobody knows if these adventurers who seemed to thrive in the bush were pleased with Nairobi's development. Messages by runner from Mombasa took a year to reach them and they appear to have learnt to live without what in the civilised world are considered necessities. But whether they liked it or not Nairobi began to look like a frontier town with its many shacks and makeshift shops, bars and government offices, oxen-drawn carts getting stuck in the mud or ploughing through red dust, officials riding mules and a few brave women trailing their long skirts in the quagmires known as roads in Nairobi.

John Ainsworth, who had also worked for the I.B.E.A. Company and then transferred to the government administration, moved to Nairobi in 1899 from Machakos in Ukamba, which had been considered as a possible capital, and where he was sub-commissioner. His first house was where the Salvation Army H.Q. stands today and it was built by A. M. Jeevanjee, an Indian railway contractor who later became a very prosperous business man. Ainsworth measured the city limits to be within one-and-a-half miles radius from his house and Nairobi city limits remained so until 1920.

By 1900 Ainsworth knew that Nairobi needed shaping up as a proper township and he became chairman of the first Nairobi Township Committee which engaged fourteen Indian policemen, ten convicts (also Indian) to keep the town clean and two lamp-lighters. Oil lamps were used to light the streets but they often broke down owing more to the vandalism of the Saturday night drunks than to manufacturers' fault.

In 1902 there was bubonic plague in the Indian bazaar and the same Colonel Patterson who had eliminated the man-eaters of Tsavo eliminated the bazaar by burning it down. The Administration had to deal with 712 claims from irate shop-owners. But nothing could hold Nairobi back. By 1903 it even boasted a Town Clerk at £200 p.a. and a Sanitary Inspector who was a very much needed and vilified gentleman.

The railway, despite all difficulties, had reached Port Florence, later renamed Kisumu, on Lake Victoria on 20 December 1901. The railway engineer's wife, Florence, who had accompanied her husband Ronald Preston throughout the years of railway building, suffering the most incredible hardships and dangers, now put aside her parasol on the lake shore, and drove the last key home in the last rail. The British Parliament drew a sigh of relief after five years and £5,502,592 actual cost which meant £7,909,294 to the British tax payer when they had finished paying the interest on the borrowed capital.

All they had to do now was find the money for the upkeep of the railway, but they did not seem at all keen to have hundreds of prospective settlers rush to Kenya to take up land and make the railway viable. The exception was Sir Charles Eliot who had become the East Africa Protectorate's Commissioner in 1900 and who had the vision to understand that exports had to be produced in order to pay for the maintenance of the Uganda Railway.

When Edward Lingham visited Grogan in hospital in Johannesburg he certainly did not have the slightest idea of what Kenya was really like, but both he and Grogan had that sense of adventure with which all early pioneers were endowed, and the decision was taken from that hospital bed to go and try their luck in the newest and most promising of British possessions.

Chapter 10

MOMBASA—NAIROBI

It was time for Gertrude to pack up again and probably she was not sorry to do so this time. Grogan had decided to investigate the promise of Kenya with Lingham and he wanted Gertrude to accompany him. It was decided to send little Dorothy, then eighteen months old, back to England with Nanny Redwood, Edith and Martin. Dorothy said to me: 'I went home with the cricket team.'[1] I suppose this means a cricket team was travelling on the same ship.

Ewart, Gertrude and Edward Lingham landed in Mombasa in November 1903. Like all other travellers then and now they must have been impressed with the green banks of the Island of War, as Mombasa was known to the Swahili inhabitants because of its long war-like history. Giant baobabs, mango and palm trees were everywhere. Since Whitehouse, the engineer in charge of the railway, had arrived Mombasa had made great progress. As the ships glided through the Kilindini harbour entrance, red tile roofs could be seen through the trees—the homes of the railway employees and government servants, although there were still no adequate wharfs for large ships which anchored out in the harbour and small craft had to take the passengers ashore.

They had travelled the two miles separating the harbour from the town of Mombasa in little trolleys on narrow rails which were pushed by chanting Swahilis past African huts built under mango trees, a great deal of virgin bush, frangipani and hibiscus. The trolley pushers followed a strict order of etiquette. If a high official's trolley came up or down the line, the pushers of the lower officials had to lift the trolley and its occupant off the line to allow the exalted personage to pass. On reaching the town the first thing visitors were struck by was the imposing old Fort Jesus built by the Portuguese in the fifteenth century to defend themselves from Arab attacks.

The Club, built in 1896, that most important of institutions wherever an Englishman set foot, stands next to Fort Jesus and here the British elite 'drank cooling, if un-iced, drinks, read the ancient papers and feasted their eyes on the splendid collection of trophies that lined the walls.'[2]

It is unlikely that Grogan and his party stayed at the Club which was then still reserved for government and railway officials and their hallowed guests. The next best thing was the Grand Hotel, a stone-throw from the Club where the Standard Bank stands now. This was the first hotel to be built in Mombasa, and Anderson and Mayer had bought it in 1902 after the Greek owner 'had disappeared in the interior'.[3] It was a very elegant white two storey building with arched verandahs on the ground and first floor and it boasted 'bathrooms', hot and cold water and twenty bedrooms and a 'Lux' system of lighting.

Conveniently attached to the hotel was the Colonial Store which was a safari outfitter and general merchant and where newcomers shopped for the khaki clothes, sun helmets and spine-pads they all felt were essential in the tropics, especially the women who arrived in their long Edwardian skirts, tight ruffled blouses and feathered hats. They went into the Colonial Store elegant London ladies and came out farmers' wives. 'Women looked like Christmas trees,' an early settler said.[4] 'Enormous pith helmets with mosquito netting hanging down over their faces, spine pads, long sleeve shirts and khaki bloomers—mid-calf skirts split in the middle.' The mother of this early settler nearly lost more than her helmet travelling up from Mombasa to Nairobi. She had got off the train at one of the many stops and a spark from the engine set her head gear on fire.

Captain G. H. (Jack) Riddell, a man of aristocratic origins, who ran the Boma Trading Company in Nairobi, which offered a number of facilities to its customers from cattle, donkeys, Somali ponies to skins, beeswax, feathers and safaris into the interior, recommended that gentlemen provide themselves with puttees, breeches, Norfolk jacket and flannel shirt. He stressed that flannel 'under garments' were best and safest for the cold nights. He even went as far as saying that although the climate in the highlands could be hot at midday, at night it was sometimes so cold that a fur-lined coat would not be unwelcome. For the sportsman, of course, he had a much longer list of requirements. Saddle and bridle, a revolver, a pair of strong field glasses, a compass, two blankets, rifles and ammunition. Like most companies of that period he could supply the customer with almost anything and any service.[5]

Grogan, who was known for his pith helmet right up to his death, always thought that the tropical sun rays were most dangerous to the European and for many years he advocated spine pads as well as sun helmets, especially for children, who, in his opinion were in greater danger from the penetrating rays. For many years it was said in Kenya that the strong sun rays had a retarding effect on human brains, and Grogan was a strong supporter of this theory. The combination of sun and altitude were thought to be deadly enemies to good health—both mental and physical.

Whilst Gertrude shopped for her unknown future in Kenya, Grogan and Lingham sought out government officials and plied them with questions about forest concessions in the highlands. These gentlemen, not unnaturally since they lived in Mombasa, knew nothing about forest concessions. All they could tell them was that certainly there were forests in Kenya but nobody knew anything about their size or the kind of trees that grew there. Besides, the forest areas were not surveyed yet and if Grogan was interested in buying forest he would have to do the surveying himself. Grogan was not put off. Timber had brought him to Kenya and timber he was going to get. Not only that, but he was going to bring it down to Mombasa and ship it to South Africa. Before leaving Johannesburg he had studied the situation in the mines and he knew that they were begging for pit props.[6] As he tramped around the port, waiting for the twice weekly train to Nairobi, a plan began to take shape. He not only needed large tracts of forest, but also a piece of land within the Kilindini harbour from where he could ship his timber. The piece of land he thought particularly suitable was M'Baraki at the entrance to Kilindini.

Mombasa was hot at that time of the year and Gertrude, despite the new clothes but still wearing the whale-bone corset that gave women of the period hour-glass waists in Europe and prickly heat in Africa, was anxious to leave for Nairobi which people claimed had the ideal climate.

The trains left Mombasa on Tuesdays and Thursdays at 4 o'clock in the afternoon and arrived in Nairobi the following day at 12 o'clock.

During the twenty hour journey the stops were many and essential as the passengers were locked in their compartments from one stop to the next.

The coaches were a wooden construction looking like a box on wheels and each coach had four non-intercommunicating compartments. The two lower bunks were covered in buttoned down green leather and where four bunks were required the back rest was lifted up at night. The coaches were painted white inside and out with brown windows. They were entered through a sliding door on a small platform and at the other end there was another sliding door opening onto a small lavatory with toilet discharging straight onto the rails, and a wash basin.[7] All essentials were there but walking about was impossible and of course, the train had to stop for the passengers to be fed. Breakfast, lunch, tea and dinner were all essential stops, plus every station and unscheduled stops when game walked across the rails.

Stations had Dak Bungalows[8] where hot meals were served and passengers could walk about and talk to other passengers who looked dirtier and dirtier as the journey progressed. Red dust, smoke and sometimes sparks from the locomotive penetrated everything. Mosquito netting, sun shades and louvres at the windows did nothing to keep the clouds of dust out. To the uninitiated it sounds a very uncomfortable journey—in fact, most early travellers were fascinated with the experience, especially as the plains were still filled with game in those days. 'Then the journey was an adventure,' Lord Cranworth wrote. 'It was raining when we started, and the roof leaked like a sieve . . . It was a thrill to see the sun set over the Taru desert . . . It was even wonderful to turn out into a dirty tin hut [the Dak bungalows] and eat stringy goat and drink tepid beer. So it was to lie snoozing and listening to the noises of the night . . . Long before dawn we were up and at the windows to get the first sight of the game . . . how we rushed from window to window as . . . some new wonder [came into sight]: an eland, a giraffe, yes, even a rhino! And then we saw natives, Masai and Wa-Kamba and Wa-Kikuyu, with real spears and real jam-tins in their ears.'

Perhaps one person who was not quite so enthusiastic about 'the adventure' was Gertrude. By all reports she was not the type of early settler to whom dirt and discomfort mattered not a jot. Gertrude had always lived in beautiful houses surrounded by every comfort and luxury—and safety. Now the stories of the man-eaters of Tsavo[9] and a more recent one about a man who was taken by a lion from such a carriage as she was travelling in might have given her a few moments of anxiety as they stopped at Kima, 69 miles from Nairobi, where in June 1900 the railway policeman Charles Ryall was snatched by a lion, dragged by his neck through a window of the carriage, then partially eaten by the side of the coach.[10]

Not a reassuring story for Gertrude but finally the 'little tucked up train on two ribbons of rust', as Grogan referred to the proud Uganda Railway, 'crawling across the Plains and still an object of wonder to the swarming game', although late, arrived in Nairobi 'the home of innumerable frogs'. He described the station as 'a mud patch distinguishable only from the enveloping mudlands by virtue of the decrepit tin shed proudly holding aloft a kitchen clock. All the world was there, true to the old time Nairobi tradition, to meet the train. "All the world" was then four strong and Newland, as ever radiating optimism.'[11]

Newland, Tarlton & Co were another firm prepared to facilitate anybody's life in Kenya. They arranged the largest safaris, they could insure your farm, house or hotel and supply you with cattle dip. It was therefore natural for Newland and others like Tommy Wood to be at the station. Besides roasting coffee, auctioneering, representing a London insurance company and many other occupations, Tommy Wood also represented the Messageries Maritimes Company on whose ship Grogan and his party had travelled from South Africa, so it was not unnatural for this prominent citizen, who was also a member of the Nairobi Municipal Council, to be at the station to meet the Grogans.

Apart from the local safari operators, Messrs Thomas Cook & Sons were on the scene offering trips from Mombasa all the way up the Nile.

In 1903 when the European population was less than five hundred, it did not take long for news to spread and there was no more interesting news than prospective settlers coming to swell the ranks. Prospective settlers with large capital were indeed a rarity and the Grogans' financial status and fame had preceded them to Nairobi. A little fuss at their arrival was therefore expected.

Lesser mortals were carried away from the station on ox-drawn carts or at best rickshaws, but the Grogans had Newland's mule drawn carriage put at their disposal. November was the month of the short rains and the carriage splashed through a sea of mud, following a zig-zag course to avoid the pot-holes and stones. The road seemed to have no limits in its width. As ox-carts got stuck in the mud, other traffic made a detour around the immobilised wagon and the road became wider and wider, and a humorous traveller planted bananas and an assortment of vegetables in the middle of the road.

The only trees in Nairobi were eucalyptus which the ever-active Provincial Commissioner, John Ainsworth had imported from Australia, being the best kind of tree for swampy land as it absorbs all the moisture around it. Some of these trees still exist in Nairobi, but where tarmacadam has covered the swampy ground, they are being cut down, only their huge roots remaining as evidence of early efforts to beat Nairobi into a semblance of a town.

When the Grogans arrived at the Stanley Hotel, that is the *old* Stanley Hotel in Victoria Street (now Tom Mboya Street), they thought they were back in one of the small wild west towns they had hurriedly passed on their travels through America. Horses, mules and ox-carts were tied to the hitching post outside the tin roofed verandah of the hotel, and beer drinking hotel guests observed the new arrivals with great interest. The hotel was no more than a simple wooden building, with a dining room, a few bedrooms at the back and of course, a bar.[12] Meeting in bars was very important and the only relaxation in those early days for the settlers who travelled for days to come to Nairobi to stock up with provisions to take back to their lonely farms. It is not surprising that on those occasions they let off steam in the most unconventional ways, one of which was shooting at the meagre Nairobi lighting system, and the other was shooting the bottles off the bars.

Once the Norfolk Hotel opened its doors on Christmas Day 1904 there was more fun to be had and more bottles to shoot.

One enormous man, W. B. Thomson who looked after the American millionaire McMillan's horses out at Juja, preferred to ride right into the bar *then* shoot the bottles off the top shelf. When he came in the Goan bar stewards were instructed to clear the bar of all bottles as quickly as possible but he was a fast shot and the damage was always considerable.[13]

The fun was not reserved to men only. A young 'lady' called Buster, the daughter of a farmer living on the Naivasha road, whenever she came into town treated the crowds to what she considered a sporting exhibition. She used to ride a six-mule-drawn-cart, known as a buck-board with no sides, at break neck speed down Government Road, her legs on each shaft, waving her long whip and splashing everybody with mud.[13]

In fact Government Road was used as a race track by anybody with a sporting instinct, but the favourite sport was rickshaw races between the Norfolk and the Stanley. Some people owned rickshaws, others hired them from the stands outside the hotels, and everybody had their favourite rickshaw boys, the pusher and the puller. The best built were the favourites, and these were engaged for one rupee a race,[14] with a promise of a bonus if they won. A particularly powerful Kikuyu pumped up and down between the shafts with excitement as bets among participants were taken before the start. Once the race had started this particular expert, cut corners, scared people off the road, ran over the wooden fronts of shops, and encouraged by his rider always arrived first at the steps of the Stanley.[15]

There is no evidence that Grogan ever took part in these sports or ever drank to excess, but he was never what may be termed as 'a serious young man'. He liked his fun—more than the average—but his fun did not run to drinking or rickshaw races, and when he arrived in Nairobi he had other things in mind.

Chapter 11

WHITE MAN'S COUNTRY

Sir Charles Eliot, the Protectorate's Commissioner, encouraged by Lord Delamere was more than willing to assist Grogan to acquire land in Kenya but there were certain difficulties to overcome.

Hugh Cholmondeley, the third Baron Delamere, known simply as 'D' first came to Kenya in 1898 when he trekked through the highlands following a shooting expedition in Somalia and Ethiopia. He fell in love with the country then and returned in January 1903 to take up 100,000 acres at Njoro which was granted to him in November just before Grogan arrived. The aristocratic flavour was beginning to be noticed in Kenya and the Norfolk Hotel, where earls and lords as well as adventurers and poor farmers congregated, came to be known as the House of Lords. Some odd goings on at the Norfolk, like the man who sat naked on the roof with a bath over his head declaring he was God, were not unusual and the aristocrats joined in the fun as enthusiastically as anybody else, but it was not all fun and games; many early farmers lost their all because they did not understand that English style farming could not function in Kenya.

Years after Delamere had died, Grogan wrote about him:[1] 'Kenya, of course, has had the normal quota of peculiar individuals, any one of whom could well have served as "funny man" in novels of adventure; but apart from a worthy lot of earnest, hard-working lovers of the land, none of us are likely to remain figures in history, with the possible exception of Lord Delamere.

'D, as he was fondly called, was a lovable blend of puckish charm and unpredictable political orientation advantaged by a short-term hereditary title—which fifty years ago still retained a narcotic effect upon a British community . . .'

There is a touch of jealousy and even bitterness in these lines. Lord Delamere's son the fourth Lord Delamere said to me: 'My father got on very well with Grogan, although they used to argue a fair deal on political ideas they didn't share. Grogan was a very strong personality. A tall, handsome man and a very good speaker, and although they often disagreed my father very much admired him.'

On a lighter note Grogan's daughters said that their father and Lord Delamere used to vie with each other for who could give the largest party for the least money.

This was much later, but when Grogan first met Delamere and Eliot, he was impressed with both men. He considered Eliot 'a remarkable personality whose diversions were confined to drinking claret and reading Chinese verse.'[1]

Eliot was a man of wide diplomatic experience, a great linguist and oriental scholar, and he was shocked by the backward naked Africans. He was told to develop the country and he considered British rule as 'the greatest philanthropic action'.[2] He wanted to civilise Kenya and found no charm in its backwardness. He believed that the only way in which Britain could be repaid for its 'philanthropic action' was through European settlement.

Until his resignation, Eliot was considered by the settlers to be against them. In fact he was very much their champion and he referred to Kenya as 'a white man's country'. He believed Kenya could become another New Zealand and he urged the Foreign Office to give land concessions to settlers and to be of assistance to them, but this was not known to the settlers who were frustrated by the difficulties facing them on arrival. They had been encouraged to come and take up land, and when they arrived they found that the land had not been surveyed and was not likely to be for years.

Applications for land poured in by mail from England, Australia, New Zealand, South Africa and even America, and every steamer brought its quota of intending settlers. But there was nothing ready for them. There was no accommodation available for the newcomers with meagre funds and John Ainsworth who was responsible for the allocation of farms, had very little patience with the aspiring settlers' demands. Like Frederick Jackson, Eliot's Deputy Commissioner, Ainsworth believed that Eliot was too easy with the settlers and that the government officials' first duty was to the natives.

The hostility between settlers and officials went on from there. New arrivals had to camp around the Land Office and named the place Tentfontein. Applicants besieged the Land Office every day pressing for allotment and survey of farms, many of them coming back from exploratory marches in districts remote from the railway, quoting place-names which did not even appear on maps, and in 1903 the Land Office was 400,000 acres in arrears with its surveys.

The aspiring farmers' frustrations mounted as their resources dwindled through the months of waiting. Many of them could not afford to wait for the vagaries of the officials to be surmounted and they left Kenya poorer and disappointed. 'Not without foundation,' Eliot wrote.[3] He also wrote to Lord Lansdowne, the Secretary of State for Foreign Affairs, that 'you cannot invite people to dinner and then lock the dining-room door.'[4] He complained that nothing was ready for these people and the Foreign Office blamed him for inviting the new-comers before the government could provide the appropriate services and officers.

In his book, *The East Africa Protectorate*, Eliot wrote: 'The fault does not lie in the land regulations, which are sufficiently liberal, but in the absolute lack of administrative organisations.'

Grogan, with his antipathy for the civil service would have agreed whole-heartedly with Eliot; in fact he wrote to *The Times* about it, but like all prospective settlers he felt Eliot was as much against European settlement as all the other officials. To protect themselves and show a strong united front the settlers decided to form an association: The Planters' & Farmers' Association with Delamere as their president.

Unfortunately for the prospective settlers and fortunately for the Africans the Government officials were anxious to see that the interests of the latter were fully protected. In 1897 the British government had already decreed that: 'A certificate will not be granted in respect of any land which at the time of the commencement of these regulations is cultivated or regularly used by any native or native tribe, but may be granted if the Commissioner, after such inquiry as he may think fit, is satisfied that such land is no longer so cultivated or regularly used, and that the grant of a certificate would not be prejudicial to native interests.'

This was confirmed on page 312 of the Official Gazette of 1902 where it stated that: 'In dealings with Crown Land regard shall be had to the rights and requirements of the natives. In particular the Commissioner shall not sell or lease any land in the actual occupation of the natives.'

The question of 'unoccupied land' created a problem in later years when Africans, and especially the Kikuyu, claimed that what the white man considered unoccupied was merely *and* temporarily vacated because of famine or smallpox or just because they felt like moving on. In fact, in 1903, the majority of Kenya's 225,000 square miles, i.e., 10.7 million acres, were uninhabited. Of these only 50,000 square miles were the fertile uplands which attracted the Europeans, but even these were very sparsely populated. In the end 16,700 square miles were allotted to Europeans.

The Kikuyu had been decimated by famine and smallpox and when Eliot arrived in 1901 it was calculated that the Kikuyu population amounted to between 200,000 and 300,000 people spread over an area one hundred miles long by eighteen miles wide. The entire population of Kenya amounted to no more than two million.

No wonder great tracts of land were unoccupied. Some were, of course, forcibly kept unoccupied by the Masai who kept their natural enemies, the Kikuyu and the Wakamba, relegated to the forests' fringes whilst they occupied the grass lands with their vast herds of cattle, and terrorised their neighbours. Border hostilities were the order of the day and inter-tribal wars were frequent. There were no overall rulers within the tribes which were splintered into many clans always fighting each other, and this was their weakness.

All this notwithstanding, it seems perfectly logical that however careful the government officials were in allocating land to new settlers, some of that land may have been left to lie fallow, or vacated because of drought or pestilence. When later the government obtained proof from 5,000 Kikuyu that their land had been allotted to whites, they compensated the original owners at the rate of one cow per 100 acres, or two rupees per acre. Although this was considered reasonable by the Africans at the time, later they changed their minds and claimed that the land in question was their 'best and most favoured land'.[5] After this a line was drawn beyond which white settlement was not permmitted, but the great majority of the tribe was left in possession of their land which was of natural high productivity.

The Masai were not so well treated. Twice they were moved from their ancestral pastures to make room for white farmers who wanted land near the railway, including Delamere, despite his protestations in defence of his beloved Masai. They were moved once from the Rift Valley to the Laikipia plains with promises of a permanent home—'so long as the Masai as a race shall exist,' the treaty signed in August 1904 stated. But when this location looked better suited to European ranching, they were moved to the southern end of the Rift Valley. Even in these modern times they have been asked to vacate some of their land in Amboselli to make room for the wild game in that part of the country. Perhaps because they were always and by nature nomads they accepted the moves, but it is hard to understand why they were so good-natured when their land was reduced in size. Considering that at one time they grazed their cattle from near Mombasa to Lake Baringo and were unchallenged masters of thousands of square miles, it is not surprising that they have been the most unco-operative of tribes in allowing the white man to tell them what was best for them.

The Masai moves came later, but in 1902, after Joseph Chamberlain, the Secretary of State for the Colonies paid a brief visit to the Protectorate, he offered some thousands of square miles to the north of the railway, in the Mau, as a national home for the Jews. The settlers, and especially the prospective settlers, were furious and Delamere, as President of the Planters' and Farmers' Association cabled the Foreign Secretary: 'Feelings here very strong against introduction of alien Jews. Railway frontage fit for British colonisation 260 miles. Foreign Office proposes give 200 miles best to undesirable aliens. Is it for this that the expensive railway was built and large sums spent on the country? Flood of people that class sure to lead to trouble with half-tamed natives jealous of their rights . . .'

This was not the end of the Jewish story. The colourful outcome, in which Grogan was involved, will appear a little later.

Meanwhile, Grogan was told that he was welcome to take up as much as 64,000 acres of forest on the Uasin Gishu Plateau which would not be advertised for sale to others until 1908.

The offer was inviting but no survey had been carried out and he would have to wait for that and for the Foreign Office to agree to the concession. Everything would be done to facilitate him, Eliot said. Ewart Grogan was not a man to wait around, nor the type to camp in Tentfontein. With Lingham and a private surveyor he had engaged, he boarded the train to Londiani, the nearest station to Eldama Ravine in the vast Uasin Gishu Plateau and there he hired ponies and mules from one of the few South African Boer traders who had roamed the land since the start of the railway. He had to penetrate the thick forest to see for himself just what the government was offering him. He had heard enough stories around Tentfontein about settlers who had been elated when given a piece of land and once they got there found it to be solid waterless rock.

From the moment he left Nairobi he was enchanted with the country on each side of the railway. Miles and miles of empty rolling acres. The immense Rift Valley which traversed the whole of Africa, its extinct volcanoes, Lake Naivasha where a Masai legend says a monster reptile lived and devoured people, and the Lakes Elmenteita and Nakuru fringed with pink flamingos. From Nakuru the railway climbed the Mau Escarpment, the air became thinner and the views more spectacular. He thought this was paradise and even before he saw his forest, he knew Kenya was going to become his life. There was only one problem. As he travelled through more and more empty lands he wondered who was going to work his forest concession. The labour problem was something all other farmers had already experienced and in the years to follow it would explode into another fight between settlers and government.

In 1933 when Africans began to clamour for land he was asked, together with other early settlers, Africans and Indians, to give evidence to the Kenya Land Commission on the conditions he found on the Uasin Gishu Plateau when he first went there in 1903.

'I could tell you something about the distribution of the people in the early days,' he told the Commission.[6] 'At that time, beyond one or two Dorobo families, in the area between the Kamasia Hills, Londiani Mountain, the Nandi and the Plateau, there were no natives at all.'

Grogan was delighted with his forest of cedar, podocarpus and olive trees, but he was not prepared to admit it to Eliot when he returned to Nairobi. What he said instead was that the size of the forest would hardly make it worth his while to start a saw mill and spend money in transporting the timber to the nearest station. He needed more land. He was right in one respect. It would take years to make the forest a paying proposition. Eliot, anxious to be of assistance agreed to grant him an extra sixty-four acres of land at M'Baraki, the piece of land at Kilindini in Mombasa which Grogan had decided on arrival he needed to ship his timber to South Africa. Now all that remained to be done was to obtain the approval of the Foreign Office and to have the forest surveyed.

Grogan found this delay irritating, but there was nothing he could do except return to England. Gertrude was anxious to spend Christmas with Dorothy, and Grogan felt she had been patient enough waiting for him in Nairobi whilst he tramped on the Plateau. Dorothy was too young at the time to remember now whether her mother was pleased at the prospect of returning to Kenya permanently when her husband declared his enthusiasm for the country, but she must have agreed because he arranged to rent a house on the Hill from a Mr Roberts who had a business in town for when they would return to Nairobi.[7]

Within days of returning from up-country he had bought an enormous piece of land the other side of the Nairobi river which is now called Westlands but is still shown on maps as Groganville and everybody knew it as such for many years.

On a small part of that land between the Nairobi River and the Gura River there was a wood and iron building known as the Manse and belonging to the Reverend W. Bennett and this Grogan bought as well and decided it was the ideal spot to build the house which he would name Chiromo. There would be no wood and iron building for the Grogans. Of course they had to ford the river to reach their promised land, but these things never bothered Grogan. He would soon remedy that.[8]

He had heard of the Manse from one of the most colourful characters in Kenya: John Boyes, known as the King of the Wakikuyu, because he was the first European to penetrate and be accepted by that unfriendly tribe. This he achieved by organising the scattered warriors of the many clans into an efficient army and by teaching them that selling their fresh produce to the railway's construction gangs would bring wealth to their tribe.

It was now time for the Grogans to get back to London and they were delighted to hear that Sir Charles Eliot was travelling on the same ship. Grogan enjoyed this erudite man's company, but when they landed in Naples and Eliot insisted that the most interesting sight in that city was the aquarium, Grogan was somewhat surprised at the reception. 'We were required to put our names in the visitors' book,' Grogan wrote,[9] 'and while Sir Charles was peering at specimens of his loved ones, an excited little Italian dashed up, threw his arms round my neck, and warmly kissed me on both cheeks, exclaiming: "Ah! so I meet the great sea-slug Eliot." Not being aware at that time of Sir Charles's pre-eminence in this incredible sphere, I was startled, but pointed out the proper recipient of the embraces.'

Chapter 12

CHIROMO AND THE FOREST

The Grogans were back in Nairobi within a few weeks having arranged for their furniture to be shipped from London to Mombasa, including a piano, lavatory bowls, handbasins, baths and most important of all: a Dover stove. These stoves had not been seen in Nairobi before and would not be in the shops until 1906. Until then cooking was done on stone fireplaces, but Martin, the cook-housekeeper, would have refused to cook in such primitive conditions. The Dover stove was a great black monster which fed on wood and was alight twenty-four hours a day. All this, plus special oak beams, leaded windows and many more accessories, Grogan ordered in England for the house he had planned at Chiromo.

Whilst this was being built Ewart, Gertrude, baby Dorothy, Nanny Redwood, Martin and Edith all lived on the Hill in Mr Roberts' house. A typical house of that period built of wood on stilts, with a corrugated iron roof, and a long verandah running along the front of it. The house overlooked the dusty plains teeming with zebra, giraffe, kongoni, wildebeest, gazelles, ostriches, lions and rhinos as far as the Ngong Hills.

The Athi plains and Ngong were also visible from Chiromo but the view was interrupted by the sprawling tin roofs of Nairobi which was growing untidily in all directions. To make sure Chiromo would never be invaded by others Grogan purchased 113 acres of land from Salisbury Bridge to where St Mark's

Church stands today. Along the left hand side of the railway and Salisbury Road, which is now known as Chiromo Road, past today's shopping centre all came to be known as Groganville.[1] So extensive and wild was the land that game, including leopard, was not an unusual sight, and Grogan built a hunting lodge (where East Church Road is now), although his hunting fever was by then almost spent after his Cape to Cairo walk.[2] On Groganville he also built a large L-shaped wood and iron building on stone stilts with a verandah and windows running all round it which he used for guests. It was so comfortable and large that a later governor, Sir James Hayes Sadler, preferred to hold dances in its enormous living room rather than in the cramped reception rooms of Government House on the Hill.[3] The Japanese Embassy is on that same piece of land now. Grogan also allowed some of the poorer aspiring settlers waiting for land grants to set up their tents in Groganville. Nobody ever said Grogan was a mean man. People could always rely on his help.

Groganville did not end there, it extended to where the Kenya Girls' High School was built much later and what was known as Hospital Hill.

Chiromo was being built by Indian fundis, some of the 724 who had decided to remain in Kenya after the building of the railway, and Grogan followed the building in every detail, but one day as he approached Chiromo from Hospital Hill he noticed great activity on the hill and enquired from a government surveyor what was going on.

'We are building a hospital,' the surveyor informed him.

All that Grogan replied was: 'Oh, how interesting. Nairobi does need a hospital,' and rode on to Chiromo.

Weeks passed and indeed the projected Nairobi Hospital was taking shape and part of it was being built on Grogan's land.

On making further enquiries Grogan was again informed that the building *was* the Nairobi Hospital. 'How very nice of the Government to build me a hospital,' Grogan laughed. His deep throated laugh and his penetrating blue eyes were the first thing people always noticed about him.

The engineer in charge was not amused and informed Grogan that he was mistaken. The hospital was a Government project on Government land.

" Better have your surveyor work out his figures again,' Grogan advised the astounded engineer. 'You'll find that part of the land you are building on is actually my land.'

When his contention was confirmed the Government engineer and the surveyor were furious. 'If you knew from the beginning that we were building on your land, why did you wait until we started building before pointing out the mistake? There's nothing we can do about it now.'

'Yes there is. Just take down that end of it,' he said pointing to the offending walls; but in the end he ceded the piece of land to the government.[4]

He had built a bridge across the Nairobi river so that Gertrude could indulge in her favourite pastime of developing a garden, but in 1905 the bridge, together with the much stronger Ainsworth Bridge, collapsed after the river flooded twice in one week. Grogan rebuilt it and Gertrude came every day from the Hill house riding in the rickshaw that Grogan had bought, being pulled and pushed by the two rickshaw boys who were dressed in a starched uniform of khaki colour and a red fez. They were neatly dressed but not as smart as some of the other rickshaw boys. There was competition in those days by some of the owners of rickshaws as to the smartness of their boys. Some went as far as having their family crest emblazoned on the uniform and the rickshaw, but Grogan was more interested in building the best house in Nairobi than such superficial ostentation.

As Robert Foran wrote later, Chiromo for those days was a 'splendid residence'. Comfort and modern facilities were Ewart's and Gertrude's main concerns, and perhaps charm, but certainly not splendour. Neither of them was in any way ostentatious but even today Chiromo would be acknowledged as a beautiful house. Built on a rise above the Nairobi river it is surrounded by extensive gardens. Gertrude transformed bush into a garden filled with the most beautiful European and tropical plants, and having found a pure spring, Grogan channelled this to supply the house with water and from the river he fed an artificial ornamental lake which Gertrude surrounded with cannas, lilies and agapanthus. Grogan was already then indulging in what became an obsession in later years: the channelling of water.

The house itself, which is now the British Institute in East Africa and part of the Nairobi University, has gables rising on each side of a wide verandah. Each gable has an 'eye' covered in leaded glass like all the other windows. The verandah is supported by square pillars and it used to be covered by a huge bougainvillaea. From this verandah the house was entered through a mahogany front door, reinforced by iron hinges and carved. It has a leaded window with thick coloured glass incorporating the initials E.S.G. and '1905' is carved on the door frame. The very large hall has an arched ceiling supported by oak beams, like the two living-rooms flanking it. An unusual feature was the parquet floors of Canadian pine. Many of the beams are carved 'Grogan Mombasa'.

Lord Cranworth, who leased Chiromo from Grogan in 1909, wrote about it in his *Kenya Chronicles*: 'I remember vividly today how attractive our new home looked as we drove up, with bougainvillaea a purple mass over the verandah and the cannas and wattle blazing in the garden . . . It was by local standards most luxurious. After amply accommodating ourselves and family, there were two or three spare bedrooms, an excellent kitchen, servants quarters and ample stables: while, best of all, there were two baths in which one could count on the water being really hot . . . At night after dinner in the dry season one could usually hear the deep grunts of a hunting lion in the distance.'

He does not describe a stone rotunda with a fireplace and a stone table in the middle, so perhaps this was added by Lady McMillan when she purchased Chiromo in 1925 after her husband's death.

Cranworth was also impressed by Chiromo's owner. Of the people he met in Nairobi when he first arrived he wrote: 'None of them made more impression on me than Ewart Grogan, a romantic figure to any young man . . . his personality loomed large among the settlers. Grogan was gifted by nature far beyond the ordinary . . . Good looking, with a fine physique and an impelling eye, he had a presence in full keeping with his reputation . . .'

Cranworth was not alone in considering that Grogan possessed qualities most of the other settlers lacked. As soon as he arrived he was invited to become a member of the Colonists' Association which had been created on 4 January 1903 at a meeting in the Nairobi Hotel at Kikuyu. The Association was an offshoot of the early Planters' and Farmers' Association which was mainly concerned with securing better conditions for farmers and an outlet for produce. The Colonists' Association on the other hand became more political and was responsible for the Highlands being reserved for European colonisation. It had the blessing of Sir Charles Eliot and through him it obtained the formation of a Land Committeee, extension of the jury system and coroner's jury. It obtained reduced rates on the railway for shipping of produce and eventually the appointment of a Legislative Council. The members were also under the illusion that the Association assisted the Administration in carrying out reforms and influenced its policies. The most important thing about the Association was its unanimous European voice and its representations carried great weight. Grogan was destined to become its president in 1907 at the worst period of his East African career.[5]

He was also a member of the Central Committee of the Legion of Frontiersmen and generally became involved in all issues, political and otherwise which affected the future of the colony and its settlers.

Some might say that he interfered in issues that did not concern him but he believed that everything to do with Kenya, and especially the Kenya settlers, concerned him.

One such settler one day came to Grogan with an unusual complaint and hoped Grogan could help him out. The settler had decided to build himself a house a little different from the rest. He wanted to use the clay on his plot and by mixing it with straw he planned to make bricks. He happily started digging clay when Charles Hobley, the Commissioner of Mines came riding by the mud track on his white mule. Hobley asked the owner of the plot what he was doing and upon being told the purpose of the digging he was most indignant and informed the surprised digger that according to the Mining Ordinance clay was a mineral and it belonged to the Government and as such it required a prospecting licence before anybody could prospect for it—let alone use it without a proper licence.

When Grogan heard the ridiculous story he was furious and immediately referred to Government officials with his favourite appellative. 'Those human silverfish feeding on their files.' At the same time he assured the prospective house-builder that he would be allowed to make his bricks very shortly.

Having contacted Hobley and received no satisfaction Grogan decided to teach the 'bumbling' government a lesson. He took out a prospecting licence and that same night, with the help of the frustrated men camping in Groganville, a load of pegs and mallets, he proceeded to stake out his claim to most of Nairobi including the Hill and Government House. Holes were appearing everywhere and Hobley became very alarmed. He demanded, in the middle of the night, that Grogan prove his right to this prospecting and Grogan gleefully showed him his prospector's licence and announced that unless something was done about this ridiculous law declaring mud to be a mineral, his men would dig up a few other towns in the Protectorate—in fact, they were already on their way and only waiting for him to send word as to whether the digging was to be carried out or stopped.

Hobley was in a cleft stick but Grogan suggested, laughing and in his most soothing voice, that there was no need to worry, all that the government had to do was change the law. 'At this time of night?' Hobley asked. 'No need to hurry,' Grogan said. 'Just assure me that the law about mud will be changed and I will take your word as a gentleman that this will be done tomorrow.'

Not as quickly as Grogan expected but the law *was* changed and clay to this day is not considered a mineral.[6]

He was not having the same measure of success with the most important issue and the reason for which he had come to Kenya. The Foreign Office was still sitting on his application for the forest concession. With Lingham he travelled to their promised concession in the Eldama Ravine more than once and on one occasion he met Captain Meinertzhagen at Londiani. In his *Kenya Diary* Meinertzhagen wrote on 23 May 1904: 'At Londiani I met E. S. Grogan (of Cape to Cairo fame) . . . On meeting Grogan I was immediately attracted to him; he had great charm, a brain as clear as crystal and a strong character. He not only means what he says but he says what he thinks . . . He is a great man and will be even greater some day.'

Meinertzhagen never changed his mind about Grogan, either during the First World War when they were in Intelligence together, or in his old age.

It was at this time that Grogan's aspirations suffered a great blow. The man who was his greatest champion for the granting of the forest concession suddenly resigned. Unfortunately for Grogan and the settlers in general, Sir Charles Eliot decided to give up the struggle. He was frustrated and disappointed that his efforts to improve conditions for the settlers had no effect on the Foreign Office in London, and in Kenya he received no support from his deputy, Frederick Jackson.

The settlers who had considered him a snob only interested in his oriental studies, now suddenly realised his worth and demanded an inquiry into the circumstances of his resignation.[7] On 27 April Grogan wrote for *The Times* a strong article defending Eliot and many years later he wrote: 'The manner of his departure was not one of the brightest pages in the history of the Foreign Office. In the Blue Book covering the incident it was claimed in support of the Foreign Office that a certain cable from Sir Charles had not, if sent, been received. The Blue Book had been badly censored by its editor, for in the appendix citing the correspondence the cable with its date of receipt was included!'[8]

The reasons for Sir Charles Eliot's resignation were many, but one that finally induced him to take a decisive step was the Foreign Office's insistence that a Zionist colony should be started on the Mau. He objected strongly to this and he wrote: 'An experiment whose success is more than doubtful, and which, if successful, is likely . . . to provoke racial conflicts.'[9]

In November 1904, on behalf of the Polish and Jewish refugees, a commission from the Zionist Congress came to see the 'Uganda Offer', as the 5,000 square miles of land on the Mau were called, despite Eliot's, Delamere's and the settlers' remonstrations. The proposal was that they would form an autonomous state, with self government and a Jewish governor, but under the protection of Great Britain.

By the time the Zionist commission arrived Sir Charles Eliot had been replaced by Sir Donald Stewart as Commissioner, and, although the Zionists were accompanied by a Foreign Office official, Sir Donald decided that they needed two experienced settlers who knew the Uasin Gishu Plateau and Trans Nzoia where the 5,000 square miles offered the Jews were situated. The new Commissioner was advised that he could find no better guides than Ewart Grogan and Edward Lingham and the party entrained for Londiani.

Grogan was impressed with the gentlemen of the Zionist delegation whom he described as 'scholarly types, but not farmers or settler-pioneer types'. When he mentioned this to the head of the delegation he was assured that the people who would come to farm the land offered by the British Government were not of their calibre but poor artisans. Grogan said nothing but this revelation was no more pleasing than the first. The artisan class was already being filled by the Indians and the few Europeans who arrived with those qualifications soon changed to other businesses or farmed.

As they tramped through the forests, valleys and over mountains it became obvious to Grogan and Lingham that the gentlemen of the delegation were not accustomed to this type of walking and soon they made camp in a glade. Grogan later swore that he had no idea that this was in a path always used by elephants. In fact, he had seen very little game in that region on his past visits, but that night a whole herd of elephants passed between the tents of the terrified Zionists. The following day they went on walking and looking at the land promised to them, but that night the camp was visited by lions who sniffed at the tents and walked around the camp as if it was their territory. Even more unusual, on the third day they met a party of Masai warriors on their way to attack their neighbours. They were arrayed in full war regalia and miles away from their lands, and upon meeting the white men they surrounded them and shaking their spears they gave their war cries. Grogan and Lingham approached them and spoke to them for a long time but the Masai were not so easily dissuaded from their fun. They broke the circle and retired a small distance away where for most of the night they kept up their war dances and Grogan thought it best to set up guards to protect the terrified members of the commission.

On the fourth day they asked to be taken back to Nairobi and in London they declared that they had seen an 'unholy land'. The British offer was turned down in August 1905.[10]

The story raised a laugh for many a month in Kenya where people were certain that the appearance of both wild animals and Masai had been arranged by Grogan. This is somewhat unlikely but it made a good story and Grogan's reputation gained strength.

When he came back Gertrude told him that her suspicions before his trip were now confirmed. She was definitely expecting another baby. This time they were both sure it would be a son and this called for a celebration. Grogan was always ready for a party and Gertrude was a wonderful hostess. He was rather inclined to hold the floor and was a great raconteur, but Gertrude did not seem to mind. She was quiet and attentive to her guests but seemed to enjoy her husband's stories about the Cape to Cairo walk even though she must have heard them many times. 'She was the sort of universal mother,' her daughter Jane told me. 'He was clever and intellectual and she wasn't musical.'[11] Nevertheless, she enjoyed his strumming on the banjo and 'banging' on the piano. May Harries (now Mrs Stocker) remembers going to Chiromo in 1905 as a girl of fifteen with a group of people. They rode the thirty miles from Thika on an ox-cart and when they arrived at the Grogans' their welcome was enthusiastic and in no time the carpets were up and everybody danced to Grogan's music. People did not always come from so far away. The Cowies had built a house just across the road, on the site of the present Casino, and they were frequent visitors. The Grogans' house was always open and their guest rooms filled with friends from up country, but Gertrude was worried about giving birth to her second child in Nairobi. She did not have faith in the few local government doctors although all the other European women gave birth in Kenya, and Grogan told her she should have their son in London.

They would all go to London for the happy event with Dorothy and Nanny Redwood—besides, Grogan had a few things to say to the Foreign Office.

Chapter 13

EXPANSION AND ACQUISITION

There was no need for Grogan to go to London to obtain his forest concession. Sixty-four thousand acres were granted to him at Eldama Ravine on a fifty year lease at two rupees per annum per acre. That is £8,500 per annum.[1] Not an indifferent sum of money in those days. One hundred acres were also granted to him at M'Baraki in Mombasa as promised by Eliot. Meanwhile he had bought seventeen acres of 'township stands'. Valuable plots in the middle of Nairobi which he either rented, or built on or just kept for future development.

All this was not enough for Grogan. At the beginning of 1905 he immediately applied for as much forest again as he had just obtained. He claimed that timber from 64,000 acres hardly made it worth his while to equip sawmills, importing expensive machinery and transporting the timber to M'Baraki.

He had, of course, applied for this extra land, as the first, with Lingham, but he had no need to use the 'dummying' method that almost all other aspiring settlers applied. The average settler was only allowed 5,000 acres and in order to increase their concessions they put forward their wives' names, or their mother-in-laws', or anybody they could think of.

Dummying was not for the likes of Grogan, Delamere and a few others. They were wealthy enough for the Government to welcome them as landowners, but when Grogan, having received his concession of 64,000, applied for a further 68,862 acres, the

Colonial Office considered this 'outrageous'. On 1 April 1905 the Colonial Office had taken over the administration of the East African Protectorate from the Foreign Office much to the delight of the settlers who thought the Colonial Office would prove more competent and amiable. They were not so to Grogan.

Having made their calculations the Colonial Office came to the conclusion that Grogan was trying to acquire the greater part of the Uasin Gishu Plateau. The proposal was considered 'the usual promoter's scheme for floating a company on the faith of Government support, as a means of catching unwary investors'.[2] The Colonial Office were not too far wrong. Grogan did later rent part of his concession to other investors, but meanwhile the Government refused to listen to his arguments.

A visit to London was therefore essential after all and as the second baby was almost due, Ewart, Gertrude, Dorothy and Nanny Redwood sailed from Mombasa and on 27 June 1905 another little girl was born and named Joyce.

Grogan must have been disappointed but he was probably too busy fighting the Colonial Office to give the new arrival much thought and the pressure he applied on the Government obviously paid off because by the time they came back to Kenya in December 1905, Grogan had obtained the extra 68,862 acres of forest land. To this he added another 71,032 acres in 1912, and although in 1909 he gave up 17,500 acres for Masai settlement, he still ended up with 186,394 acres which was more than any other settler, including Delamere who had 115,627 acres. Very few others had more than 20,000 acres. The Government might not have liked giving away so much land to the rich individuals but they needed them to support the smaller landholders.

In England he ordered the most up-to-date sawmilling machinery but, as in Kenya, his interests were not exclusively business. Politics were always in the forefront, and the 'Indian Question' was a predominant part of those politics for the rest of his life.

Trading in Kenya was mostly in the hands of Indians from the beginning but in 1905 they were not satisfied with that slice of the country's wealth. They wanted land and they wanted it in the White Highlands, and when the Aga Khan visited Kenya that year the Indians asked for his help. The White Highlands ran from Machakos to the Mau and the Aga Khan advised the Indians not to press for land in that region but to be satisfied with the other areas open to them and which they considered inferior. This was later proved wrong by many white farmers, including Grogan, who cultivated thousands of acres south of Machakos, but in 1905 the Indian demands became so insistent that a Land Committee was set up with Delamere as President and Grogan one of the members.

As a member of the Land Committee Grogan was asked to give evidence to a special commission in London and he argued 'very strongly against any further immigration of Asiatics because the relationship of the white man to the black man in the country was reciprocal and complementary,' he said.[3] 'If you open the doors to the Asiatic peoples you are going to introduce a wedge which would prevent the European from expanding and the African from rising.'

Twice he wrote to *The Times* that year[4] expounding his views on Indian immigration and the paper picked up his theme and made it the subject of long articles. He also wrote three articles for *The Times* on Argentina and New Zealand comparing them to Kenya and its potentials.[5]

Whilst in England, an article written by him was published in the *Empire and the Century*. In 'The Nile As I Saw It' another side of Grogan comes to the fore. In describing the beauty of Lake Kivu he is almost poetic.[6]

The Grogans were back in Kenya in December where the Commissioner, Sir Donald Stewart, had meanwhile died in Office. There was much work to do for Grogan. The forest concession, which he had named Equator Saw Mills, had to be organised. Sawmills had to be built at strategic points and equipped and the right kind of men found to run them. From the very beginning Grogan, like Delamere, was instrumental in bringing out to Kenya a great number of settlers from England, New Zealand and Australia, and during his last visit to England he had engaged two young Englishmen to run his sawmills. Of course these men and the labour recruited from neighbouring tribes had to be accommodated, and the first trees felled in the forest were used to build labour lines and a primitive dwelling for the two young managers. A log cabin was also built for himself and Lingham.

The transport of the timber from the forest to Londiani station was another problem to be solved and for this oxen had to be brought from Nairobi and carts built on site. Not the quickest method of transport even in the best of weathers. The huge carts used for the transport of timber and drawn by twelve to eighteen oxen on dusty and rutted tracks, were often bogged down for days during the rainy season. Grogan used to refer to these tracks as the 'Red Sea' when the red earth turned into a muddy sea during the rainy season and the name was adopted by the pioneers who arrived much later and had the same problem.

When the first pioneers began to take up farms in the Eldoret area,[7] if they were lucky and the weather was favourable, it took them two or three days by oxcart to cover the sixty miles from the station at Londiani to Eldoret, but if it rained, it could take them a fortnight. As a 95-year-old lady reminiscing to me said: 'When we got stuck and the oxen couldn't pull us out of the mud, we just sat on an ant hill until the road dried out.'[8]

Not an economical way of exporting timber, and in 1905 Grogan was already hatching a plot on how to talk the Uganda Railway's authorities into building a railway line to Eldama Ravine. It took almost twenty years for him to obtain what he wanted, but as usual he never gave up the fight and the whole thing became a scandal in the early twenties when a number of people accused him and Lord Delamere of furthering their own ends.

Perhaps because of the difficulties involved in transporting the timber Grogan did not make the fortune he expected out of the Equator Saw Mills. This did not deter him and he proceeded to develop his property at M'Baraki within the Kilindini port of Mombasa. Again he invested a great deal of money in building the first deep water pier at Kilindini with the *podo* trees from his forests and importing cranes and lighters. For years his wharf was used as a coal depot where ships unloaded the coal needed for the railway and in this way he paid for some of his expenses. The Africans carried the coal in karais[9] on their heads and the faster they went the more money they earned as they were paid one 'pice' (the equivalent of one penny) per karai. A supervisor stood at the end of the pier with a great bag of 'pice' and paid the men as they passed with their full karai.

These were years of intense work and great financial investment of Gertrude's money, but there was a pleasant interlude when on 14 March 1906 King Edward VII's younger brother, the Duke of Connaught and his bookish German wife arrived in Kenya with their daughter Patricia. The Duke was at the time involved in a passionate affair with the famous American beauty Leonie Jerome, Jennie Churchill's sister, but she was not in the royal party. The Edwardians kept up 'proper' appearances, but more interesting to the Grogans was another member of the party. Gertrude's brother-in-law, Robert Baden-Powell. Grogan had met Lord Baden-Powell during the Matabele war and he was now delighted to welcome him on his first visit to Kenya.[10]

The Grogans with their daughter Dorothy were at the Nairobi station with other prominent citizens of the Protectorate to welcome the illustrious visitors, and the four-year-old Dorothy presented a bouquet to the Duchess. The *East African Standard* reported that Miss Grogan 'looked perfectly charming' as she presented the bouquet, but Dorothy now says: 'I must have hated that and probably thrown a tantrum as usual.' Like her father, she had a will of her own. She was known to the Africans as *mtoto ya simba* (child of the lion), and Grogan was known as *bwana simba*.

Another welcome arrival in 1906 was Grogan's sister Dorothy with her husband Wilfred and their two children Patrick and Geoffrey. Wilfred C. Hunter was an associate of the Chartered Institute of Secretaries and an M.A. Cambridge and in Kenya he became a well known personality both in business and in politics. As Lord Cranworth wrote in his *Kenya Chronicles*: 'He was a man whom everyone felt that they could instinctively trust, and he possessed a large fund of shrewd common sense . . .' His wife Dorothy was apparently very different from her brother Ewart. According to Lord Delamere, 'she was quiet and very nice, but strait-laced and respectable.'

The Hunters settled in a house in Groganville and Wilfred started his own accountancy business in a little tin office not far from where the Nairobi Cathedral now stands which was then outside Nairobi. One of his first clients was his brother-in-law who elected him secretary of the Upper Nairobi Township Estates Ltd., which was Groganville and the other properties Grogan owned in Nairobi. Hunter also became secretary for the Kilindini Harbour, Wharf and Estate Company Ltd., which was the 'umbrella' company for M'Baraki and the forest concession; and he was Chairman of Longonot Ltd., a recently acquired farm on the shores of Lake Naivasha. In fact, Wilfred Hunter was either agent, secretary, accountant or chairman for all of Grogan's businesses. But he did not work exclusively for his brother-in-law; he had other clients like Lord Delamere, for whose estates he kept accounts, and in 1912 he was largely responsible for the building of the Muthaiga Club and became its first president.[11]

Meanwhile Grogan was busy accumulating property and developing. The Longonot farm, which was situated between the extinct Longonot volcano and Lake Naivasha, covered 20,000 acres including six miles of lake frontage and here Grogan sank four wells and also pumped water from the lake to fill troughs for sheep and to irrigate the extensive vegetable gardens. His inventiveness in the use of water was always in the forefront, and with Delamere he was the first to import merino sheep from Australia together with a New Zealand manager for the farm, F. S. Clarke, and a pure bred Shorthorn bull. Also at the same time as Delamere he imported the first pigs which thrived at Longonot. In 1911 it became the largest supplier of pigs for the new bacon factory on the Escarpment.

Perhaps the most important innovation for Kenya at the time was trout. The Brown and Rainbow trout which is now so popular with fishermen and gourmets alike in Kenya was first imported by Ewart Grogan. Having studied the cold rivers of the Highlands he decided that they were ideal for trout and an order went off to Dumfries in Scotland for thousands of ova and a gillie to look after them. The expense was enormous and Grogan established a Trout Acclimatisation Society to which Frederick Jackson, S. L. Hinde and a few other enthusiasts contributed £10 each, but the bulk of the cost and the responsibility for the success of the scheme was Grogan's. The ova were nursed all the way from Scotland to Mombasa and from Mombasa to the headwaters of the Gura river in the Aberdare range at an altitude of 11,000 feet and there a hatchery was established and on 21 April 1906 the *East African Standard* proudly announced the success of Grogan's enterprise. Soon trout was released in the Kenya rivers and thrived on the watercress imported by Grogan's friend Geoffrey Buxton. It was planted on the watershed of the Gura river and, like the trout, it spread to all Kenya's rivers. Grogan wrote[12] that some years later at a lunch party given by Frederick Jackson, S. L. Hinde, 'a notorious provincial commissioner, despite my presence, recited in great detail how he had introduced trout into Kenya. Jackson listened patiently for the end of the recitation, stood up, put his eyeglass to his eye, and said: "Hinde, you are a damned liar", and left the room.'

As if all this was not enough, he bought two farms at Limuru, then still known as Limoru or Lamoru and after planting the non-indigenous black wattle he rented them out. When he was accused of speculation he was indignant. The *East African Standard* reported that as a member of the Land Committee Grogan had said: 'It is absurd to attempt to prevent speculation. Transfer should be facilitated. Land in new countries is simply raw material and is not sacred as in old countries.' He also thundered against the appointment of a new Commissioner of Lands. Colonel J. A. L. Montgomery, a retired Punjab government servant, was hardly suited to the problems of Kenya, Grogan and others opined, and instead of liberalising land regulations, this gentleman tried to introduce a higher land rent and shorter leases. This infuriated the settlers and Grogan, who was much applauded after a speech on the subject at the next Colonialists' Association meeting. Also at this meeting the Indian Question was not spared his harsh sarcastic comments. In fact, he never missed a chance to rail at the Indians' aspirations using any argument to prove his point, one of which was their dirty habits. At that meeting he was not loath to mention the new outbreak of plague in the bazaar and the discovery of the body of a dead child in a dustbin.[13]

The Europeans' clamourings received some satisfaction when the Secretary of State, Lord Elgin, in July 1906, pledged to continue refusing the Indians rural land in the Highlands.[14] This was announced by the Governor[15] Sir James Hayes Sadler and Grogan's friendship with this administrator began on a good note. His friendship with governors was an on and off affair depending on how the Crown's representative behaved towards the settlers. For the time being the Grogans were seen at parties at Government House and the press, as the world over, reported their presence and Gertrude's outfits. For such occasions clothes followed the European fashions and it was not rare for women to import them especially for parties and the races.

The Nairobi Swamp was regarded by all Nairobi citizens, whether African, Indian or European, as an area to be avoided. Only mosquitoes thrived there. Frank Hall had built a causeway across it (now part of Race Course Road) in 1899, and Arab and Kamba caravans used it as a camping site many years before, but nobody would refer to it as a salubrious or a useful area. Grogan thought differently. It may not have been salubrious but it would certainly become useful he thought. He could see that eventually Nairobi would spread to the Nairobi river and past it, and the swamp lying on each side of the river would have to be controlled some day to allow for the town to expand. So without further ado on 5 December 1906 he bought the whole 121.4 acres of it, from Ainsworth Bridge to Race Course Road, and named it the Gertrude Swamp. Another odd thing about it, most people thought, in view of Grogan's animosity towards Indians, was his choice of partner: a Mr Sharif Jafer, but Grogan never said he disliked all Indians. In fact he liked the warrior races like the Sikhs but disliked the Hindus and their aspirations to grab the Highlands from the Europeans, and anything he said about them was just fuel to his arguments.

Anyway, he now had an Indian partner and he obtained from the Land Department a 99-year lease on 119.3 acres and an 88-year lease on 2.1 acres.[16] Another incomprehensible quirk of officialdom, he thought, but he was well satisfied with his purchase. Now all he had to do was dry out the swamp. An enormous undertaking, but with his usual determination and more money he began to fill portions of the swamp and rent them out to Indian market gardeners who built miserable hovels housing whole families within a few feet of corrugated iron and any material that came to hand. They also fertilised their gardens with human excreta and when the Government Health Officer learnt this, Grogan had something to answer for. He promised to speak to his tenants but people in Nairobi went on contracting dysentery and the cause was thought to be the swamp grown vegetables.[17]

Grogan was not interested in the swamp for the rents it could bring or what he could make from the quarry and the clay he had discovered there; he always thought much further than most people. He knew the swamp would be valuable one day—even if it took twenty years—which it did.

The Nairobi side of the swamp was known as Grogan Road until recently, and an article in the *Nation* of April 1977, headed 'Crooks, Cooks and the Ghost of Colonel Grogan' describes part of the swamp today as not very different from the swamp seventy years ago. By the polluted Nairobi river, the *Nation* writes, today as in Grogan's day, you will find shanties made of cardboard and plastic. The plastic is an innovation and some of the activities too, but even Grogan would not be surprised at the development there today. He would say he always knew it would come.

Business, or rather investments, were going well but Gertrude worried Grogan. For some time she had suffered intense pains in her ears and his old 'Nile days' friend Dr Milne diagnosed mastoiditis, a serious infection of the inner ear.

Dr Milne had married Eleanor Cole's sister Alison and was now a government doctor destined to become the Principal Medical Officer in 1913; people referred to him as Daddy Milne because of his kindness, and his family as 'savage' probably because he was so fond of disappearing into the bush to hunt. Perhaps because of his urge to go hunting he postponed doing anything about Gertrude's mastoids and recommended instead a holiday at the coast. In those days, and even now, 'a lower altitude' is supposed to deal with all manner of ills.

Chapter 14

THE FLOGGING

Upon their return from Mombasa Dr Milne observed that Gertrude's condition was not improved and he recommended an operation. In those days a very difficult and dangerous operation which could result in death or deformation of the face.

Dr Milne informed Grogan of the dangers and also that there was a new operation performed on such cases in England but the delay involved in travelling to England meant certain death for Gertrude whose infection of the inner ears was dangerously spreading to the meninges. Grogan could not stand watching the appalling pain she was suffering and he could not take the risk of allowing her to travel to England so with her consent he asked Dr Milne to arrange for an operation.

She was operated on at the small European Hospital on the Hill and at first the operation seemed to be successful, and the muscles of her face were not affected. Grogan was delighted and promised her a holiday at Naivasha as soon as the doctors released her from the hospital.

Meanwhile the settlers began to believe that the only man who could represent them with the government was Ewart Grogan. An 'urgent whip' was sent round for a general meeting of the Colonists' Association on 23 January 1907, and at this meeting Grogan was elected President by ninety-five votes as against fourteen given to a Nairobi solicitor. He now held the highest non-government post in the Protectorate where there was no parliament or any kind of official representation for the settlers. The only organ which could put pressure on the government was the Colonists' Association and Grogan was considered the ideal person to apply the necessary pressure. His motto was 'politics not personalities' but it was his personality which inspired the politics.

On 16 February he was also nominated to the Nairobi Township Council and he was already a Visiting Justice of the local jail which he considered a disgrace. He did not recommend improvements; he recommended a fresh start and the building of a new jail which was not carried out until 1911. Little did he know at this time how close he would come to that jail in the very near future—and not as a Visiting Justice.

When Gertrude was released from the hospital they all went to the Longonot farm in Naivasha and there it was soon evident that Gertrude's operation had not been the success it had first appeared to be. The pains began again and Grogan quickly brought her back to Nairobi. Although Dorothy was only five years old at the time she remembers how her mother screamed through the intense pain when they got back to Chiromo and her hands had to be tied because she was beating them so hard against the brass rails on the bed that they bled. Her daughter Jane, who was born in 1911, still remembers the scars. Another operation was recommended and this time she nearly died. They were not able to bring her out of the coma after the operation and Dorothy remembers bringing roses and sweet peas which her unconscious mother could not see, and her distraught father standing by the hospital bed clamouring for the doctors to do something.

Dorothy Hunter, Ewart's sister, and a friend, Miss McDonald, were told by Grogan they could visit his wife for a short spell and they took his rickshaw to ride to the hospital. For some unknown reason three Kikuyus, instead of the usual push-and-puller, went with them and the ladies soon realised they were all drunk. With frightening yells and much laughter the puller threw the shafts of the rickshaw up in the air and the women bounced up and down as the rickshaw hit the ground to the delight of the other two. The women were screaming and telling the Kikuyus to stop and let them off, but the whole thing was too amusing for the three rickshaw boys and they ran on as the women hung on for their life. When the boys finally stopped they pulled the frightened women roughly out of the rickshaw and left them to walk home.

Grogan was at Chiromo having just returned from the hospital where Gertrude was still in a coma, when the hysterical women turned up and told him the story. He was furious. He grabbed his kiboko, a whip of hippo hide, and went out to look for the three offenders. These were nowhere to be found, nor was his headman and his syce.[1] He started to walk to Wilfred Hunter's house, and then decided it would do no good to involve him, so he walked to a neighbour's house. Captain Sydney Fichat was an accountant and an estate agent, he was also Vice-President of the Colonists' Association and Grogan wanted his advice. It was by now 6.30 on the evening of 13 March 1907. Fichat was sitting on his verandah enjoying the traditional sundowner drink when Grogan stomped up the steps and said: 'Fichat, I am very angry.'

'What's the matter now,' Fichat asked. 'Land Office again?'

'No, more serious.'

After Grogan had told him the story Fichat warned him that he could get into trouble if he took the law into his own hands. He advised him to go home and sleep on it. Grogan agreed and asked him to come to Chiromo on his way into town the next morning.

The next morning Fichat arrived whilst Grogan was having breakfast and he calmly told his friend that he had followed his advice. He had slept on it and decided to flog the boys—in public. He was going to do this to show the government that if they could not keep law and order he would make sure that no native would touch his women ever again. He was tired of his servants' insubordination. They were becoming more and more difficult to handle and the police were totally ineffectual. He had to do something to stop this state of affairs, he decided. Whereupon he went out, found his headman and syce and the three rickshaw boys who had sobered up and returned home during the night. He tied their hands behind their back and locked them up in a shed. Returning to the dining room he informed Fichat that he was going to take the boys into town and whip them in the most public place he could find. The wives of the three boys began to cry because they thought their husbands were going to be killed[2] but this did not deter Grogan. He was considered a fair employer, supplying his servants with food, clothes, good accommodation, good pay and medical attention. When Gertrude's home remedies did not work, he took his servants to his own doctor rather than send them to the Native Hospital,[3] and unlike most other people he allowed them to have their families at Chiromo.

As in all small towns the news spread quickly. On his way to town Captain Fichat met Newland near Mrs Elliott's tea rooms in Government Road, and Newland met Mr Russell by the Travellers' Club who met Mr Low, until the whole town had heard of Grogan's intentions and excitement mounted as the story was repeated and embellished. It was no longer a case of drunken rickshaw boys frightening two European women, it was indecent assault and people looked forward to Grogan doing something effective about it. There had been cases of indecent assault, robberies and insubordination and the police did nothing to control the Africans. On top of this the government did nothing to help the settlers find adequate labour. In fact, they told the Africans that there was no need for them to work for the Europeans if they didn't want to. It was an explosive situation and this was a good opportunity to show the government that the settlers were no longer prepared to take this treatment lying down. Grogan would see to that.

Meanwhile, by 9.45 Grogan was walking from Chiromo to town followed by the three rickshaw boys with their hands tied behind their backs and reinforced by a Masai, a Mkamba and a Kavirondo. 'I brought three different tribes so that each might explain to their own people that it was a dangerous thing to insult white women,' Grogan said at the trial.[4] 'I walked past the Police Station, through the bazaar and down Government Road. I was still undecided. I nearly flogged the boys outside the Police Station and then I thought of Mr Isaacs, the Collector, or the Sub-Commissioner's office, but I changed my mind again and came down the street. I was surprised to see a lot of people coming from different directions towards me.'

He came to the Town Magistrate's Court which was within the Town Hall (where Regal Mansions in Moi Avenue stands now) and decided this was the ideal spot. By then a great crowd had collected and they clambered over the two cannons outside the court and trampled the grass and flowers. During the trial different witnesses assessed the number of people present as being between 40 and 250.

When Mr E. R. Logan, the Magistrate, gave evidence he said that he arrived at the court at 10 o'clock on the morning of 14 March and from his window he saw a number of Europeans coming towards the court. He sent his clerk to find out what was going on but the Goan clerk came back without a satisfactory answer. 'Being under the impression that unlawful proceedings were about to take place, I thought it my duty to go outside and protest against what was going to be done,' he said. 'I stood at the top of the steps [of the court] and found a large crowd of Europeans gathered at the foot of the steps. I should say forty to fifty persons more or less. At the centre of the crowd there was an open space. Lying on the ground I saw two natives. One of the natives was huddled up in a heap. The other one was lying, I think, at full length and the accused Mr Bowker was bending over him. By Mr Bowker's side was standing Mr Grogan. I called out to Mr Bowker and said, "Mr Bowker what are you doing?" I received no reply. I then said, "Gentlemen you are not allowed to take the law into your own hands. The proper course is to make a complaint to the proper authorities." I said this in a loud voice so that everybody present could hear. The accused, Captain Grogan, then said: "If we did what will happen? Will they be advised not to do it again?" I replied, "If anything is proved against them I imagine it will be more severe than that." Captain Grogan said: "What will they get?" And I answered that without knowing what the offence was I could not say what the punishment would be. That was all that was said. I waited a minute or two on the steps of the verandah and then seeing that the men were determined to do what they intended I walked back to my room. Not very long afterwards I heard the sound of blows.'

There is no record to show that despite the sound of blows Mr Logan took any action. He claimed he had no police on the premises and that he 'was completely taken by surprise', but he was able to tell the court that he had definitely seen the accused Mr Grogan, Mr Bowker, Mr Low and Captain Gray.

At this point, another accused, Captain Fichat cross-examined Mr Logan for the benefit of the crowded court and asked him if he would be surprised to hear that there were *three* Africans lying there. Logan had to admit that he was surprised, and the crowd was delighted. Fichat also asked him if when he came out on the verandah he had 'proclaimed to everyone who he was'. 'No, everyone knows who I am,' he replied as the public laughed.

According to Grogan's evidence, when Mr Logan came out on the steps he asked what Grogan was doing and he had replied, 'I am going to beat these boys.' 'Why?' Logan asked. 'Because I wish to do so,' Grogan claimed he had replied. 'What for?' Logan asked again. 'For insulting my sister and a lady friend.' There was a lot of noise but Grogan heard Logan say words to the effect that the Africans should be properly charged and Grogan answered that he 'was sick of being made a fool of and this was a matter I dare not leave to the authorities.' It was difficult to hear anything, he stated, but after a few more words Logan turned away.

Captain Smith of the police arrived just before the flogging and in his evidence he said: 'I pushed my way through the crowd and put my hand on Grogan's arm. As I did so the crowd closed in and hustled me outside.' He said he was in uniform at the time and Bowker was one of the people who pushed him out. There was nothing for him to do but go for reinforcements. The crowd was angry and he could tell that alone there was nothing he could do.

Grogan also realised the crowd was growing angry. In his evidence he said: 'I was afraid some scene might occur and I spoke to the crowd as loudly as I could and said that I did not want any interference. It was purely a personal matter and as I thought the crowd had got a false idea, I stated that it was nothing indecent and I asked them to give me their word not to touch the natives and their general assent was given.' He then asked Mr Campbell Cowley who could speak Kikuyu to interpret to the Africans why he was doing this and 'to warn their people that white men could not stand any impertinence to their women folk in any part of the world.'

After the ineffectual Mr Logan had retired to his office and Captain Smith had gone for reinforcements there was nothing anybody could do as Grogan, Bowker and Gray whipped each African twenty-five times.

In his evidence Grogan said: 'I gave one of the boys twenty-five. When I finished the whip was pulled out of my hand, the crowd closed in around me and I did not see what followed. I saw the natives brought out and when I saw the crowd disappear I knew there was no risk of any further trouble and told the boys to go off home. I then went to the Travellers' Club and had a drink. Later I went to T. A. Wood's room to attend a meeting.

My object in flogging these natives in public was that my natives were getting out of control owing to the total inadequacy of the punishment inflicted. I look upon any matter connected with the safety of my women folk as so important that I do not consider it justified, as a family man, to leave it to the vagaries of the law and the application thereof, and I wish the natives to understand, and it should be generally understood that any action of that nature involves a far greater risk than "horsetooth mealie".' By this he meant prison where the prisoners were fed this type of mealie.

The newspapers followed the case avidly and during the trial the *East African Standard* wrote: 'Captain Grogan was undoubtedly justified in using physical force as the provocation was of a kind no man will brook, and it does not matter whether the assault was committed on a native or a European. We have never heard of any man who had appealed to the law to punish his wife's insulter.' The newspaper also advocated the removal of 'those officers who had allowed the natives to reach such a pitch as to make it possible for them to insult a white woman . . . Blood beats and in a tropical climate the Caucasian is apt to be intemperate.' The newspaper claimed that it was curious that the four accused had been the most prominent in the criticism of the administration. It claimed they were being penalised for different reasons than the flogging.

Just before his death in 1979 Lord Delamere, the 4th Baron, remarked on the famous flogging and he said: 'Grogan was not a ruthless man, he was charitable and generous to the Africans. He always helped all sorts of people but we now forget that flogging was a very common form of punishment in those days. Starting with school, in the army or in the navy and in the prisons, flogging was an accepted form of punishment and it still is in the Kenya prisons today.'

The difference of course was that the flogging Grogan and his friends had carried out was done by private citizens and not by the authorities. He *had* taken the law into his own hands and he expected trouble, not only from the authorities but from the Africans. An emergency meeting of the Colonists' Association was held and Grogan pointed out that there was unrest among the natives. It was resolved that a local defence force be formed and that the Government be asked to supply rifles and ammunition to whoever required them. The Committee then proceeded to pay a visit to the Acting Commissioner, Frederick Jackson, the Governor, Sir James Hayes Sadler, being on leave in England. This was a large deputation including Burn, Fichat, Bayldon, Roberts, Watkins and Bailey and led by Grogan. It seems that Jackson agreed to give an immediate order for the distribution of arms and ammunition and to appoint a committee who would organise a scheme of defence.[5]

A massive amount of correspondence passed between Jackson and Elgin from the first telegram on 15 March, the day after the flogging, and Mr Churchill, the Under Secretary for the Colonies, had to answer a series of questions in the House of Commons.

There was a great excitement in the town and when Grogan returned to Chiromo he sent the three rickshaw boys to the native hospital, where their backs were not only treated but also photographed and the resulting photographs sent to the Foreign Office.

The newspapers in England gave the flogging almost as much publicity as the Kenya papers, and opinions as to justification for Grogan's act were very mixed. Meanwhile, Jackson, in a despatch to the Colonial Office, denied that 'there was any foundation for reports of an African rising,' and in fact there were no incidents.

The accused were summoned to appear on Monday, 25 March at the Magistrate's Court and on that date there was a preliminary investigation into the case of the Crown versus Captain Grogan, W. Russell Bowker, W. MacLennan Wilson, Major W. A. Burn, Captain S. C. Fichat, Captain Thord Gray, Reverend O. A. Bennett, Walker Dunn and Ernest Low. The summonses against Walker Dunn, MacLennan Wilson and the Reverend Bennett were withdrawn after the Crown Advocate, Mr R. M. Combe, stated that these gentlemen although present took no active part in the proceedings.

The trial lasted until 6 April and the odd thing is that during his evidence Grogan never mentioned the stress he was suffering over Gertrude's condition and he did not allow his lawyer, Mr B. G. Allen, to mention the fact in mitigation. Grogan knew he would be punished and he wanted no special treatment, he wanted to make a point. Gertrude meanwhile had come out of her coma and Grogan was greatly relieved but not at all worried about the outcome of the trial.

The Magistrate, Mr Dolbey had decided at the preliminary

hearing that he would not press the charges under Sections 144 and 147 I.P.C. which referred to rebellion and armed riot for which there was insufficient evidence, but he would try the accused under Section 143 which referred to 'unlawful assembly'. It appeared later that jurisdiction did not allow him 'to split the offence for the purpose of giving himself summary jurisdiction.' Another mistake was that they were tried without the benefit of a jury and without the right of bail. But the strange thing was that the accused were not charged with assault.

During the trial the court was crowded but when it came to V. M. Newland's turn to give evidence he asked that all ladies be made to leave the court. Cross-examined by the Crown Advocate he assured the court that he felt justified in having taken part in the 'unlawful assembly' because like Grogan he was tired of being made a fool of by the government. 'Only four months ago,' he said, 'a native exposed his private parts to a female of my family and this is not the first case of indecency.'

Dr Milne, who had been present at the flogging, also gave evidence, but when it came to Bowker's turn the Crown Advocate was booed by the spectators and reprimanded by the Magistrate. The Crown Advocate stated that during his defence Bowker had said: 'I deliberately flog niggers on sight.' The Magistrate corrected the Crown Advocate by saying that Mr Bowker's defence was: 'I always flog niggers on sight who insult white women.'

The result of the trial was fourteen days simple imprisonment for Bowker and Gray plus a fine of 450 rupees (£30).

'The worse case of all,' the Magistrate said, 'is that of E. S. Grogan who originated the whole affair. I have been careful in conducting his defence to weigh the reasons for his actions which he has put forward but I do not find any justification of any sort or kind which can be urged on his behalf, owing to the position which he occupied, as a man to whom the Government ought to have been able to look for assistance for the keeping of law and order. In fact, from the evidence in this case it is clear that he had used his influence towards the others. The order of this court is that he be imprisoned for one month of simple imprisonment and pay a fine of 500 Rupees (£34) or an extra month of simple imprisonment in default of payment. Conviction and sentences under Section 143 I.P.C.' Had he been found guilty of assault he would have been given six months and 1,000 rupees fine.

The newspapers and the settlers were indignant. The Standard said there was no recourse in law where women were insulted by Africans.

The English papers also reported the verdict and Mr Churchill had to answer questions in the Commons again, and as a result he cabled the Acting Commissioner to investigate whether Grogan's health was suffering in jail and instructed Mr Jackson to do everything possible to make his imprisonment comfortable with regard to his health and proper standard of humanity, but, he added, that persons who were guilty of misconduct in primitive countries are liable to suffer. He assured the Commons that provision had been made to build a prison for Europeans in Nairobi.

But not soon enough to house Grogan, Russell Bowker and Gray. The three European prisoners were an embarrassment to the Government. There was no prison to house them in and they could not be detained in the native prison which Grogan had only a few weeks before declared a disgrace. The only alternative was a small government bungalow on the Hill, which was later always referred to as 'Grogan's prison', and Churchill need not have worried about comforts and humanitarian treatment for the prisoners. The first night they were locked up in the house they were serenaded by a large group of Nairobi citizens. They were always allowed visitors and special dishes of food were sent in to them throughout their imprisonment. To show their contempt for the Government's action, the Colonists' Association refused Grogan's resignation and re-elected him to the post of President on 20 April.

On the same day the *Standard* appealed to the Governor to return from his four months' leave and it warned him that he would find the Kikuyu less settled than before. He would also find that there was a great deal of passive resistance against labouring for the white man throughout the tribe. 'Fifty thousand Kikuyu spears are restless,' it warned.

In fact, nothing happened but Grogan was busy in the house on the Hill writing out instructions to his lawyer for an appeal. He also sent telegrams to the Secretary of State, Lord Elgin, and a long, legally worded defence of his case. In the first paragraph he claims that 'no charge of assault, brutal or otherwise, was ever formally preferred against me. Therefore I had no occasion to bring evidence to rebut the false allegations of brutality made in the Acting Commissioner's cable.' He also wants to know why Lord Elgin has refused a request by the European community to appoint a Commission of Enquiry into the case. He lists the technical points as to why the case should not have been tried by a Magistrate without a jury. He also mentions the fact that Jackson was afraid of being accused of taking revenge against Grogan otherwise he would have not suggested the case be tried in Mombasa where Europeans were not likely to make trouble.[6]

He also wrote a letter to *The Times*[7] ridiculing Churchill's statement in the Commons that 'great improvements have been made in the jails at Nairobi and Mombasa and further improvements are in the contemplation.' 'Mr Churchill has not visited the Nairobi jail and therefore must be relying on official reports from this side,' Grogan wrote. 'I am a visiting justice of the Nairobi jail (and this) has been condemned by several medical boards. Quite recently there was a serious outbreak of beri-beri among the prisoners. The only improvement which has been made within the last eighteen months has been the boring of a hole for ventilation . . . So much for the recent great improvements.'

The flogging incident had a number of repercussions. The Colonial Office had decided at last to establish a Legislative Council in Kenya and now it considered postponing it because the whole settler position was being re-examined. The new council was to have six official members, including the Governor, who had meanwhile returned to the Protectorate, and two unofficial members who would be chosen by the government. Even before the opening of Legislative Council on 17 August, it was known that Lord Delamere and E. S. Grogan would be nominated. The opening of Legislative Council went ahead as planned but Grogan was not in it. He had been substituted by J. C. Baillie who died before the Council opened and A. A. Baillie was nominated in his place.

Grogan was not surprised by this, nor was he surprised when the Appeal Court reversed the verdict of the Magistrate's Court. Under Criminal Appeal No. 2 in July, Presiding Judge Barth examined the evidence of the previous court and found that the Magistrate 'cannot try summarily when he is not competent to hold a summary trial,' he said.[8] 'It is a rule of law often laid down that a Magistrate must not whittle down the offence disclosed in the evidence in order that he may procure jurisdiction . . . In my opinion,' the Appeal Judge summarised, 'the Magistrate erred in dealing with the case himself on the offences alleged, and the evidence thereon and the finding and sentence must be reversed. The only point that remains to be considered is whether the accused should be committed for trial or not. In view of the fact that the accused has already suffered the term of imprisonment to which he was sentenced, I refrain from ordering a committal, and acquit him.'

This did not mean that Grogan had learned not to fight the establishment. As far as he was concerned they were as guilty of illegitimate deeds as before he went to jail. The Government was now trying to reduce leasehold terms to twenty-one years and the terms were 'received with marked disapproval by all classes of the white community'[9]—to put it mildly. The Colonists' Association, through its President E. S. Grogan, appealed to the Governor to change the rules and Grogan also wrote inflammatory letters to the press. To the *East African Standard* he wrote: 'The entire clause reeks of the amateur who has not even borrowed a primer on the subject, who believes the World is straining at the leash, hungering for the pest-ridden lands of Central Africa. The measure is the cheerful outcome of the ignorance of Downing Street.

'Will the Commissioner for Lands inform us whether he really believes that a man will turn aside the assisted passages and free land grants of self-governing Canada to pay an import duty of £50 upon himself for the privilege of coming to East Africa, where taxed, voteless, voiceless and the butt of every jack-in-office (a sort of fifteen century Russian serf) he may carve a farm out of the wilderness in order that when it becomes productive he may hand it back to the Government as a gift.'

He then sent a dissertation on the economics of settlement to the Colonial Office giving details of the expenditure needed to establish pastoral farming, of money already spent without rewards and many other details, ending his dissertation by saying that land monopolists existed 'almost exclusively in the minds of academics. The actual person wants interest on his outlay and strives to obtain some return by sale or development.' The Colonial Office were not impressed, they knew what they were saying when they spoke of land monopolists. The correspondence between Grogan and the Colonial Office went on for two more years.[10]

Grogan was angry. There were too many aspects of Kenya which disappointed him and perhaps the biggest disappointment was being excluded from the Legislative Council. Now that Gertrude was better and out of danger, he decided it was time to leave Kenya—at least for a while—but perhaps for good. The way Kenya was governed disgusted him, however much he loved the country. Churchill was due to visit Kenya in October and the one person he did not want to see was Churchill, much to the relief of the Government officials who dreaded a confrontation. It was perhaps a good thing a confrontation never took place as Churchill stated that Kenya could never become 'a white man's country . . . in the sense that Canada [is] a white man's country', which was completely opposed to Grogan's and Delamere's thinking. Churchill also advocated that holdings of over 100,000 acres should be considered illegal and the holders fined £25 per day. That would have gone down well with Grogan!

A great sigh of relief must have gone up from all civil servants, from the Governor down, when Grogan, Gertrude, the children, Nanny Redwood and Martin the housekeeper embarked for England on 28 September. Edith, the maid, had married a postmaster and stayed in Kenya.

Chapter 15

ELECTIONEERING IN ENGLAND AND WRITING

Kenya had not heard the last of Grogan. As soon as he arrived in London he was interviewed by a number of newspapers such as *The Times*, the *Daily Mail*, the *Evening Standard* and a representative of the *East African Standard*.

On one of his pet subjects, the Indian question, he wrote to *The Times* on 20 December 1907 warning his readers that if 'Asiatic immigration' was allowed to expand, the whites would be 'frozen out'. 'If we do not face the issue now and agree on some *modus vivendi* there will surely be a series of explosions which cannot but end in a gigantic conflagration,' he wrote, from the New Oxford and Cambridge Club.

When the Grogans arrived in England they stayed with Gertrude's sister Helen Baden-Powell in Palace Gate. Gertrude was expecting another baby and Helen insisted they should stay until the birth despite the fact that Grogan did not like his brother-in-law. He kept busy with his controversial correspondence and a plan for a new future.

When he was still in Kenya, Joseph Chamberlain, the respected British statesman who had been a Colonial Secretary and was the leader of the Unionist Party, had invited Grogan to stand for election in Newcastle-under-Lyme and now that Kenya was of no immediate interest to him, he began to consider Chamberlain's offer seriously. He had talked about the possibility to Delamere before leaving Kenya when the latter had taken over the leadership of the Colonists' Association, and Delamere had been enthusiastic at the prospect of having Grogan in the House of Commons.

There was a lot to do and a lot to learn, but meanwhile he could not forget Kenya's problems nor did Kenya forget him. The *East African Standard* reporter who interviewed him in London referred to him as 'a man who may have a considerable influence in moulding [Kenya's] eventual destinies . . . and the acknowledged head of the non-official white community.'

Asked if he believed Kenya was a white man's country, he answered most emphatically that it was, both from a climatic point of view and because of the availability of land; 'yet the newcomer is told by the officials, appointed presumably to settle the country, that there is no land available. A population of four million natives has a total area equivalent to a quarter of British India with a population of two hundred millions. This anomaly cannot surely be permitted to endure much longer. . . . Nowhere would it be safer to embark on a scheme of sending the surplus hands and mouths of the industrial community back to the land.'

As for the administration of justice he could speak from experience and 'it leaves something to be desired,' he said. 'There is much to support the impression that there is one law for the settler, another for the official and none at all for the native or the Indian. It works out as follows: the settler is jumped on; the officials explain; the native runs away; and the Indian is rarely found out.'

The Indian question could obviously not be spared his comments. He said, amongst a lot of other things, that the British Government 'invariably claim for the Indian the rights in other people's countries that they specifically deny him in his own . . . [the immigrants from England] have contributed eight millions as against Indian immigrants who have contributed nothing . . . It is most obviously the duty of the Government to give preference to the white who has fought and paid and to the native who was in possession. The Asiatic can never be other than a menace to the welfare of both.'

He listed seven points of improvement in the administration of Kenya including 'a change from the unjust system of hut tax . . . (for the natives)' and he summed up by saying: 'No taxation without representation'.[1] This was to be his motto, adopted by the rest of the settlers, for many years before the Government decided to allow the country to elect their own representatives in the Legislative Council.

In Kenya, meanwhile, all was not well with the new Legislative Council. In April 1908 Delamere asked the Governor, Sir James Hayes Sadler, questions on the labour situation and the Governor answered equivocally. Delamere tried to pin the Governor down and having failed he led a group of two hundred settlers to the Governor's office where he was thought to have retired. Not finding him there, Delamere and the two hundred marched to Government House, but the Governor refused to see them. An ugly scene ensued when the demonstrators threatened to break down the door and the police had to be called to disperse them. The result was the suspension of Delamere and Baillie, the only two nominated members of the Council, for leading 'an organised demonstration of an insulting and disorderly character against His Majesty's representative in the protectorate.'[2]

Grogan was accused of many misdeeds in his life and references to his participation in this demonstration appear in many books and newspapers. In fact, quite a number of people are convinced that Grogan was the leader and very probably he would have been had he lived in Kenya at the time, but he was in London and the *London Standard* asked his views regarding the demonstration. 'It is quite evidently a strong outburst of public indignation which has come to a head over the proposed new labour ordinance,' he told the press. 'There has been a growing distrust in the administration of the Protectorate . . .'

'[The suspension of Delamere and Baillie] represents nothing but the negation of right of free speech . . . These gentlemen have been expressly nominated by the Governor to give a community voice in the council . . . The Governor's action in requesting their removal is another example of local official panic, and it proves the absolute necessity of selecting for the post of Governor for this class of Protectorate a man with *self-governing*[3] colonial experience. At present, the white community who are heavily taxed have not even an admitted right to criticise the expenditure of their money.'

'Self Government' were words which would now recur in Grogan's and Delamere's speeches at regular intervals, and

Grogan was convinced that this was Kenya's only hope of success until a few years before the country's independence.

The Kenya labour question was being discussed in the British Parliament and Grogan did not fail to write to *The Times* commenting on Churchill's speech about the problem. In his letter of 4 August he insinuated that Churchill knew nothing of the problem after a few days' visit to the Protectorate. He wrote this letter from Camp Hill near Newcastle in Staffordshire where he had bought a house in order to be within the constituency he intended to run for.

Gertrude had stayed on in London with her sister and there another daughter, Cynthia, was born on 27 August 1908. Her godfathers were Lord Baden-Powell and Dr Milne, who was on holiday in England. Grogan might have been disappointed at not having a son yet, but in that period up to the First World War, the daughters remember him as a 'marvellous father'. He used to hide soft toy animals in their beds, tell them stories and draw them pictures. Throughout his life he loved children although after the war he changed towards his own.[4]

In Camp Hill he had more on his mind than electioneering. He was writing a book on economics which he called *The Economic Calculus and its Application to Tariff*, and dedicated it to Lord Delamere 'who is responsible for the germination of much of the theory herein contained'. The bibliography included a long list of books on economics, Karl Marx's *Capitalist Production*, Charles Darwin's *Origin of Species*, United States Labour Bulletins, Sir William Petty's economic writings, Adam Smith, Ricardo, Malthus, J. S. Mill and many more.

'There is a growing feeling that the classical system of economics has failed to justify its claim for recognition in the domain of Science,' he wrote, and proceeded to examine the reasons why. From the theory of human evolution he elaborated on the structural and organic units and analysed the objectives and the laws, the stress of man as non-man, agriculture, grazing, communications, population and money. He gave a large part of the book to free trade, protection of workers and unemployment and sums up with Britain's position in all these spheres. Throughout he illustrated his theories with elaborate tables extending them to energy and calories applicable to workers' output.

The book is a detailed study of the economic situation in Britain which obviously cannot be examined here but was recognised by the experts of the period as a valuable addition to the study of economics and it is still used today as a reference book in the British Library of Political and Economic Science at the London University and many other universities and libraries throughout England.

The book was published in August 1909 and during his electioneering in Newcastle-under-Lyme he used some of the information applicable to the workers in his speeches to the electorate, of course, simplifying the language to bring it to the level of his audiences.

Although women had no vote as yet in England, a great number of them attended his meetings and enthusiastically backed Grogan. His good looks, penetrating blue eyes and forceful manner and speech attracted the women pottery workers who painted themselves blue and red and shouted such slogans as: 'No one shall up us but Grogan' along the streets of Newcastle-under-Lyme.

Years later[5] he told the story of how one of these women, 'a virginal virago', attacked him with the challenge: 'Hey, mister, what about votes for women?' and he answered that he was in favour of votes for married women and also an additional vote for every baby they had. He was never asked about the women's vote again, but nevertheless remained popular with them despite his opponent's campaign against him. One of the stories circulated by the other parties was that Grogan had thrown two policemen down a well and they had drowned,[6] but no evidence was ever produced to confirm the story. Unfortunately for him, another story—the flogging of the Africans—was easily confirmed and used. His enemies made great capital of it and even his daughters, Dorothy and Joyce suffered for it at school where they were taunted for being the daughters of the man who beat natives. Churchill was one of the accusers who did not let anybody forget who Grogan was.

Dorothy and Joyce also suffered in another context for their father's election. Grogan used to take them on a donkey cart through the streets of Newcastle-under-Lyme shouting: 'Vote for daddy', but although this method of electioneering appealed to some of the electorate, others did not care for it and sometimes the two little girls would arrive home screaming and in tears because they had mud thrown at them.[7]

Even baby Cynthia was involved. She was entered for a baby

competition and she won it. 'I think I lost him his seat because of that,' she said.

There must have been more reasons for losing the election, but lose it he did in January 1910 to Mr Wedgwood who was, after all, a better known figure in the pottery world of Staffordshire.

Grogan went back to his writing and in May of that year his *Tariff, The Workers' Charter* came out after many requests for the publication of his campaign speeches. In the book, as in his campaign, his motto was: 'Complementary exchange is good for the worker, competitive exchange is bad for the worker.' He also wrote that workers must be protected or they would leave the country.

This small book (138 pages) was very clearly written and obviously meant for all classes of people. It went into a second edition in 1911 and like its predecessor it is still a reference book.

Chapter 16

EMPIRE BUILDING

Despite all his activities he was longing for Kenya and on 28 June 1910 he was back in Nairobi for a short visit to check on his investments and the general situation.

One of the first things he did was to buy his Indian partner out of the Swamp. He paid Mr Jafer £3,000 and the Swamp was now entirely his.

There were not many changes in Kenya. Nairobi's streets now had electric light but they were still dusty and full of pot holes or muddy and rutted. One change which did not displease him was the change in governors. The previous year Sir James Hayes Sadler had been transferred and replaced by Sir Percy Girouard, a Canadian, which seemed a strange appointment to most settlers, but not to Grogan. Could it be that the British Government was actually considering the possibility of giving Kenya self-government? Why otherwise choose a Governor from a self-governing country?

Grogan was welcomed back by many people and especially by the members of the Colonists' Association. He immediately started where he had left off in 1907 when he had proposed a scheme for a political federation of all the European associations in the country, such as the Colonists, Pastoralists, Coast Planters, etc., and about which nothing had been done during his absence. Now his forceful personality convinced the members of the necessity to start the Convention of Associations which was created on 25 July 1910.

Dr Gerald Anderson was a very young boy then and worked as cub reporter for his father, the editor of the *East African Standard*, and often reported Grogan's speeches at the Colonists' Association. 'Whenever there was trouble Grogan was asked to speak,' he said. 'He could say an awful lot in an hour. He had a gift for public speaking. A very intelligent man and one of the greatest of East Africa. When speaking he always knew how far he could go without tripping over the snares. He was nearly always elected amongst the leaders. He used to talk at quite a different level from other people. He had a mind above the petty things of life, and he was a fearless man, not foolishly so, but sensible. He had a silver tongue.'

During his short stay in Kenya he was absorbed by what people came to know as his 'political child'. The Convention of Associations was also known as 'Grogan's Big Noise' and was destined to become the most powerful body in Kenya politics. Although it started with the Governor, Sir Percy Girouard's blessing, subsequent governors often wished he had vetoed it for the trouble it caused the Government in the years to follow.

In December 1910 Grogan was back in England and ready to let the Foreign Office have more of his opinions on Indian immigration. A report was being prepared by the Committee on Emigration from India to the Crown Colonies and Protectorates and Grogan was invited to give evidence.[1]

As he was no longer interested in contesting a parliamentary seat for Newcastle-under-Lyme, he sold the house in Camp Hill and bought a huge establishment at 52 Draycott Place in London. It was referred to as 'No 10' by his daughters, had been a dance academy and spread over the whole corner of Draycott Place and Draycott Avenue and rose four stories high. Grogan enthusiastically set to transferring the dance academy into a comfortable family home. It was a modern house for those days. Over the double arched entrance a shield carries the date '1907'. Grogan transformed the ground floor into a ball room. Two drawing rooms and the dining room were on the first floor and a large number of bedrooms on the other floors. His study/library occupied the corner of the top floor and above that were the mansard windows of the staff floor. From the outside it could be mistaken for a town hall but the daughters have happy memories of this huge house where dinners and balls were held regularly. The important part of the house for Grogan was his study and large library. According to his daughter Jane, it had every conceivable book on every subject imaginable. Grogan would sit there for hours in his carpet slippers, but he was not averse to his daughters using the library, in fact he was rather pleased when he discovered Jane pulling down an encyclopedia. She was terrified when he came quietly upon her in his carpet slippers, but he soon reassured her by saying: 'Thank God I have a child who reads. Any time you want to read you can come up here and take any book you want.'

This was much later in Jane's life. She was born on 22 December 1911. Yet another daughter for Grogan who so wanted a son.

Although he had lost the elections at Newcastle-under-Lyme, on 15 April 1911 he was elected President of the Working Man's Empire United League and invited to lecture at the potteries in Staffordshire. At the first public meeting the Chairman, Mr W. Wilson, explained that the object of the new league was to provide facilities for the debate of matters of Imperial interest. 'The future of our country and of our children depends upon the future of the Empire, therefore our policy must not be party but national and the leader must be an Empire man and Captain Grogan has done us the honour of accepting the presidency of the League.'

In his speech, as in many speeches before and after, Grogan sang the praises of Kenya and encouraged young men to go out and make their home there. Invariably after such meetings a number of men would approach him and ask for more details of this fabulous land and many of them took his advice and made Kenya their home. Some more successfully than others.

He always stressed in his speeches that the British had made the Empire and it was up to the British to go out and cultivate this wonderful land. Throughout his speeches there were cheers from the audience every time he mentioned the Empire. The British were not ashamed of their Empire in those days—far from it. Grogan was a very popular speaker with the workers and for a few months the meeting halls where he lectured were thronged with people of all classes.

On 20 February 1912 he was back in Kenya for another quick visit. At this time another change of Governors took place. The Canadian Girouard was replaced by Sir Henry Conway Belfield and a mass meeting was held in Nairobi asking for Belfield's appointment to be reconsidered on the grounds of inadequate previous colonial experience. To show what a lot of notice the Colonial Office took of the Kenya settlers' demands, Belfield stayed in office, longer than any other Governor, until 1917.

Grogan was back in London in April 1912, but he had meanwhile encouraged a son of his half-brother, Harold Grogan, to go out to Kenya. Harold Grogan was a surveyor and Kenya needed surveyors, and when he mentioned to his uncle that he disliked working in the City and wished he could work in the country, Grogan said: 'Why not try British East Africa. There is plenty of fresh air there.' 'That settled me,' Harold Grogan wrote.[2] 'I never hesitated but sailed on 6 September 1912 for Kilindini.' He never regretted it and remained in Kenya until his retirement in 1964.

In London Grogan became a member of another association: the 'East African Association' whose members were all Kenya men such as Lord Cardross and Lord Hindlip and whose purpose was to interest prospective British investors in Kenya and also help Kenya settlers whilst in London.

Grogan's activities in England were not absorbing enough for his thirty-eight years. Even an invitation to stand for Parliament again did not attract him. He wanted to return to the land which he now considered his home, as he said to the *East African Standard* reporter who interviewed him before he sailed on the *Carisbrooke Castle* on 7 November 1913 with Gertrude, Dorothy and Angela Sharp, the daughter of Arthur Sharp who had accompanied him for part of the walk through Africa.

Joyce, Cynthia and Jane were left with the trusted Nanny Redwood at Draycott Place and there were enough aunts and uncles to keep an eye on them until a decision was taken in Kenya as to whether the children should be brought out or Gertrude go back to them. Angela Sharp could meanwhile teach the eleven-year-old Dorothy.

The Grogans were back in time for the opening of the Muthaiga Club on 31 December 1913. This new club was created for the non-officials as opposed to the Nairobi Club on the Hill which was mostly for Government servants and which the settlers resented using as they were often at loggerheads with the officials. Also, the aristocrats among the settlers thought the standard of the Nairobi Club was very poor. At first the Muthaiga Club was not popular with officials or the commercial population of Nairobi because it was considered too far out—three miles by rickshaw—from the centre of Nairobi. It was a country club and the settlers were delighted to have it to themselves, although they could hardly make it pay. It was a rich man's toy.

Major J. A. (Archie) Morrison had come out to Kenya to hunt and, like many visitors before and after, he had fallen in love with the country. Whilst staying at Chiromo as a guest he told Grogan's brother-in-law, Wilfred Hunter, and Freddy Ward that he wanted to develop a residential area with a country club close to Nairobi. Ward drove Morrison in one of Ali Khan's barouches through winding country paths to Muthaiga and he fell in love with it. Next morning Archie Morrison made arrangements with the Standard Bank of South Africa which had just opened and consisted of one room, a table, three chairs and a safe. To Ward's and Hunter's astonishment, Morrison handed Mr J. J. Toogood, the bank manager, a cheque for £60,000 and appointed Ward and Hunter to be his representatives in the enterprise as he was going back to England. The future of the Muthaiga Country Club was assured.

Muthaiga is the Kikuyu name for the Greenheart tree bark from which the Kikuyu used to make medicine and also poison for arrows. The construction of the Muthaiga Club, which came to mean many things to many people, from champagne parties to involved extra-marital affairs, was not an easy matter. A highly qualified architect, H. E. Henderson, who subsequently built many important buildings in Nairobi, had to be brought from England and he, in turn, brought a stone carver, a master builder and a plumber. As cement was difficult to obtain, murram and lime were used for the pink stucco on the outside of the Club walls, which are still such an important feature of the Club.

Finally the Club was opened and although only fourteen guests partook of the New Year's Eve dinner, the Club cellar boasted Lafitte, La Tour, Hocks and Moselle wines, port and the best brandy. The chef was from the Bombay Yacht Club and the stewards were Goan. It also boasted a band but the first year it lost £1,300.[3]

Nairobi was progressing in some ways but in others it was still a cowboy town. When the new *East African Standard*'s premises were gutted by fire on 21 August by the time the ox-drawn fire engine arrived it was almost completely burnt out. Like a Hollywood film set, the *East African Standard* had a stone façade and the rest was a wood and tin structure. Having finally arrived on the scene, the firemen then discovered that their hose could not reach the nearest stand-pipe which was in the Indian bazaar, hundreds of feet away. A number of hose pipes were then joined together and promptly burst, but when eventually a trickle of water was produced it was too late for John Cowan, an employee of the *Standard* who perished in the fire.

This was the sort of thing which infuriated Grogan. The Government couldn't even organise a proper fire department, but there were compensations. The Theatre Royal advertised a variety show with 'vocal and conjuring and bioscopic pictures', and the town flocked to it, crossing the newly laid out 6th Avenue (now Kenyatta Avenue) which was a mud field. When the road was being planned as a 200 foot wide avenue, Delamere was indignant. 'What is my wife going to do when she has to go across that muddy black cotton soil field just to do a bit of shopping on the other side,' he said. Grogan answered him that the only hope for a well planned town was wide streets.[4] He could always see a little further than anybody else.

Chapter 17

THE FIRST WORLD WAR

On 4 August 1914, at the beginning of the war, the Grogans were staying at Turi in 'a funny little hut' Grogan had built close to his forest concession. Word of the outbreak of war spread very fast despite difficulties of communications and Grogan insisted they should all get back to Nairobi as quickly as possible. They reached Londiani by ox-cart and there was great confusion at the station as all the farmers in the region were also determined to reach Nairobi and to join up.[1] Some of them were too impatient to wait for the train. They loaded their horses with a few necessities and their guns and rode off to Nairobi. None of them knew what they were going to join up, but as in England, the outbreak of war in Kenya was met with great enthusiasm and every man wanted a part in it.

Grogan knew very well what he was going to join up. He found Colonel Richard Meinertzhagen already busy organising an Intelligence section and he offered his services. Meinertzhagen, who had first met him in 1904 at Londiani, and had written enthusiastically about him in his diary, was a great admirer of his and he was delighted to have Grogan in his group. Not for them the confusion of the mounted volunteers, one of whom was Grogan's young brother Quentin.

There had been a hurried call for volunteers—anybody who could ride a horse and use a rifle—but there was nothing organised for them yet, so they organised themselves under the leadership of individuals of their choice. Nairobi House, the Volunteer Forces H.Q., was besieged by men anxious to defend their country. Some joined Bowker's Horse, others Arnold Scouts, the Plateau South Africans, the Legion of Frontiersmen or Monica's Own, named after the Governor's daughter.

Nairobi was in a state of excitement and confused activity and nobody knew what was going to happen. Were the Germans in Tanganyika going to attack? Should the settlers attack the Germans? Others said, like many in England, that the war would be over by Christmas. It would not affect East Africa at all, they said, because it was unthinkable that the two white races should fight each other in black men's countries, and yet others were of the opinion that Tabora on the other side of the border should be occupied immediately. There were also the pessimists who expected an overwhelming force of Germans to swoop down on Nairobi at any minute. These self-styled experts said the Germans had a great army, unlimited weapons and aeroplanes. In fact the Germans in Tanganyika had one plane which had been brought there for the recent Dar es Salaam exhibition and no more regular troops than the British in Kenya, who had two King's African Rifles battalions spread around the Northern Frontier and Uganda, amounting to no more than 2,400 askaris and white officers. One of these pessimists reported spotting a German plane over Nairobi and there was panic followed by nervous laughter when the plane turned out to be a rather large bird. A verse appeared in the papers:

I thought I saw an aeroplane
Upon the Athi plain.
I looked again and saw it was
A Kavirondo crane.

Meanwhile the defenders of King and Country, the volunteer mounted units, filled the hotels and clubs. There was a lot of esprit de corps, but no discipline at all. They all wore just what they thought the situation required. Pith helmets, bush hats and worn out double terai were very popular, preferably with all kinds of feathers stuck in them. Riding breeches, shorts, long khaki trousers were topped with any kind of shirt, but the favourite was a khaki jacket with the sleeves cut off to enable the wearer to shoot more freely. This type of jacket has remained in the East African wardrobe as a must for all who think of themselves as practical 'men of Kenya'. Coloured handkerchieves tied around the neck were a help when dust choked the wearer.

There was plenty of dust as some of these keen mounted volunteers practised on the ground opposite the Norfolk Hotel armed with rifles and even lances. One man in every four was left to hold the horses and mules, whilst the 'company' ran to attack the 'enemy' and blazed away. When the order came to retire and mount, very often all they saw was a cloud of dust as the mules and horses had bolted at the first shot.

Eventually this motley crowd was collected into one unit which came to be known as the East African Mounted Rifles and fought all through the war distinguishing itself many times for its bravery and resourcefulness. The men's knowledge of the country and local conditions gave them the advantage over the imported troops from India and Britain, South Africa, Rhodesia, Nigeria and even the West Indies.

The Germans in Tanganyika did not waste any time speculating. They captured the frontier post of Taveta and were across the border at Kajiado and a hastily put together force of Mounted Rifles and K.A.R. men was sent to confront them.

The East African war which came to be known as 'the last of the gentlemen's wars' was nobody's idea of a gentleman's war at the time. 'Africa was rude,' as Grogan had said many years before, and the suffering of the men on both sides was not due so much to the fighting but to the peculiar hazards of fighting in Africa. Rain, mud and mosquitoes plagued the men for months at a time; followed by scorching sun and intense heat, dysentery, blackwater fever, tick fever, jungle sores, jiggers, armies of red ants called Siafu and scorpions; and always hunger if not actual starvation. There were no roads and the few motorised vehicles shook to pieces before they had gone many miles. The oxen or mule transport were decimated in the tsetse fly areas and as many as 50,000 horses, mules and oxen died before they could bring the much needed supplies to the men at the front. Shortage of water was always a great problem and both sides used a simple method of protecting the few water holes available. Almost every water hole had a notice nailed to the nearest tree: 'Poisoned Water'. They all soon learned to ignore such signs but many water holes *were* contaminated. By the end of 1916, 15,000 men had been invalided out with malaria, dysentery, blackwater fever and the many other varieties of diseases peculiar to Africa. Wild animals were another hazard. Lions were a particular menace to mules and oxen which were devoured if left unprotected. On one occasion a patrol of the E.A.M.R. advancing towards an enemy stronghold was met by seven lions, not the enemy, and a pitched battle with large baboons was fought when they were mistaken in the dark for the enemy. Hyenas developed a liking for leather saddles and giraffes became entangled in the wires of field telephones. To fool the enemy, both British and German troops painted many of their horses and mules with zebra stripes but this only fooled the real zebras.

The small East African force was being quickly swelled by 30,000 Indian troops, 20,000 South Africans, British and other colonial forces but they had to fight a formidable adversary.

Colonel (later General) von Lettow-Vorbeck was a 44-year-old regular German soldier who knew that, unlike his opponents, he could not get reinforcements from Germany because of the British naval blockade in the Indian Ocean. He had to rely on the few whites in German East Africa and the Schutztruppe: his black askaris who worshipped him and for whom he had great regard. He trained them for the only possible method of fighting left to him. The hit-and-run method. With a total strength of a thousand men he defeated a British force of 8,000 at Tanga, the second most important town and port after Dar es Salaam. In fact, when the attack started on 1 November 1914, he only had 400 men but quickly moved troops by train from Moshi 190 miles away. Von Lettow himself did his reconnoitring on a bicycle, chain-smoking as the battle progressed. By 4 November the Indian Expeditionary Force had to retreat abandoning arms and equipment on the sands of Tanga. The British generals' incompetence was blamed for the shameful defeat.

Despite this victory, von Lettow soon realised that to save men and materials, and to divert enemy forces from Europe, he had to fight a guerilla war and this continued until the very end of the war.[2]

Grogan was active on another front. As soon as he had enlisted in the Intelligence, he arranged for Gertrude, Dorothy and Angela Sharp to return to England because Gertrude was anxious to be with her other children. Now that the war had started it was difficult to obtain passages to England, but after a short stay in Mombasa with Dr Henderson and his family, Gertrude left and Grogan immediately handed over Chiromo to be used as a hospital in conjunction with the European hospital next door on the Hill which was already becoming crowded. 'The hospital was a wonderful place during the war,' an ex-patient said.[3] 'People climbed out of the windows, went to town to get sozzled and the rickshaw boys, who knew where everybody lived, brought them back drunk.' One of the popular bars was The Hole in the Wall owned by a Mr Todd in Victoria Street. The bars were open eighteen hours a day including Sundays and did a roaring trade.

Grogan took a cottage at the Muthaiga Club for 150 rupees per month (£10), which he used between assignments. Members were not allowed to keep cottages on an indefinite arrangement, but the committee decided to allow him this concession in view 'of the public work he was engaged in'. They even agreed to build a covered way between his cottage and the main club so that he would not get wet during the rains.[4]

The 'public work' he was engaged in was officially liaisoning the British command with the Belgians in the Congo and unofficially arranging a spy net-work in the north of Tanganyika. His chosen code name for his Intelligence work was 'Simba', the nickname the Africans had given him years before.

Although the British had entered the war against Germany to honour a treaty with the Belgians, the Belgians had no intention of feeling any obligation towards the British in East Africa when they were attacked by the Germans. The Governor General of the Belgian Congo had been instructed by the home Government to stay neutral—come what may.

Fortunately for Grogan's intended mission, the Germans crossed Lake Tanganyika in their small steamer *Hedwig von Wissman* and destroyed telephone lines and canoes. They also sunk the only Belgian boat worth the name on Lake Tanganyika, the steamer *Alexandre Delcommune*.

Grogan arrived in the Congo just after these events, and on 27 October 1914, a meeting took place at the Belgian Headquarters at Kibati between himself and his old friend from the Nile days, Commandant Henri. They were delighted to see each other again but Grogan was anxious to press for Belgian support against the Germans. It is not clear whether Major-General Tighe, commanding East African troops, had instructed him to make any promises to the Belgians but Grogan did anyway. He promised Henri that the British would send two motor boats for the Belgians to use on Lake Tanganyika, and the *Mimi* and *Toutou* were sent from England to the Cape and overland (by train and ox-cart) to the lake. They were commanded by Commander G. R. Spicer-Simson and armed with a 3-pounder gun and a machine gun. They arrived in October 1915 and by Boxing Day *Mimi* had immobilised and captured the German steamboat *Kingani* and refloated it to use against the Germans. She was renamed *Fifi*. Eventually, by February 1916, these little boats with their girlish names, after sinking the *Hedwig von Wissman*, had complete control of Lake Tanganyika.

Grogan had won the first round. By February 1915 the Belgian Minister for the Colonies instructed Major General Tombeur, who was in charge of Belgian operations, to gain command of Lake Tanganyika, to deter the enemy from invading Belgian territory by compelling him to defend his own and to occupy Ruanda and Urundi which were in German hands and the Belgians coveted as part of the Congo.

'Concerted action is not immediately possible,' Grogan reported back to Major-General Tighe,[5] but the Belgians were now prepared to use their 15,000 men, including 250 Belgian officers, to defeat the Germans—but not before October 1915.

This was disappointing but it did not stop Grogan's continuous intelligence activity. It gave him time to infiltrate German East Africa and to disrupt at least part of the German war machinery. He travelled very light and with only a few Africans who knew the local dialects, but part of his luggage was counterfeit money: the simply printed paper rupees the Germans used as currency in Tanganyika. The Tanganyika currency was already devalued because of the war and this inflation did not help matters. Meinertzhagen was doing the same further south, but it is said that Grogan paid for the printing of the counterfeit rupees he was distributing. The Africans on the German side were more than pleased to accept his money although they declared themselves loyal to their German masters. They informed Grogan that each German farm owner was training his natives into fighting soldiers ready to join von Lettow whenever he called for them. At a meeting in Nairobi Grogan said this 'sounded very terrible' to his ears, even more terrible than the German attempts to recreate a 'navy' on Lake Tanganyika.

On 1 July 1915 he reported from Mwanza on the German side of the lake that the place was full of German engineers who were there to mount guns (which had an 11,000 yards range) from the *Königsberg* onto the *Mwansa*, an old tug on Lake Tanganyika.

The S.M.S. *Königsberg* had given the British navy quite a run in the Indian Ocean. The cost to the Royal Navy of chasing the elusive *Königsberg* for almost nine months was staggering, tying up twenty-seven fighting ships during which time Grogan's M'Baraki coaling wharf at Mombasa had supplied them with 38,000 tons of coal. Finally the brave *Königsberg*, which was hidden in the Rufiji delta to carry out essential repairs, was discovered and destroyed in July 1915, but her guns went on fighting the battle. They were dragged by oxen over hundreds of miles to be mounted on the *Mwansa* on Lake Tanganyika, on trains and throughout the colony bringing devastation wherever they were used.

Grogan's headquarters was in Entebbe in Uganda from where he sent his reports signed 'Simba' and where he stayed with an old foe, Frederick Jackson now Governor of Uganda. Both Grogan and Jackson seemed to have forgotten the animosity of the 'flogging incident'.

Many years later Grogan wrote[6] in glowing terms about Sir Frederick Jackson and his abilities as an administrator, remarking that 'his wonderful touch with the African out-manoeuvred Carl Peters [the German colonizer of Tanganyika] in establishing British dominance in Kenya and Uganda . . .' He also found Lady Jackson striking and charming and he mentions their kindness in allowing him to use Government House as a motel in his comings and goings during the war.

The liking was obviously mutual because in his book *Early Days in East Africa*, Sir Frederick Jackson wrote that there was a lot in common between Ewart Grogan and himself. 'A man of great ideas, but a little too much ahead of the times,' he wrote. He gave the example of how one evening walking near the swamp at Entebbe Grogan explained how he would drain the swamp and turn it into a sugar plantation, and Sir Frederick thought this would perhaps happen fifty years hence.[7]

In his book Jackson is most emphatic about their being 'old and good friends. At one time there was a little rift between us, and a feeling of soreness on both sides, but that all passed away long ago,' he wrote, referring to the time when he was all in favour of having Grogan jailed for flogging Africans. In his book he also praised Grogan for his 'resolute fighting spirit' during the war, and added that 'he saved the situation more than once when relations were very strained . . .'

Relations were certainly strained on a number of occasions with his Manyema porters in the Congo. He knew they were good porters from the days of his walk, but he also knew their weaknesses, such as stealing and having a preference for human flesh. In 1962 when interviewed by the *Star* he said: 'In World War One our men sometimes ate the Germans they killed. Fortunately I was always on the skinny side myself.' His sense of humour got the better of him when he telegraphed his H.Q. in Nairobi: 'Herr Smidt missing—believed eaten.' This habit of the Manyema was also reported by other officers when the Belgians eventually joined in the occupation of Tanganyika and they had to watch the graves of recently buried soldiers which the Manyema were liable to dig up during the night to feast on the corpses.

He also felt he was back in the good old days of his walk when food ran out and to keep his porters fed he had to shoot elephants which were their favourite food after humans. There was no way in which food supplies could reach him and his men when he was engaged in secret missions inside Tanganyika. Like his walk, the war for him was a very lonely business and only his resourcefulness and experience kept him alive.

Chapter 18

PATRIOTIC SPEECHES AND INTELLIGENCE WORK

In August 1915, during a short visit to Nairobi, Grogan was shocked to discover that the first enthusiasm for the war had died off and, encouraged by the Government, the settlers who had volunteered were now returning to their farms where the Governor told them their contribution to the war was far more important than at the front now that British troops and colonial troops were pouring into Kenya. The military, on the other hand, complained that the civilians and the Government gave them no help at all.

Having assessed the situation, Grogan had long talks with Colonel Meinertzhagen and together they went to see the American millionaire Northrup McMillan who had already done so much towards the war effort. The twenty-four stone Northrup McMillan was at his Juja farm near Donyo Sabuk which he kept as a game sanctuary and 'where game in thousands abounds', Meinertzhagen wrote on 22 August 1915 in his unpublished diary.[1] 'I found Grogan a charming companion. He probably knows British East Africa better than most men,' he wrote. 'I should imagine he is a far sighted business man but rather speculative. He is enthusiastic about the future of the colony but has no high opinion of the modern class of settler, many of them are not workers. We are hatching a plot to try and wake them up. In most cases they follow the Governor's lead, too apathetic about the war.'

The plot consisted in finding a way to arouse the enthusiasm of the settlers again, and to shake up the Government into doing something positive about the war. McMillan and Meinertzhagen voted Grogan as the ideal person to prepare and deliver a speech at a public meeting in Nairobi. No one else in Kenya had Grogan's power of swaying the crowds, and with his friends' encouragement he sat down to write a few notes.[2] He never wrote his speeches nor carried notes when he spoke, but sometimes he prepared himself by jotting down a few thoughts.

On Tuesday 7 September 1915 'the Theatre Royal was packed from the door to the ceiling, and had it been possible to get on the roof, there is no doubt that this would have been taken advantage of,' the *East African Standard* wrote. It was the greatest meeting in the history of British East Africa, they added. There was an orchestra and patriotic songs were sung. McMillan as Chairman introduced Grogan by saying that he was known by all and more than anybody else had the interests of the country at heart. He then read telegrams of support for the speaker. The salient points of Grogan's proposed speech had passed from mouth to mouth in the past two weeks. Everybody knew that he proposed to stress that the administration, professional, industrial, commercial and military resources of the Protectorate should be organised on a war footing within a comprehensive system. He would also advocate a War Council *and* conscription. It was surprising that he was applauded so enthusiastically when he spoke of conscription, which had not even been adopted in England yet.

In his speech he gave a convincing picture of how well the Germans in Tanganyika were preparing for war; adding that he knew this from having taken a few walks around that territory.

'I ask that we play our full part in this war,' he said, and reminded the audience that it was possible to wander into any club or hotel and see a dozen men between twenty and twenty-five 'passively reclining in chairs with illustrated papers on their knees.' The audience laughed and he added: 'I ask every one of you to go up the Hill amongst the elite and there you can see growing up a host of pretty gardens, tennis courts and such paraphernalia whilst at the front people are doing their duty and in Nairobi nobody is doing anything. Government offices are filled with gentlemen earning large salaries compared to the troops and doing nothing for the war effort. I feel, and I am sure you feel with me, that this is not the time for attending to two-penny-halfpenny bits of business and thinking of shambas[farms].'

He related how in the streets of Nairobi a young farmer had asked him why the settlers couldn't let the British and the South Africans do the fighting whilst they looked after their farms. His answer to the young farmer was that his outlook on life was that of a rabbit, not even a grey rabbit, but a white one, looking through the bars of the cage and waiting for someone to bring a lettuce.

Someone in the audience asked him whose fault all this was, and he answered, 'It is our fault. Many men have played their part, but many have not. We have to realise that this war is on an entirely different basis [from any other war] and we have to rely on the country making no distinction between settlers, officials and military, remembering that we are all British subjects.' There was a great burst of applause here, and he went on, 'We have to organise for this war on a basis of sacrifice. We cannot expect any man to go out and fight whilst others stay at home and make money. We have to keep in front of our noses that our first duty to our pride and self respect is to cleanse this country of the invader . . . we are all British,' he repeated, 'and when history reviews its position, and the war is over, and we have to go before the bar to say what we have done; when the women and the children of this generation and the next will discuss the war and the children will ask: "What did your daddy do?" Let no one present shrink from hearing this question asked. When the question is asked from Home, let us be sure of the answer and then we will hear: "Well done thou babe of the Empire".'

By all reports it is a wonder the small Theatre Royal could stand all the applause, stamping, cheering and singing.

Meinertzhagen, who was also on the speaker's platform, together with Russell Bowker and the Chief Secretary, wrote: '[Grogan is] an accomplished speaker [he] impressed his audience . . . The resolution was acclaimed and passed without a dissident note . . . That it has not done so before is to a great extent due to apathy on the part of the Governor and his tin-god administration. . . . Grogan's speech put matters very clearly and very truly. I look on this moment as the turning point in the history of British East Africa. The colony has found itself . . .'[3]

Belfield was not a popular Governor with the settlers and the troops. On one occasion, Meinertzhagen wrote, Belfield invited the Mounted Rifles to go to Government House, then drove fast past them covering them in dust on his way to the station. Meinertzhagen was also bitter, like Grogan and most settlers, about the Governor's refusal to allow Government officers to take part in the war effort and allowing them to take their leave in England as they always did.

On this occasion there was nothing Belfield could do about the overwhelming popular opinion instigated by Grogan. A War Council with Grogan as a member was elected and conscription agreed upon.

Sir Gordon Clovell, the Chief Medical Officer, after attending the meeting wrote about Grogan's 'fiery eloquence', but there were also a number of critics. A civil servant in the Secretariat by the name of W. J. Monson 'who cannot refrain from blossoming out into verse on the slightest provocation ridiculing everyone and everything military,' Meinertzhagen wrote, published a sarcastic poem about the meeting of 7 September.

Grogan, who never missed an opportunity to hit back at Government servants, wrote an open letter of withering sarcasm and undisguised contempt for the stay-at-home civil servants who had the gall to use their 'pretty wit' against brave fighting men.

In later years Grogan was often referred to as Kenya's Churchill, 'the leader who might be ignored or rejected when all seemed well, but who could not be done without in times of crisis. During the First World War he was the inspiration and the driving force behind the popular movement which eventually resulted in the country being reorganised on a war footing. Kenya was in a state of muddle then with the Government entirely unable to cope.'[4]

Having played his part in the reorganisation of the country, Grogan went back to the Congo where General Tighe had asked him to arrange a meeting between Sir Frederick Jackson and Major General Tombeur. On 6 February 1916, the Belgians agreed to start their offensive providing they could be supplied with 5,000 carriers, a number of British officers and an ox train of 100 wagons. Nothing was concluded at this meeting and Grogan went back to Uganda with Jackson, only to receive instructions a few days later by the new Commander to arrange another meeting between Sir Charles Crew and Major General Tombeur.

The British East African Expeditionary Forces command was given to Jan Christian Smuts on 23 February 1916. A South African Boer was a surprising choice as Commander of a British force, but Smuts soon came to be admired and respected. He had experience, physical energy, courage and a remarkable memory. He was also remote, cold and unsympathetic, but he had a will to conquer. 'Slim Janie' as he was nicknamed, meaning 'Sly Janie' in Afrikaans, had one objective. To 'surround and annihilate' von Lettow in the shortest possible time.

Grogan, who had been at Cambridge with him, was pleased to be serving under such an experienced man. The first thing Smuts asked him to do was to approach the Belgians again. Later, Grogan says,[5] Smuts asked him 'to maroon two of his generals in the remoter approaches of the Congo,' but he does not give their names.

At the next meeting with the Belgians, General Crew and Grogan agreed to supply 5,000 carriers and 100 ox-wagons from Uganda and the Belgians agreed to contribute 1,000 men. The British used 175,000 African carriers during the war known as the East African Carrier Corps and without them the war could not have been won.[6]

From the time Smuts took over the command the Germans retreated but never surrendered. They fought their relentless guerilla war and kept the British forces from joining the European war until the very end.

Grogan stayed with the Belgian forces entering Kigoma in August 1916 and Tabora in October. He entered these towns in disguise before the troops arrived to report on German defences and movements and was often involved in hand to hand combat when he was discovered and could not get back to his lines. A dangerous way to live for which he was mentioned in three Dispatches,[7] given the Distinguished Service Order,[8] and made an Officer of the Order of Leopold at the end of the war.[9] His admirer, Meinertzhagen, wrote in the *Army Diary*: 'His reports were masterpieces and his ability and courage, both moral and physical, placed him very high in my estimation . . . A most lovable man.'

A most lovable man to Grogan was the famous 63-year-old hunter Frederick Courtney Selous who was killed next to him on 4 January 1917 at Behobeho. Courtney Selous acted as guide to the British forces and despite his age he was, like Grogan, always in the vanguard.

In January 1917 when Smuts was invited to the Imperial Conference in London, Grogan, who had by then been promoted to the rank of Major, started a collection to present Smuts with a Sword of Honour, 'in appreciation of splendid work done in the East African campaign.' Grogan gave the largest contribution of 300 rupees (£20).

During this visit to Nairobi, he was also present at a mass meeting on 16 February held at the Palace Theatre.[10] Although he was not a member of the Legislative Council, two unofficial members, Delamere and his brother-in-law Wilfred Hunter, invited him to speak at the meeting.

'I am grateful to be invited to say a few words,' he said, 'but I really don't know what about. If I spoke about subjects close to my heart, you would still be here in the morning.' Nevertheless, he seemed to know what he was talking about and they *were* subjects close to his heart. He spoke of Kenya's unpreparedness for war. 'Nothing saved this colony from disaster except the German failure to realise the full extent of our Administration's neglect . . . The Government thought the war was a rude interlude—probably organised by settlers.' He also emphatically insisted that Kenya should be represented at the Conference of the Empire to put up their case as 'at home they regard us as four footed agitators.' He added that they needed somebody at the Conference who could stand up for their rights. This, eventually, turned out to be Grogan, but he finished that speech by saying: 'Meanwhile let us get on with the war.'

People always attended his speeches partly to hear the truth frankly spoken but also to be entertained, and Grogan never failed them.

He was busy fighting and spying on the Germans but the political aspect of Kenya was never very far from his mind, and in 1917 the future Kenya Constitution occupied a great deal of his writing and his thinking. He started bombarding the newspapers with a series of letters advocating control of the country by the Legislative Council with an unofficial majority.

The first letter, written on 17 December 1917 and known as the 'Dodoma Letter',[11] was signed by fifteen other settlers engaged in the war and it carried the usual Grogan flavour. 'May we register emphatic dissent from the findings of the Select Committee on Elective Representation,' he wrote. 'The framers of the report have started with the principles of "one man, one vote" and attempted to combine "one interest, ten values" . . . This is not representation, it is sheer autocracy . . .'

The Committee's report recommended that a Government majority in the Council be maintained and Grogan wanted to know why, when 'the Colony finds its own sufficient revenues even under its present flaccid method of administration . . . The minimum measures of our rights which we must demand are: a) An absolute democratic franchise for adult Europeans who are bona fide British subjects, b) Provision for adequate Indian, Arab and native representation subject to the unalterable principle that political control shall remain with the Europeans, c) Complete control by the Legislative Council, with an unofficial majority, of all expenditure of national monies and of all internal policy, subject only to the veto of the Governor and of the Home Government.'

He ended up by writing: 'Let us stand pat on this and East Africa may cease to be the Cinderella of the Imperial sisterhood.'

The 'Dodoma Letter' was followed by the 'Christy Minstrel Letter' and a sixty-five minutes speech at Royal Theatre, called 'Grass Fire Speech', ending up with a letter of 1 March 1918[12] criticizing the unofficial members (Delamere, MacLennan Wilson, Clarke, Hoey and Grogan's brother-in-law Hunter) for their ineffectual stand on the Constitution when he wrote: 'Are we to elaborate a House of Commons or a Reichstag?'

When members of the Legislative Council declared that Grogan was not their mouthpiece, he replied: 'This is hardly kind to my powers of literary expression!' He added that the Government took advantage of the absence of the majority of settlers, 'in spite of solemn promises,' to rush highly controversial legislation on the country. 'The pity is that the unofficial members should have been coaxed into the position of accessories to the crime,' he concluded.

As in all his speeches and letters, he ended by saying: 'Meanwhile, let us get on with the war.'

For the time being Grogan was not fit enough to do so. He was in Nairobi recovering from another attack of blackwater fever. Most people died of this disease. This was the second time he had contracted it and yet he not only survived but had the energy to pursue his many interests, which, by all calculations, at this time began to veer from simply the political, economical or even military. Women began to enter his life in earnest. He had not been with Gertrude for four years and it can hardly be possible that a man of Grogan's energies and vitality could sit back and wait to rejoin his wife.

I have assured the people involved that no real names of lovers, girl friends and illegitimate children will be mentioned in this book, therefore I will give each of them fictitious names.

Grogan's first real love affair was with a much younger woman (she was about twenty-six and he was forty-four), who was married to an architect. It is believed that Mrs 'Brown' was a volunteer nurse at the Military Hospital when Grogan was recovering from his last attack of blackwater fever. She obviously helped him recover and with recovery he plunged straight into Kenya politics again.

Sir Henry Conway Belfield, the Governor, had been disposed of in 1917 and the Honourable Charles Bowring was Acting Governor when on 29 January 1918 a mass meeting was held in Nairobi to appoint delegates to a committee to ask the Colonial Office to appoint Sir Percy Girouard as Military Governor. Delamere, Grogan, Hunter and fourteen others were appointed and cables were sent to the British Prime Minister and Lieutenant-General Smuts, Sir Percy Girouard, the London Chamber of Commerce and the Press Association. Even an Indian, Mr Mangal Das, who was an unofficial member in the Legislative Council, wrote to the papers supporting Major Grogan's motion requesting the appointment of Sir Percy Girouard, and for his troubles he was thoroughly slated by the Indian community who maintained that *all* governors were anti-Indian. To which Mr Mangal Das replied that: 'So long as Indians are not united, so long as they do not conform to the present day requirements of civilization, it is immaterial what Governor we have.' He also stated that a lot of Indians present at the meeting had promised Grogan support and then changed their minds.

Like most requests to the Colonial Office by the settlers, this one was not successful and Grogan went back to the war against von Lettow. Von Lettow had lost German East Africa to Smuts, but with only 300 white officers and 1,400 Schutztruppe he forced the British to chase him into Portuguese East Africa and back into German East Africa when the surrender of the Germans in Europe put an end to his fighting. His was the only German force who never surrendered.

The war was over in Europe on 11 November 1918 and on the 14th Grogan was present at an open air service near the Scottish Church, and a march-past when the Acting Governor Charles Bowring took the salute, supported by General Llewellyn, Delamere and Grogan who gave a 'stirring address'. The K.A.R. band played, there were sports and in the evening bonfires and a torchlight tattoo to celebrate the Armistice. Now people could go back to normal life—except perhaps Grogan for whom life was never what most people considered 'normal'.

Chapter 19

LOVERS AND MONEY

Ewart Grogan was in no hurry to get back to normal life. According to his daughters 'he disappeared completely' during the war and they never heard from him. He did not seem to be anxious to rejoin his family even after the war ended, although he was at the Peace Conference in Paris on 30 November 1918, and it seems incredible that he did not pay at least a quick visit to his family in London.

Lord Milner had invited Grogan to accompany him to the Conference in St Germain-en-Laye as adviser to the British and South African Supreme Economic Council. He was also Milner's adviser on African Boundary questions, 'to the great annoyance of the Colonial Office representative,' Grogan wrote later.[1] 'His secretary and I were compiling a memorandum for him in our office when Milner, then Secretary of State for the Colonies, called me to a map of Africa on the wall and said: "The Chief [Lloyd George] has given the Juba River to the Italians. Where is it, and has it any significance?" Thus are empires made and unmade.

'My other task was a memorandum on the Congo Basin Treaties for Botha and Smuts . . . The memorandum made a good case for a free-trade area (despite the Congo Basin treaties) comprising the Union of South Africa, Rhodesia, Tanganyika, Kenya and Uganda . . .'

Grogan was back in Nairobi in January 1919 and immediately

called a meeting of the Convention of Associations, of which he was President and which had not been operating during the war. There were many questions to discuss: Land settlement, the Indian question, popular representation, native registration, labour bureau, taxation, currency treaties, native education, medical services, the police etc. 'The businesslike manner in which the programme was carried out speaks wonders for the ability of the chairman and his executive,' Cranworth wrote.[2]

The Convention of Associations was referred to as the Settlers' Parliament, and Grogan, as its president, referred to himself as 'the baddest and the boldest of a bold bad gang'.

He was certainly bold. At this meeting he stated that: 'The white man must be paramount but we must make the native a useful and contented citizen . . . give him reasonable education, especially technical, industrial and agricultural. The workshop on the farm should be the school of education. We must educate the native to come out of the reserve and work. He must be taught to read and write not literary training and freehand drawing.' He was also convinced that the day was 'not far distant when the settlers of Kenya and their families will be able to assume full control and occupation of every post—save perhaps the Governor's—in the Civil Service.'

The *East African Standard* was as usual there to report his speeches in which they were especially interested since he had become a director in 1918 by buying one hundred shares for 1,500 rupees.

A new Governor was about to arrive and the members at the Convention of Associations briefed Grogan on a speech of welcome to be delivered by him at the dinner for General Sir Edward Northey on 12 February.

The dinner turned out to be a disaster. A drunken European had got into the kitchen that afternoon and ejected all the cooks until the police arrived, with the result that the guests got little more than 'soup, whisky and aerated water'.[3] As for Grogan's speech which lasted 122 minutes, this turned out to be a 'violent and insolent tirade', according to Lord Emmott in the House of Lords.[4]

In the two hours 'tirade' Grogan attacked every issue that had plagued Kenya since its inception, and if Northey did not agree with the settlers they would fight him, he added. On the other hand if the Governor was in accord with them he could count on loyal co-operation. The people were entitled, he said, to know whether Sir Edward 'was going to be merely a telephone exchange for Downing Street'.

Sir Edward Northey showed considerable restraint and diplomacy in answering Grogan. He thanked the President of the Convention of Associations, he sympathised with both settlers and officials and hoped for co-operation. 'My brain is rather in a whirl after Major Grogan's speech,' he said, but he had listened with great attention and interest although he had not expected such straight speaking and hoped the people present would not expect immediate answers. During his speech Northey referred to Grogan as Kenya's Godfather and hoped they could co-operate in the future.[5]

Grogan's anxiety over what kind of Governor Northey was going to be is partly understandable when one considers Kenya's post-war economic situation which was none too healthy. An Economic Commission had been appointed on 27 March 1917 with Grogan, Delamere, Bowring, Wood and Hunter as members, to examine and report on the economic policy of the Protectorate after the war. Now that the war was over the 'Comic Commission', as the Economic Commission came to be known by its detractors, was very concerned with the economic collapse which followed the war and a new threat to the currency which was still the Rupee, but there was now talk of revaluation which could bring the country even further on the road to collapse.

Within a few weeks of his arrival, Sir Edward Northey was presented with the report from the Economic Commission which he forwarded to the Colonial Office and which was discussed in the House of Lords almost a year later.[6] Grogan's old friend, Lord Milner thought the report 'purely deplorable' the way it abused the Indians, but no action was taken to relieve Kenya's economic situation. No wonder the settlers always felt they were dealing with a brick wall.

Meanwhile Grogan's personal expenses were rising. After fifteen years of negotiations the Government finally agreed to grant him another fifty acres at M'Baraki at a time when he would have liked to sell rather than buy. The expensive overhead steam cranes and the pier were all in need of repair after the overactivity they had suffered during the war, and Grogan said: 'There I was, having completed this magnificent project, with my legs hanging over the pier without enough money to buy bread."[7]

He was obviously exaggerating, but the whole of Kenya was sliding into a depression and Grogan's absence from his business interests during the war had not helped. His troubles were not just financial.

Mrs Brown's husband had died of yellow fever and now she was pregnant. There was no doubt that the child was Grogan's and he was in a quandary as to what to do about it. He was never a man to keep a secret for long and in July 1919 he went back to Draycott Place in London—with the pregnant Mrs Brown. Poor Gertrude was 'hysterical with grief', her daughter Jane said, and naturally she refused to let her husband's lover come and live in her house, although Gertrude was so kind that she went to see the young woman in hospital when she gave birth to a little girl whom I will call 'Mary'. I don't have Grogan's reactions to the situation but he obviously faced his responsibilities because he always looked after the mothers of his illegitimate children, and in Mrs Brown's case he settled her on a farm in Sussex, always contributed to Mary's upbringing and at his death he left her a large trust.

From what the daughters have told me, it seems that when Grogan went back to London he was not a well man. Cynthia remembers him looking quite grey at the age of forty-five, still unwell from his attack of blackwater fever and 'very odd'. Apparently he would go off in his T Ford and suddenly stop and say to a policeman that he could not go any further. 'Now we would say that he had a nervous breakdown,' Cynthia said. 'He was probably very worried about money as well because he didn't have any until he sold the Kilindini block,' she added.

He was indeed a changed man. No longer was he the loving father, punctuating his talk with a laugh, drawing pictures for the children and hiding soft animal toys in their beds. The war had changed all that. Cynthia who was then eleven years old remembers him as 'terribly unkind and sarcastic. I remember at an enormous luncheon party he stared and stared at me and then said: "Have you been to the zoo lately. No? Well, next time you go look for the ugliest animal and you'll see what you look like. A tapir. You'll see your cousin sitting in the cage and it's got Tapir written on it." I burst into tears and my mother said: "How could you be so unkind?" and he said: "I didn't mean anything." He was very cruel and then he would give you all you wanted and put a present at your place at breakfast. Even when we grew up he would say: "I'll get a pencil and I can make your face quite attractive if I try." And after that he might give you a hundred pounds. He was an extraordinary man. He thought he could buy your affection.'

Apparently he hardly ever wrote to his daughters. He only wrote to Cynthia once and once sent Dorothy a four page letter when she went to boarding school, telling her to concentrate on geometry. He was never very interested in their education—that was all left to Gertrude—but he insisted that Dorothy should go to Cambridge and he was shocked when she said she wanted to study medicine at Oxford where women were allowed caps and gowns, and he exploded: 'Oxford? Oxford? don't talk to me about Oxford.' Despite the fact that Dorothy had his fiery character and they had many disagreements, she is the one who remembers him with a measure of affection—perhaps because she knew him in better times. On the other hand, Jane cannot forgive him for making her mother suffer so much. She was very young at the time and she can only remember her mother crying. 'It was not fair to such a lovely defenceless woman,' she said.

By all accounts the war had changed his entire personality as far as the family was concerned, but to the rest of the world he was still the forceful, intelligent, witty and charming man he had always been, and this is what he appeared to be at Caxton Hall in London on 8 July 1919, when the Overseas Settlement Committee invited him to speak to prospective Kenya settlers.

Instigated by Grogan in the War Council, a Soldier Settler Scheme was started in 1919. Two hundred and fifty seven farms of 160 acres each on the Uasin Gishu Plateau were allocated free to ex-soldiers and disabled officers by a selection board in London and Nairobi. There were 2,200 applicants and the farms were drawn by lottery. Some drew good land, others dud and soon after he occupied the land, one ex-soldier advertised his farm as a stone quarry, and many others lost their farms because of the depression and the change of currency.

In his speech at Caxton Hall to thousands of prospective settlers Grogan did not pull any punches. He told them exactly what to expect in Kenya, from a description of the country to geology, rainfall, soil, suitability of crops, the pros and cons of coffee cultivation, sisal, cattle, maize, wheat and social conditions.

He did not forget to prepare the future farmers for what to expect from Africans, 'the proletariat of the country, upon which everything fundamentally and finally depends,' he said. 'We are in this fortunate position that, as distinct from South Africa, with their tragic racial history, there is no antagonism or real dislike . . . the conditions are kindly between the European settlers and the great native population . . . I see no reason in the world why those quiet relations should not be permanently maintained —I think they will.'

Quite another matter were the Indians with their continuous demands for land and the Government with their blind attitudes. He told them about climate, tropical diseases and of course, about the dangerous sun rays. These were not the only dangers he advised them against. Too small a capital would spell disaster for any future settlers, as indeed it did for many who did not listen to his advice. He warned them about the labour crisis and said the Kikuyu were intellectually like Scotsmen 'therefore one must not be misled by mere appearances . . . I am perfectly certain that we have an intelligent lot of natives individually— I mean really intelligent and amenable to tuition. Many of them are ambitious and would like to acquire wealth, and when properly organised . . . I believe we have a resident population in British East Africa which will enable us to achieve the most stupendous development.' But he warned them that when they got to Kenya they would not find 'the natives all sitting in a row waiting to do a job. You will have lots of trouble.' In fact he warned them of so many drawbacks that it is a wonder any of the prospective settlers ever went to Kenya. But they did. The speech and the clear answers he gave to their many questions convinced them that Kenya was indeed a 'white man's country'.

'When they came they brought their grandfather clocks. They didn't bring them to chop up for firewood,' a friend of Grogan said recently. 'If you bring out your grandfather clock you presume that it's going to tick for another two hundred years.'[8] Hundreds of people came to Kenya encouraged by Grogan or to work for him.

On July 19 *The Times* reported that Major Ewart Grogan DSO had delivered a lecture on British East Africa at Caxton Hall which had proved so popular that a large number were unable to obtain admission and, therefore, Major Grogan would repeat the lecture the following Monday and copies of the lecture were available at the hall. The pamphlet ran to twenty-eight pages. He was never short of words.

Nor was he short of words in the fight that began over the rise in value of the rupee. For many years it had remained stable at 1s. 4d., but at the time of the Soldier Settler Scheme it had risen to two shillings, a fifty per cent increase. Settlers were alarmed as their bank loans and mortgages went up. And it looked as if the situation would get worse. Grogan bombarded *The Times* and the Kenya newspapers with letters and articles. In this campaign for the Kenya settlers, many of whom began to go bankrupt, he was helped by the Governor, Sir Edward Northey, who met him in London at the beginning of 1920 and together they consulted the Colonial Office with no real success. The rupee rose to 2s. 6d. and there was panic. Bank managers were besieged by desperate clients as Grogan went on battling for the stabilisation of the rupee, and eventually in June 1920 it fell to two shillings and there it stayed.

In 1920 the East Africa Protectorate became the Kenya Colony and regional electorates were established now making it possible for the settlers to hold elections and appoint representatives to the Legislative Council. The electorate knew what Grogan was doing for their welfare and although he was in London the *East African Standard* voiced the general feeling and, under the headline 'The People's Leader', asked for Grogan to come back and take the leadership.[9] Grogan was not ready to return to Kenya and he appointed an agent to stand on his behalf for the Kiambu Constituency where he was defeated. The people wanted Grogan not an agent but he was busy in London with the rupee question which Northey, now back in Kenya, had entrusted to him. He was also fighting another innovation of the Colonial Office. They wanted to start an Income Tax system and Grogan fought with all his economic knowledge. So much so that the introduction of Income Tax survived barely two years.

He was also busy writing about an air route through Africa. The Editor of *The Times* had suggested that he give his views on what could be done in the scientific exploration of Africa with the aid of the aeroplane, and this he did—and more—on 9 February 1920. A detailed map of the route and landing places was published with the article. All this was twelve years before the Imperial Airways started their services through Africa.

In his article Grogan wrote that it was a shock to him to

realise 'that it is twenty years yesterday since I emerged from the first traverse of the African continent from Cape to Cairo. Now the reverse journey is to be made by flight, while I am still forty-five.[10] It is a startling epitome of the pace of our time. In the economic sphere it is impossible to exaggerate the significance of the coming of the aeroplane . . . Many of [Africa's] areas have large populations of primitive natives, who require only the stimulus and organising capacity of the European to become important contributors to the world stock of essential foods and raw materials and reciprocally important consumers of the manufactures of Great Britain.' This he wrote sixty years ago when most whites discounted Africans as 'important contributors'.

'In Africa, the European,' his article continues, 'is the yeast that leavens the inert dough of Africa's peoples; he is the mysterious factor (undiscovered by Marx), which raises to infinity the *per capita* effect of the individual effort. Rapidity of movement and intercommunication between these European stimuli is the first essential of African progress. The car, wireless, telegraphy, and the 'plane are facile means whereby the physical obstructions to communications can be overcome; and their advent heralds a new era for all Africa . . .'

There were not many in 1920 who believed in the usefulness of the aeroplane, and certainly not flying through Africa. Grogan was a man of vision whom his contemporaries often thought of as an impractical dreamer.

Chapter 20

THE INDIAN CONTROVERSY AND REBELLION

The rupee question brought Grogan back to Nairobi in January 1921, and with Sir Edward Northey's support he pressed for a new coinage, but all the Colonial Office did was to issue 7,561,000 florins to the Kenya Treasury which threw the economy into an even greater chaos, and confused the Africans in particular who did not understand the changes and were convinced the whites were swindling them.

The crash that Grogan had predicted was upon them. Ninety per cent of the settlers and new enterprises lived on overdrafts and the revaluation of the rupee meant ruin. 'But alas, in this crisis not all the Colony spoke with one voice,' Lord Cranworth wrote.[1] 'The sane portion led by Major Grogan, Berkeley Cole, and, to his eternal credit, the Governor, demanded with incontroversible argument that the old value of the rupee must be restored. This was strenuously opposed by all the banking interests, and not unnaturally by some of those with fixed salaries. The utmost that could be offered, it appeared, and that as a favour to a beggar, was stabilisation at two shillings.'

The division of interests in the Colony was known as 'ratting' by those men who saw their life work thrown away. By the stroke of a pen, the cost of production and of the country's administration was increased by fifty per cent. At the same time the price of primary produce began to fall. Whoever owed money, and most people did, had their debts doubled and very few could survive this kind of crash.

Nature too seemed to be in league with the bankers. Three years of drought withered the farms and what was left was eliminated by swarms of locusts twenty miles long. Despite this destruction of food not a single African died of starvation as in past famines. The Government saw to it that they had enough to eat.

There was nothing that could be done about nature's punishment but the 'sane portion' was not prepared to bow their heads to the banks' attempt at destroying them. A delegation which included Grogan and Cranworth embarked for London to consult with the Bank of England. 'The banking representatives yawned in our faces, and when we had finished we were dismissed in two sentences to the effect that we could take it or leave it, since their minds were made up,' Cranworth wrote.

This was unacceptable and Grogan stayed on in London where Northey joined him in June to continue the battle. A change from rupee to a decimal form of sterling was finally approved in November 1921 and the value eventually fell back to 1s. 4d. New 1, 5 and 10 cent pieces of copper-bronze alloy were minted with a hole in the middle to enable Africans to string them around their necks, or other favourite places. The new cents became very popular ornaments for the African women.

Grogan's private affairs did not seem to suffer the volcanic upheavals of his public life. He had established Mrs Brown and their daughter in Sussex and often saw them, but life at home in Draycott Place with the loving Gertrude continued peacefully. 'He loved her in one way,' his daughter Jane said. 'She was obviously not the right person for him.'

Gertrude Chapman, Gertrude Grogan's niece from New Zealand, recently wrote: 'I remember her in the 1920s, when I often went to Draycott Place to supper. That lovely oval face and smile. She loved a bit of romance. Either her own or other people's. At seventeen I was rather frightened of Uncle Ewart but I thought he was the best looking man I had ever seen! Grey hair and piercing blue eyes! No wonder Aunt Gertrude fell for him and found him exciting.'

In London he gave many parties and 'he was absolutely sensational, witty and amusing, although not often with his family. He had to be heard and admired, but he could take or leave people. He was very self-sufficient. He had a very forceful character so he was always the centre of attention.'

He certainly seems to have captivated Northey's attention, despite his 'tirade' at the welcoming dinner, and the Governor very much depended on Grogan's help and advice during his visit to London in 1921 when they appealed to Churchill, now the Secretary for the Colonies, to curb the incessant Indian demands. The previous year two Indian elected representatives had been allowed into the Legislative Council, but they were not satisfied. They argued that 8,000 Europeans had eleven members and 22,000 Indians only had two—they wanted twice as many representatives as the Europeans, they wanted free immigration and land on the Highlands. All of a sudden the settlers 'had visions of hordes of "Bombay failed" arriving to swell the electorate, Indian District Commissioners, heads of departments, Indian judges and even an Indian governor.'[2] The local newspapers had an orgy of headlines: 'Defending our Homes', 'No Betrayal of Kenya', 'Kenya's Ultimatum', 'A Solemn Warning', 'The Preservation of Trust', 'The Long Reach of Bolshevism'.

Bolshevism was an ugly and frightening word and everything concerning the Indians smacked of Bolshevism. They were having mass protest meetings and it was obvious, to the people who are always in the know in these circumstances that the agitation was directly related to Moscow. The agitators were smuggled into Kenya from Russia, they said. The aim was the disruption of the whole British Empire. Indian merchants were boycotted, Northey was dispatched to London to present the settlers' case. He was given a farewell dinner and a great crowd was at the station to see him off, but not a single Indian was seen there.

Whilst he was gone a European rebellion was feared and some hot heads suggested the settlers should reach for their rifles, proceed to Mombasa and see that not another Indian landed at the port. 'Valour and determination resounded from every bar in the colony', MacGregor Ross wrote. Meanwhile the Convention of Associations asked for subscriptions 'to enable immediate action to combat this danger'. A vigilante group was organised, a petition was sent to the King, and the East African Women's League petitioned the Queen, the Princess of Connaught and Mrs Smuts. 'We, the women of Kenya, humbly implore your assistance to protect us and our children from the terrible Asiatic menace that threatens to overwhelm us.' Speeches referred to the receivers of stolen goods, sellers of intoxicating liquor to the natives, engineers of subtle propaganda of disloyalty and Bolshevism. 'We must prepare ourselves to defend our rights,' they said.

Their 'preparedness' achieved nothing. General Northey came back from London with good news for the Indians. They were to have four representatives in the Legislative Council and one in the Executive Council, but Northey, who had done so much for the colony, was to be discharged in June 1922. Churchill told him Kenya did not need an army man as Governor. He left on 28 August 1922 and Sir Robert Coryndon arrived three days later, but the Indian controversy went on until 1923; so much so that a plan to kidnap the Governor and senior officials and keep them in a remote farm until settlers' demands were met, was discussed. They expected the police and the army to be on their side. Steps would be taken to collect all white women and children on certain farms and the missionaries were asked to assist in keeping 'the natives quiet'. Indians would be taken to the railway station and dispatched to Mombasa for shipment to India.

Word of this plan reached the Government and HMS *Southampton*, HMS *Cairo* and HMS *Colombo* arrived in Zanzibar, seven hours away from Mombasa. This did not discourage the settlers. Up-country farmers were asked to swear their willingness to fight, contribute their guns and vehicles. HMS *Colombo*, meanwhile, arrived in Mombasa and the crew played football matches with the local whites. Sports were always important in Kenya. Cricket matches carried on between Indians and Europeans at the Nairobi Club, whilst in England Parliament was asked to consider sending the Guards to Kenya and an Indian station master sent a telegram to his superiors in Nairobi stating: 'Dear European, sportsman killed by lion stop Brought on station for forwarding Nairobi stop Shall I consign at goods rate or passenger.' Life went on.

It all seems comic opera material today but it was then a very explosive situation which very slowly burnt itself out but not without leaving deep bitterness on both sides. The Indians had won five seats in the Legislative Council and Europeans like Grogan, who was very involved in the near-rebellion after he went back to Kenya in September 1921, never stopped fighting them. One of Grogan's contentions was that the Kenya Indians had no right to their demands considering what they had contributed during the war. He maintained that the only local Indian contribution had been eight hanged for treason and 800 blacklisted as spies. He said that during the war in the Congo an African said to him, 'We dislike the Indians so much we don't even eat them.'

As if a slump, locusts, drought, Indian demonstrations and a planned European rebellion were not enough, in June 1921, the Kikuyu began to make themselves heard. Led by Harry Thuku, a switchboard operator at the Treasury, the Young Kikuyu Association began holding meetings to voice their grievances. Most offensive of all to the Kikuyu was registration and the 'kipande' (identity card). At an excited meeting of 5,000 Harry Thuku told the crowd to load their kipande on lorries and dump them in the drive of Government House. He waved telegrams over the heads of the listeners and told them that these were the King of England's replies to his telegrams. The King was behind them, he said. He used Post Office Box 65 which was the Treasury box and when this was discovered he was sacked, but this did not deter him. The Kikuyu paid their contributions and his campaign went on. He travelled through Kikuyu country by car and by train to Kisumu to obtain the support of the Kavirondo and other tribes in that area. One of his points of contention, with which Grogan was in full agreement, was that thousands of Africans had worked as carriers in the war and had been promised rewards. Now instead of rewards they were threatened with cuts in wages and escalated taxation.

Hostility towards the white man increased after every meeting and the atmosphere was seething with disquiet when the Government decided to arrest Harry Thuku and his brother. Two thousand supporters followed Thuku to the tin police station in Government Road and stayed there all night. The following morning members of the Young Kikuyu Association went to all European houses, offices and shops and called the Kikuyu workers out on strike. Thousands more surrounded the police station and the King's African Rifles reinforced the police. The crowd mostly consisted of curious bystanders, but a few people made inflammatory speeches and were arrested. The Acting Police Commissioner suggested a delegation of six Kikuyu went to see Sir Charles Bowring in the absence of the Governor who was in

Mombasa. They were assured of a full hearing for Thuku when the Governor came back, but rumours were rife in the town and the worst was expected although the crowds around the police station were quiet except for the prostitutes who kept up a continuous racket.

Then suddenly there was a shot followed by a burst of rifle fire for 20 seconds. It transpired that no one had given orders to fire but when a European policeman went into the crowd to arrest a demonstrator who was throwing stones, he was either tripped or thrown to the ground and the askari with him nervously pressed the trigger and the firing became general. The policemen had been on duty for nineteen hours and they were as excitable as the crowd who ran for cover leaving behind twenty-five dead and wounded. Harry Thuku's supporters quickly spread the news that the police were massacring the Kikuyu whilst the Reverend W. I. Wright, who was outside the police lines, held a prayer meeting. During the shooting he had been surrounded by the screaming prostitutes who believed a man of God would save them.

Grogan and the Convention of Associations tried to throw the blame on Indian agitators. It was discovered that Harry Thuku had taken tea with Mr Desai and other Indians the day before his arrest. Thuku was tried, convicted and held in jail, but his movement, which went underground for the time being, continued until the independence of Kenya, despite the fact that the Europeans were lulled into believing that once Harry Thuku was out of the way, peaceful cohabitation with the Africans would last for ever. At the time Churchill said: 'Settlers have every right to bank on Kenya developing as a typical British Colony.'

A few days later Grogan was appointed to the Bowring Committee with Delamere, J. E. Coney, representing the producers, two nominees of the Chamber of Commerce and one Indian Legislative Councillor, Shams ud Deen, who remained a friend to Grogan for the rest of his life. The committee was to recommend how Government expenditure could be reduced and production stimulated. Always very important questions to Grogan.

On the same day, 27 March 1922, he was sworn in as an elected member to the Legislative Council for Plateau South which covered the Uasin Gishu Plateau with the exception of

Trans-Nzoia. This was the first time he was elected and from then on he was elected again and again until independence. Throughout his political career he devised ways to stimulate the economy of the country which, he said at the Extraordinary Session of 22 May, 1922, 'was in a rapid state of decomposition'.

A light note was introduced by Grogan and Delamere when the Governor, Sir Robert Coryndon, opened the proceedings with a prayer. As he started saying: 'Oh Lord,' Delamere is said to have stood up and bowed. As he continued: 'God Almighty,' Grogan also stood up and bowed.

On the Indian question, the economic and financial situation Grogan kept the readers of *The Times* well informed—from his point of view, and *The Times* thought enough of his financial knowledge to ask him to contribute articles on financial matters.

The Kenya Government also thought enough of his financial knowledge to repeal the Income Tax experiment which he said at a time of depression would mean enormous costs to the Government and the community in preparing income tax returns and it would be too much to impose on people who already paid Poll Tax at £35.10s., per annum (Africans paid 7s. 3d. and Indians £6 4s.) and high import duties.[3]

The settlers were grateful to Grogan and an anonymous contributor wrote to the *East African Standard*:

> God moves in a most mysterious way
> His wonders to perform,
> He plants his footsteps on the sea
> And sends our Grogan along.

The Legislative Council members also showed their appreciation of Grogan by asking him to attend the Geddes Committee which was sitting in London to recommend the reduction of Kenya Government expenditure, and he sailed on 16 December 1922.

Chapter 21

PRIVATE LIFE AND PROPERTIES

Since returning to England after the war with Mrs Brown, Grogan's visits were longer and very frequent and it is obvious that his attachment to Mary's mother was still strong. He did not leave Gertrude for the younger woman, but in the next four years he only went back to Kenya twice and this for short visits, although, apart from his romantic attachment, there was very little to keep him in England. As he makes it obvious in an article written in 1923,[1] he loved Kenya passionately and to leave it for such long periods there must have been a greater attraction in England.

Away from Kenya did not mean away from its problems. He kept in very close contact and British newspapers and publications considered him the expert to be consulted on all Kenya problems. It is not surprising, therefore, that the *National Review* asked him to write an article on the Indian question in April 1923. 'Kenya: The Logic of Facts' is a long article going back to the origins of Indian settlement in East Africa with figures and dates and his customary forceful arguments. 'No Indian ever played in Africa the part of a Livingstone, no Indian ever moved to Africa to tame the wilderness, no Indian touched African soil except and not until some other race had imposed safe and ordered existence upon the spot . . . the Indian part has been exclusively that of a trader and usurer,' he wrote. 'The Indian artisan is now sufficiently entrenched and organised to resist the employment of Africans in the higher grades of work . . .' He also wanted to know why the 'untouchable cast' in India were considered vermin by their own nationals, but in Kenya, where there were thousands of untouchables, these claimed adult suffrage. He reviewed every aspect of the Indian question not forgetting the part the Indians failed to play in the recent war. Grogan would never forgive them for that.

On 18 April 1923, he also addressed the '1900 Club' on Kenya's affairs, and on 27 June he was invited to be a member of the Joint East African Board affecting the economic development of the East African colonies.[2] Grogan also wrote an article for *The Times*[3] on free trade and the cost of open markets, and on 12 December he was invited to address a luncheon at Jules Restaurant where seventy guests celebrated the centenary of the hoisting of the British flag at Mombasa.

His own affairs seemed to be improving—he thought—but a series of letters to and from Sir Robert Coryndon,[4] the new Governor, show that the sale of M'Baraki took a lot longer to be concluded than Grogan expected. Despite Coryndon's friendly attitude to Grogan, the deal took four years to be finished and gave rise to bitter debates in and out of the Legislative Council. In Kenya public opinion over the sale of M'Baraki was divided. Some, including Lord Delamere, did not think that the way the matter was being dealt with was 'a credit to anybody', and the Government thought buying M'Baraki was 'fulfilling an Imperial necessity and an act of Empire building'. Grogan was not going to wait for any Empire builder to make up his mind. His letters to Coryndon, which started with 'Dear Robert', became less and less friendly and ended up with 'Dear Coryndon' telling him in no uncertain terms that he was not going to be fooled with any longer, he was going to accept other offers.

An Indian, Mangal Das, was getting his own back. He wrote to Sir Charles Bowring that Grogan was offering M'Baraki to Ambrose Smith for a lot less than he was asking the Government. Others pointed out that the pier was riddled with teredo navalis and about to collapse, but finally the sale was concluded with the government in December 1925 for £350,000. Sir Robert Coryndon did not see the sale through; he had died after an operation on 9 February 1925, but not before Grogan had extracted another promise from him.

The Uasin Gishu railway which had been on Grogan's agenda ever since he obtained his forest concession had been considered and shelved many times. The existing line went from Nakuru to Kisum by-passing the Uasin Gishu Plateau where transport was still carried out by teams of oxen, which seemed to be more numerous than ever during the rainy season and sometimes the strength of the oxen and the mud pulling in different directions dismembered the wagons. Grogan and Delamere wanted the railways to build a line between Nakuru and Turbo and they were bitterly criticised for feathering their own nests as the line would be passing right through their properties at tremendous expenditure. Questions about the line were asked in the House of Commons[5] and when Churchill, the Secretary of State for the Colonies, was asked to produce the surveys, he replied that the cost of the printing would not be justified, but finally a Parliamentary Commission was appointed.

The 146 miles of railway between Nakuru and Turbo was completed in 1925 and it cost £1,400,000, and although there was no doubt that Grogan and Delamere derived great personal advantages and profits, so did the rest of the country and particularly the Uasin Gishu farmers.

Meanwhile, Grogan added one more property to his long list of possessions in 1924. He could never keep money for very long. Money was for spending and spending in development was his passion. Even before he sold M'Baraki he bought Ventors, a beautiful Elizabethan property near the village of Rusper, six miles from Horsham in Sussex. The house was originally a monastery founded by a monk called Ventors. It was large and rambling with panelled walls, a library and two drawing-rooms, one of which was turned into a 'dance room', as he called it because it was not as grand as the ball-room at Draycott Place, but musical evenings and dances were held there.

The house was all 'corners and nooks' and almost every bedroom had its own sitting-room, but, most important of all, it had three bathrooms. A married couple, a housemaid and a kitchen maid ran the house. Faithful old Nanny Redwood had finally retired after the war when all the children went to school. Cynthia and Jane were at the Holy Child Convent in Hayfield, near Tunbridge Wells, where Grogan's sister Hilda was a nun known as Sister Mary Simion. Although Dorothy and Joyce went to another school, North Follend Lodge, Joyce was obviously influenced by her aunt as she became more and more interested in becoming a Catholic and a nun.

When she first expressed this wish at eighteen Grogan was shocked and he refused to give her permission to do such a thing until she was twenty-one. Joyce was twenty-one in June 1926 and in September she became a nun at the Holy Child Convent in Mayfield where her aunt Hilda had been for years. Joyce had obviously inherited his determination and in later years he admitted that he was rather proud of his nun-daughter.

For some time Ventors claimed his interest. It had a hard tennis court and a grass court. The gardens grew more beautiful under Gertrude's supervision but the adjoining 100 acre farm, known as Peter's farm, fascinated Grogan. At that time he considered himself an English farmer although he still dressed like a Kenya farmer. 'He was always off on his own in a field doing some simple labour dressed in khaki with big rubber boots, rather impatient with visitors who bored him,' one of his nephews wrote.[6]

He loved experimenting but others had to take over the everyday tasks.

One of the men he picked in Kenya was young Ferdinand Cavendish-Bentinck, known as C. B. and later Duke of Portland. When Grogan met Cavendish-Bentinck he was Private Secretary to the Governor in Uganda and Grogan told him he was wasting his time working for the Government. By 1925 C.B. was working for Grogan running his Equator Saw Mills from an office in Sadler Street (now Koinange Street) where Dobie's are now. 'Grogan was a generous man but in those days we didn't count money by the month or the week,' the Duke of Portland said when asked how much Grogan paid him. 'If Grogan liked you he treated you very well. He liked me and I liked him. He helped a lot of people in this country. I got on very well with him and I was with him for many years. He left me entirely to my own devices. He was far seeing and intelligent, a courteous man and extremely well mannered with everybody. He mixed at all social levels.' At that time, the Duke of Portland said, the Africans referred to him as *Bwana Chui* (the leopard) because he had 'very bright blue luminous eyes which the Africans said could see in the dark.'

When Ferdinand Cavendish-Bentinck went to work for him Grogan lived in a small wooden house in Muthaiga where

Gertrude's Garden Children's Hospital now stands, as he was hardly ever in Kenya and as in 1925 he sold Chiromo to Lady McMillan after her husband died. He extended the house in Muthaiga later but it never amounted to much although it had certain features which only Grogan could have thought of, such as the bunker-type concrete room he built for himself in the garden so that he could enjoy his privacy when the family came to live in Nairobi. One of the features of the concrete room was a bath that he could step into straight from the bed. The structure he built at the gate reminded people of gallows and the Muthaiga house was always known as 'The Gallows'. 'It looked as if it could hang half a dozen people at a time,' his grandson David Slater said.

Cavendish-Bentinck was only one of many who worked for Grogan. In the Equator Saw Mills alone he employed 30 Europeans and 1,500 Africans. The East Africa and Rhodesia directory of that period describes the company as 'by far the biggest timber-milling concern [and] the largest undertaking of its kind in the colony.' It operated nine mills in the forest concession and various subsidiary companies. Grogan had his trees regularly tested in England and some of his cedar reached 150 feet in height and 15 feet in girth. He had furniture made from his olive trees which created a sensation at the Ideal Home Exhibition in London in 1926.

Of particular interest during a visit in 1925 when he sold M'Baraki, was the proposed new Government House. A new Governor had arrived, Sir Edward Grigg (later Lord Altrincham) who planned to build a house 'suited to the light and climate of Kenya and worthy of the large expenditure proposed.' The large expenditure (£80,000) was exactly what Grogan had in mind when he addressed the Legislative Council, although he was not an elected member at the time. '. . . the expenditure became a matter of violent controversy when the building was started,' Sir Edward Grigg wrote.[7] 'I was young in those days, and I made one speech on the subject in the Legislative Council which was too controversial for a Governor. I was provoked to it by some really offensive jibes directed at me in a much publicised speech by Colonel Ewart Grogan, always an Irish firebrand in Kenya and now its Grand Old Man.'

In 1925 people began to refer to him as 'Grogs'. There was no specific reason for the name and he was not very fond of it, but it stuck to him in Kenya. Nobody called him 'Grogs' in England.

In London he continued writing on economic matters and particularly on the gold standard and he was pleased to note that 'the free gold standard operated independently of the intelligence of our great bankers.'[8]

The British newspapers were always interested in his views and doings, particularly when he was involved in controversial issues such as the address he gave at the Theatre Royal in Nairobi on 4 August 1926, on the eve of the introduction of the budget when Kenya's public was 'restless and anxious.'

Soon after his return to Kenya the Chamber of Commerce invited him to review the financial situation and give a speech. As always he thoroughly prepared himself for the task. He had a pamphlet printed and distributed to every member of the audience before the meeting opened, clearly stating Kenya's financial situation. The title of the pamphlet and the speech was 'The March of the Siafu', the killer red ant of Africa.[9]

Grogan was back in Kenya and there was plenty to talk about when he was around—and not just in the political and financial fields. Grogan was a very 'private sort of man' as the Duke of Portland said. He never talked about his marriage or his affairs, but the rest of Nairobi did.

Chapter 22

LOVERS, TORR'S, TAVETA AND LEGISLATIVE COUNCIL

'Are you married or do you live in Kenya,' 'A sunny country for shady people,' 'Men are men and women are wide open spaces,' were all sayings which referred to a group of people known as the Happy Valley crowd. The Happy Valley was a moveable feast which originated in the Naivasha-Ol Kalau-Wanjoki Valley-Timau-Sabukia area, but moved from there to Nairobi and Kilifi on the coast, or wherever there was a party. The people who belonged to it were mostly remittance men and women, often supported by their families in England in order to be rid of them. They were not interested in farming, although most of them had farms. They were interested in having a good time and they dominated the Kenya scene in the twenties and thirties. They were inspired by a few leading lights such as the aristocratic lady who had seven different husbands in her life-time. She also had a beautiful house near Njoro furnished with a grand piano and antiques brought from her ancestral home in England, and very interesting parties went on there most of the time. Swapping of husbands and wives was part of the fun and before the weekend started the names were drawn from a hat and everybody went off to different bedrooms, but not before a grand dinner, a lot of drinking and, on occasion, some cocaine sniffing. Being Kenya a certain amount of hunting of animals was also a favourite sport and those who favoured that kind of hunting went off with the other chap's wife, which method divided the group very conveniently. But the aristocratic lady did like to keep some semblance of propriety. Therefore, when the hunters were expected back she posted a trusted servant by a gong on the hill overlooking the plains and when the gong was struck all the non-hunting husbands and wives in the house went back to their respective rooms to welcome their spouses.

All this was very hard on the children who were despatched to boarding schools in England as soon as they could say: 'Da-da' as the distinction between the various da-das was not always easy for them. It is said that one of these children said to another: 'Do you know so and so?' 'Yes, why?' 'Oh nothing, they were just some of my mother's husbands.'[1]

Grogan knew most of the Happy Valley crowd but he had nothing to do with them. He was a very private man and he kept his own happy valley to himself. He did not believe in sharing his women.

He had come back to Kenya with his daughter Dorothy in 1926 and his daughter Cynthia had joined them in 1927, but their presence did not inhibit his romantic inclinations. His new love was 'Kathy'.

During the First World War Kathy had worked in the dairy at Windsor Castle when young girls volunteered to take menial jobs in place of the men who went to war, and after the war, still as a teenager, she applied for a job on one of the largest farms in Kenya. The employer expected to see a young man and when a teenage girl with bobbed brown hair and khaki trousers stepped off the train at Nakuru, he told her she had to go back to England. Unfortunately Kathy had no money and the aggravated employer had no choice but to keep her, at least until she found alternative employment. She soon found a permanent post. An older farmer from Njoro married her and by the time Grogan met her, through the husband who was a friend of his, she was an attractive and enterprising 26-year-old who was learning to fly and who became the first woman (even before Beryl Markham), to receive a licence.

Kathy was half Grogan's age but he was a very youthful fifty-three and the love affair continued until the Second World War. In fact, Grogan never quite broke off with his past lovers, they always remained good friends, especially the mothers of his illegitimate children. This did not stop him having other affairs in between, one of which was also with a 'flying woman'. He seemed to like adventurous women then and quite a lot of them had red hair. Some of them went as far as dying their hair red to appeal to him.[2]

By the time Kathy became pregnant with Grogan's sixth daughter she had left her husband, but later she remarried him and they were all friends when little 'Jenny' was born. In fact, Jenny recently said that Grogan and the man she believed to be her father were at the hospital exchanging jokes at Kathy's bedside as to whose child Jenny was. A true Happy Valley situation. Grogan was still hoping for a son although many years later his wife Gertrude said: 'God knows what sort of life the poor boy would have had. Just as well he didn't have one.'[3]

Perhaps he would have been more demanding with a son than he was with his daughters. Dorothy worked for him when she came back to Kenya and she says he was a very demanding employer, but when she had virus pneumonia he kept bringing bottles of champagne to the hospital making her very popular with the patients and unpopular with the doctors. He was also a typical Victorian father when it came to his daughters' morals. In England they were not allowed to go out without a chaperon even to a *thé dansant* and coming out to Kenya on the *Madassa* in 1926 when Dorothy was twenty-four 'he was a nightmare,' Dorothy said. 'He used to say, "time for bed" and as we had two adjoining cabins, down we went and up I went again.'

His illegitimate daughter Jenny, who believed him to be her godfather until she was eighteen, loved him dearly and he obviously returned her love because he was as attentive as a true father to her. In the eight years that she was at a boarding school near Nairobi he was the one to take her out at half-term and holidays, filling his car with her friends and taking them to Brackenhurst and Torr's Hotel. Jenny called him 'Bunnyman' because he always wore a big topee with ventilation holes in it and when she was very small, he used to say to her: 'If you look very hard through the holes you will see a little bunny running from one hole to the other,' and she used to stare at the topee for hours. She said that the man she thought was her father was a wonderful and kind person but always busy and having rows with her mother. It was Bunnyman who gave her the love she needed.

The love affair with Kathy seems to have rejuvenated Grogan

1a William Grogan

Jane Scott Grogan

2a Grogan aged two

2b Grogan aged fourteen

3a Gertrude

3b Grogan aged twenty-four

3c Grogan at the end of the walk in 1900

October 17
1900

BALMORAL CASTLE.

Dear Sir

The Queen desires me to thank you for your kind thought in presenting to Her the Union Jack which you carried on your remarkable journey from the Cape to

to Cairo. Her Majesty is glad to possess so interesting a memento of your famous journey; a journey which, the Queen understands, no other traveller has hitherto succeeded in accomplishing.

4a Extract from Queen Victoria's acknowledgement of Grogan's Union Jack

Government Hou
Bulawayo
7th Sept. 190

My dear Grogan/

You ask me to write you a short introduction for your book but I am sorry to say that literary composition is not one of my gifts, my correspondence and replies being conducted by telegrams.

I must say I envy you for you have done that which has been for centuries the ambition of every explorer namely to walk through Africa from north to sout the amusement of the whole thing

and by saying that your success has given me great encouragement in the work that I have still to accomplish.

Yrs
C. J. Rhod

4b Extracts from Cecil Rhodes' lett to Grogan 1900

5a Chiromo, 1905

Sir Charles Eliot and Mrs. Joseph Chamberlain in
ombasa, 1909 (*By kind permission of the Kenya Railways*)

6a Grogan, Gertrude, Dorothy, Joyce and Cynthia at Camp Hill, 1909

6b 52 Draycott Place, 1911

7a Grogan with Northrup McMillan, 1914

7b Captain Grogan, 1915

8a Torr's Hotel, 1928

8b Grogan, 1932

8c Girigan with Kilimanjaro in the background, 1947

because he was again plunging into Kenya affairs and investing. His business interests were vast and in June 1926 he registered a holding company by the name of East Africa Ventures, known to the wits as East Africa Vultures, which included seventeen companies ranging from the forest concession to insurance, mining, rice mills, prospecting, irrigation and sisal.[4] The directors of the company varied through the years but Ferdinand Cavendish-Bentinck was an alternative director for Gertrude and the others were Lord Egerton and Lord Francis Scott and Mr Percy Wheelock was the Company Secretary. In 1928 he started his most ambitious project. An hotel worthy of the London West End, it was said.

On the corner of Sixth Avenue and Hardinge Street (now Kenyatta Avenue and Kimathi Street) Grogan owned a plot of land from the early days and for a long time he had thought of it as the ideal site for an hotel. He consulted the architect Harold E. Henderson and together they designed an hotel which bore 'a resemblance to the Stockholm Town Hall, one of the most beautiful buildings in Europe.'[5] George Blowers was the builder and Grogan owned a tile and brick works in Grogan Road by the swamp (where the Globe Cinema stands now) which supplied the red bricks for the new building. These were made of clay mixed with stone.[6] Arched, leaded glass windows, a massive oak front door and a terrace on the first floor with seats and flower boxes completed the striking exterior. Inside there were features that no other hotel in Kenya had seen yet. By the entrance hall there was storage not only for luggage, but pets as well and on more than one occasion patrons 'stored' their lion cubs there whilst they met their friends for tea or coffee, or stronger beverages in the palm-court style semi-circular lounge on the ground floor, a corner of which was known as Tom's Corner after the Irish barman Tom Whisdom. This corner was always very popular. The trains from Mombasa ran three times a week and arrived in Nairobi at 8.30 in the morning, and 'by 10 o'clock the lounge at Torr's hummed. The poor old Stanley never had zing—it was more like the wild west.'[7] Torr's was very sophisticated and people flocked there. A band played at lunch time on the balcony of the first floor dining room and on Saturday mornings in the lounge. It also played dance music every night in the ballroom under the direction of Sid Zeigler. The only hotel in Africa to hold dances every night.[8]

Two circular staircases led from the ground floor lounge to the first floor balcony supported by graceful pillars and sixty-four bedrooms on three floors were serviced by two lifts. A first in Kenya. The top floor, another lounge, was known as the Pompeian house because Grogan had insisted the architect copy his sketches of the houses in Pompeii he had admired so much during a visit with his second 'flying' lover.

Unique and very popular were the French and Swiss chefs keeping the dining room and the grill on the ground floor continually full.

The most popular guest was Grogan himself. At eleven o'clock on most mornings he held court in the lounge. People knew he was there by the topee hanging on the left hand coat-hanger by the stairs and they knew they would always get free drinks or lunch from Grogan.[9] The women particularly flocked to his table. 'All the women sat around him because they thought he was marvellous. Having drinks or lunch with him. My wife was fascinated by him,' Humphrey Slade said.

He was always very generous with the people he liked and never thought of the expense. He had built the hotel with a large loan from the bank and he had leased it to Joe Torr, who had first come to Kenya as Sir Northrup McMillan's baker, and then with his wife Lilly had owned a small confectionery business where simple meals were also served. Grogan leased them the hotel for £900 a month and named the hotel after them; but although Joe and Lilly were very hard workers, they had no experience of large hotels and according to Lilly they lost a fortune—£20,000, she said. Four years later they gave up, but Torr's Hotel never made any money for Grogan either until the Second World War.

Lilly Torr remembered Grogan as a very enthusiastic dancer although 'he couldn't dance for toffee,' she said.[10] One of his regular dancing partners, who sometimes sported a monocle, was of course Kathy and for her he always requested 'Miss Otis Regrets', but she was not his only partner. He danced with a lot of women right up into his old age 'and he was quite a flirt and held the women so close you couldn't put a finger between the two, but he never used the hotel to sleep with his women.'[11]

His next project was sisal in which he had been interested ever since visiting the early German experiments near Tanga in 1910. In 1928 he bought 21,135 acres of semi-arid unoccupied plains in the Taveta district for four shillings an acre from a group of Africans who claimed it as their own but did not occupy it. The first time he went to see the land he realised the potentials for sisal cultivation despite the fact that everybody told him he was crazy. The Africans did not even want it and certainly not the Indians who had refused an offer of it at the same time as he became interested. As he said later: 'The Indians never wanted land. They wanted political propaganda.'[12]

Grogan knew Taveta was a risk, in fact he always used to say that farming in Kenya was 'a violent oscillation between wild optimism and imminent bankruptcy,'[13] but he felt sure he could make that arid plain bear fruit with the aid of water he was convinced he could channel from the snows of Kilimanjaro.

The first time he went to inspect the land years before he bought it, he went in his Ford, locally known as a flying bedstead, and he wrote:[14] 'The car sparks merrily in the hot dry air; we roll over long downs of red earth tufted with withered grass and speckled with clumps of thorn trees. To the east hang, like purple fog, the vague shapes of the Pare Mountains, and along their base the white waters of Lake Jipe and the heavy green of forest clumps dance in confused mirage. To the west the long red ridges climb and climb and climb, massing to immense buttresses which stay the slip of the vast upper cliffs that support Kilimanjaro's crown of ice twenty thousand feet aloft . . .' He obviously loved the country and nobody could talk him out of it. To his first purchase he added 22,000 acres of Crown Land in the Ziwani area in 1937 which he increased to 32,000 five years later. He also bought 30,456 acres in the Lake Jipe area and eventually ended up with 120,000 acres of sisal, citrus fruit, grazing and even a fish farm where telapia were bred in artificial dams covering one hundred acres.

The first sisal bulbils were planted on 3,634 acres soon after he purchased the land but these were not good times to expand. Capital was short as the Great Depression of 1929 caught up with Kenya. Grogan lived on borrowed money from the banks and to remind himself of his debts he named a place in Taveta, Montagu Norman Corner after the Governor of the Bank of England. When he put in sisal in 1929 it sold at £40 a ton. By the time it came in it was £11 a ton.

The country was not faring better than him. On more than one occasion, when representatives of the Bank of England visited

Kenya, they consulted Grogan, and as *The Times* wrote on 29 January 1929, the settlers needed Grogan's financial expertise again and he was elected to the Legislative Council representing Nairobi North.

Development was very dependent on the smooth running of the railway, Grogan said in Legislative Council on 22 October 1929. He had barely been sworn in by the Governor, Sir Edward Grigg, when he attacked the officials and particularly the Acting General Manager of the Railways whose estimates were being discussed. The poor man was not spared Grogan's famous sarcasm or witticism. 'The honourable mover of this motion [applying for further grants of money] has plastered himself and his associates so adequately with bouquets that it is difficult to find a place to put another, but . . . he can only be likened to a picador in a bullfight who waves a red flag in front of the bewildered and infuriated beast and then skips out of the arena leaving a formidable array of toreadors to deal with the animal . . . This railway, for which we pay, behaves like Jekyll who as Hyde gives solemn assurances . . .'

At this point the Governor had to call for order and instructed Grogan that he had to address the chair and not individual members. 'Yes—bad habit of mine—Your Excellency. My apologies,' Grogan said, but continued to instruct the Acting General Manager of the Railways on how to reduce rates and increase profits. He also advocated the building of better roads to encourage tourism and, when in England, he had tried to interest the Colonial Office in making available loans for the purpose. Since the First World War he was also in favour of Game Reserves to attract the tourists, although in 1906 he had spoken against such reserves saying: 'Is Kenya a zoo or a settlers' colony.'[15] With Delamere they decided that the best symbol for Kenya would now be wheat in the fields and trout in the streams.

Since the war the Legislative Council had moved from the Railway Institute to a new and imposing building known as Memorial Hall in 6th Avenue which was built in memory of the settlers who had died during the war.

Grogan was the most popular speaker in Kenya but not with the officials who had to do battle with him, such as the Government Treasurer who on 8 November 1929, submitted draft estimates of expenditure for 1930. Grogan listened attentively and when he stood to speak he first of all extravagantly congratulated the official on his thoroughness and then added: 'But I cannot help feeling that the gentleman has missed his vocation, because anybody who is in fact budgeting for a deficit, is certain to have a very wide sphere in modern finance in the City of London.' Laughter punctuated this speech and he continued: 'Anybody reading this budget would naturally assume that this was the financial happening of Utopia.'

The Governor always had to call for order when Grogan spoke, but Grogan continued to give sound opinions and suggestions, at the same time assuring the officials that he had nothing personal against them, in fact, he stated that some of them were his best friends, but he was aggrieved to see them lost in 'their fantastic system of recording accounts, filling forms and spending nine tenths of their time in useless paper work like *babus* (Indian clerks)'. He wanted the Government to 'come down out of the clouds' and make contact with the actual bread and butter life in Kenya. After a long debate his recommendation to reduce expenditure by £150,000 was passed, and Grogan won another battle.

Chapter 23

FINANCES AND AIR TRAVEL

From 1931 to 1936 Grogan did not seek re-election to the Legislative Council. There were other pressing matters which required his attention. In 1931 the Government planned to re-introduce Income Tax although the country was still struggling through the depression. At a meeting on Income Tax Grogan said: 'The playboy who runs a string of horses and gives champagne dinner parties should be skinned alive, but the farmer and developer who ploughs money back into Africa is unjustly taxed. In an inter-racial country Income Tax is a social folly, and its incidence inequitable.'[1]

He held meetings all over the country and was enthusiastically applauded everywhere. At a conference between Government officials and settlers it was decided to send Grogan, Captain A. C. Anderson and representatives from Uganda and Tanganyika to London to try and convince the Secretary of State, Sir Philip Cunliffe-Lister (later Lord Swindon), of the error of his economic policy. At the invitation of the Colonial Office, Grogan and Anderson submitted a memorandum on the tax question which was discussed during the course of long meetings with officials of the Colonial Office who did not challenge any part of the argument, but nevertheless remained convinced that it was time to introduce Income Tax into East Africa.

It was not just Kenya's economic chaos which concerned Grogan, but England's as well and from Draycott Place he wrote a series of letters to *The Times* on trade, the gold standard, gold reserves, and the financial crisis.[2]

'This way lies the collapse of civilisation,' he wrote in one of the letters about sterling prices of commodities.[3] 'The social function of currency (legal tender) is not to provide nuts for national banking squirrels to hoard, but to provide a stable measure of value so that citizens can make contracts with one another with assurance that such contracts will mature in the terms of their intention. The citizens' pound disappears just as effectually if attacked in the rear by rates and taxes or on the flanks by unemployment and bankrupt industry as by frontal explosion of all buying power of uncontrolled inflation . . .'

He could have been writing this today and it would apply as well as in 1932.

The Conference on Income Tax continued through 1932 and Grogan was also a member of the Expenditure Advisory Committee, but a more diverting invitation reached him at Draycott Place at the beginning of January. There was great excitement in England over the first flight the Imperial Airways were planning for 27 January between Croydon and Cape Town, and the man who thirty-two years before had walked through most of the route and in 1920 had advised on the feasibility of flying over that same route, was now invited to be the first passenger on the eight and half days' flight. He boarded the first aeroplane carrying air mail to Cape Town, consisting of 20,000 letters and 150 parcels, which left Croydon for Paris and from Paris flew to Brindisi. From there mail and passengers were loaded onto a flying boat to Cairo and on to Cape Town.

The Times sent Grogan a telegram of heartiest congratulations 'on your unique double achievement in being the first man to tramp from Cape to Cairo and the first passenger to fly on the regular air service in eight and a half days thus epitomising thirty-two years of progress of transport in Africa.'

Newspapers in other parts of the world carried the story and British newspapers interviewed him before and after the flight. In an interview with the *Daily Express* he said: 'It seems beyond belief that a man could have that double experience in a lifetime. It shows how fast the world is moving. This time I shall accomplish the journey in luxury and comfort in an armchair, looking down on the great continent through which I struggled with so much hardship . . . When I am dining at an airport hotel I shall think of the raw vulture I was jolly glad to eat at one stage of my pioneer journey from Cape to Cairo. I shall think of the man who struggled out of the terrible Nile swamps, bearded, tattered, exhausted, his boots tied up with string, and only ten rounds of rifle ammunition left and a liver that was an abiding curse.'

He reminded the readers of the trials of his walk thirty-two years before when he used 'every means of then-known transport, (except camel), horse, mule, wagon, dhow, canoe, gunboats, but mostly my two good feet, and some part of the way through the Nile swamp, on my stomach.'

His companions on this 'wonderful experience', apart from the crew, were F. G. L. Bertram, the Deputy Director of Civil Aviation, and a Director of Imperial Airways, and Air Vice-Marshal Sir Vyell Vyvyan.

By August 1932 he was back in Nairobi to report on the tax situation and making speeches all over the country.

The readers of *The Times* and the people who flocked to hear him in Kenya enjoyed his oratory, but the Government became more and more incensed, particularly when people met in clubs, the streets or the hotels and told each other: 'Come and hear the *silver tongue* talk about the robbers'.[4] There was nothing the Government could do about it. Grogan's arguments were often acclaimed by individual Government servants, but even so, he was not the most popular individual with the Kenya Government. Lord Delamere had died in 1930 and now the settlers looked on Grogan as their natural leader and defender.

His trips to London were still frequent and little side trips were not unusual for him especially when a woman he admired was involved. Lady Evelyn Cobbold wrote [5] that she was travelling on the same train as Grogan on one occasion from Calais to Genoa on the way to Brindisi to catch a boat bound for Kenya. At Genoa, where the temperature was sub-zero and despite the fact that Grogan was suffering from a bad cold, he went off for a walk during the short train stop without a coat. By the time he got back to the station the train had gone with his luggage. Lady Evelyn was concerned about him and on arrival in Nairobi she enquired about his fate only to be reassured that Grogan had arrived in Kenya long before her. When he had discovered that the train had left Genoa without him, he had merely hired a car and driver in Genoa and driven to Brindisi faster than the train could get there and caught an earlier boat than Lady Evelyn's.

In London in January 1933 he wrote about the madness of the gold rush in Kenya[6] when people left their farms in hordes to dig for the gold which had been discovered in Kakamega. Unfortunately for the hopefuls the gold amounted to no more than a few nuggets and the disappointed farmers went back to their debts and Grogan's *silver tongue* still battling against Income Tax. He was not only concerned about the Europeans but also about the Africans. He demanded that the Government reduce the Africans' Hut and Poll Tax by two shillings, saying that 'so crushing has the burden of native tax become that an administrative officer is ceasing to be regarded as the dispenser of wisdom and equity, but is fast becoming known as Bwana Kodi which means My Lord Tax. If wide and substantial relief is not soon forthcoming . . . the psychological reaction will develop very serious problems.'[7]

In July 1935 he wrote a twenty-seven page pamphlet entitled 'Trusteeship', which was also serialised in the *East African Standard*, explaining in clear and great detail Kenya's economic and financial position. He wrote in terms the settler could understand: the fallen price of his produce and the value of his money and he did not forget the losses incurred by the African producer. 'There is the fast growing conception,' he wrote, 'in the native mind, of the administration as a baronial invasion rather than a benevolent and beneficent penetration . . .' But he stated that in a way the African farmer was better off because he could never lose his land whereas the white farmer could have his land alienated by the bank.

The last few pages were under the heading *J'Accuse* and he made it very plain whom he accused. The Secretary of State, Sir Philip Cunliffe-Lister and the Governor, Sir Joseph Byrne 'and such local persons in any position of responsible authority who condone or support their inaction.' He claimed that whilst civil servants enjoyed 'salaries and emoluments exceeding £1,000 per annum' the farmers had to sell their produce in London at less than pre-war prices and 'are fast losing all their capital and in many cases are reduced to a state of such complete pecuniary destitution that they can pay cash for nothing at all. At least one has already committed suicide rather than face the indignity of imprisonment for not being able to pay his natives.'

The country's problems were not his only concern. By 1935 he had plenty of troubles of his own. The banks were tired of waiting for Grogan's repayment of loans and they were foreclosing rapidly. They did not care what was dearest to a man's heart. What they held as collateral they sold and the bank in Kenya held Kingatori, Grogan's jewel among all his properties, a beautiful coffee farm near Kiambu. It hurt him greatly to see it go and perhaps it hurt him just as much to have to sell Ventors in England to try and rebuild his shaky finances in England and in Kenya.

At this time he suggested to Gertrude that she should come with Jane to live in Kenya. Dorothy and Cynthia were married by then and Joyce was happy in her convent, but Jane was still single and Grogan claimed he could not remit money to England for their support any more.

Poor Gertrude did not know the shock that awaited her on arrival in Kenya. Grogan was extending his timber and stone house in Muthaiga known as The Gallows, to make it more comfortable for Gertrude and Jane, therefore, they lived for a few days at the Muthaiga Club when they first arrived.

Within twenty-four hours of their arrival a 'kind' friend informed them of the existence of Kathy and her daughter Jenny. The shock and pain was great, but Gertrude, in her lady-like manner tried to ignore it, although her daughter Jane was too close to her mother not to realise the suffering and for this she hated her father and never forgave him. Jane, who had never known her father at his best like Dorothy, now took on her mother's cause and row followed upon row with her father, until in 1936, in sheer desperation she told Peter Elliot, the man who wanted to marry her: 'If you want to marry me get me out of here,' and, without telling her father Peter and Jane travelled to South Africa and married in Durban.[8] 'To me it was frightful that anybody should treat such a defenseless woman as my mother was, like that—she lived for him to the end,' Jane said.

Always a curious mixture of callousness and generosity, despite his daughter's elopement, Grogan gave Jane and Peter a farm at Njoro, as he gave Dorothy a farm at Limuru and land near the present Gertrude's Garden Children's Hospital; and Cynthia a farm at Turi. His daughters never denied his generosity to them, but they found it impossible to forgive him for what he did to their mother. 'Father as a father was nobody's idea of heaven,'

Jane added. 'But as a grandfather, all his grandchildren thought he was absolutely marvellous. He was incredibly generous to us. He did a lot of very generous things and never talked about them. He helped a lot of people and educated friends' children.'

Whatever relationship he had with other women, he always remained attached to Gertrude, but Nairobi's gossips were not kind about their relationship. The word went around that yes, Grogan had walked from the Cape to Cairo to win her hand, but he would have gladly walked all the way back to be rid of her.[9]

In October 1935, when Gertrude and Jane arrived in Kenya, the British Round Table invited Grogan to write an article on Kenya's political and economical position 'in view of the disturbed political situation.'[10]

Among other things he reminded the reader that the Colony's debt to England was £17,205,600, on which interest charges amounted to £1,065,918. He maintained that every man and woman in Kenya was a loyal subject of the Crown, but the Crown bled them 'after all, [we are] of the same kith and kin as the ordinary citizens in Great Britain,' he wrote. 'It is the European settler who has built up Kenya, not, as some would have us believe, at the expense of the African, but very much to his advantage . . . Having supplied the driving force and the necessary finance for the development of the country . . .' He ended up by saying that the settler 'feels it would only be in accordance with the principles traditional to our race were His Majesty the King to be graciously pleased to see fit to grant to him some at least of the functions of responsible government.'

Neither the King nor the British Government saw fit to grant the Kenya settlers any such function and Grogan was off to London again in October 1936 to speak to the Secretary of State.

Chapter 24

LEGISLATIVE COUNCIL AND WAR

Grogan had been re-elected to the Legislative Council in May 1936 representing the coast. Among other elected members were his friend and employee Major Cavendish-Bentinck representing Nairobi North, as well as Kathy's husband representing another region. Almost a family affair. There was never any animosity between Grogan and his lover's husband—in or out of the Legislative Council.

Grogan always had perfect manners. His mother's Victorian up-bringing had left a lasting impression and he never used swear words, but he always went straight for the jugular vein in his speeches, as during a meeting before his last election when he advised the electorate to choose the best of the three candidates on the podium, including himself. He started by telling them in generous language that the first candidate was a religious man and a teetotaller and if they wanted a teetotaller in the Legislative Council, they obviously deserved him. The other candidate was the man who provided them with bread—a very hard working man, although Grogan said he could not explain to the audience how this honest man got his flour through the back door of the bakery at 40 shillings and three hours later it came out of the front door at 400 shillings—but by then it was baked, of course. 'So if you believe that this kind of man is honest, you deserve him too,' he added.[1]

Governors and civil servants were always a ready target for

his caustic tongue. Sir Joseph Byrne had not even sworn him into Legislative Council, when on 2 May Grogan told the House that they suffered 'from the difficulty of having a Governor's post of a kaleidoscopic nature because the Governor occupied many positions and the characters are as follows: First, there is the suggestion of the King, a sort of evanescent, intermittent halo which flows to and fro across the brow of the occupant of the post. Secondly, he is the Speaker. He is also the Prime Minister, which is the Governor's function in the Executive Council. He is, in addition to that, Permanent Under-Secretary of all departments of state. He has also to act as a sort of Beau Brummell, controlling the social relationships of the Colony and he is Field Marshal of the local army. At intervals he may appear as honorary president of the trade unions of the country. Finally, and generally speaking, on many occasions he appears as the sane, simple person that God made him.' He did say, however, that to give the present Governor his due, he had arrived at a catastrophic period for Kenya and therefore Sir Joseph had all of Grogan's sympathy.

At this point the whole House was laughing and the Governor said he wished 'the honourable member would try and confine himself to the motion.' Grogan answered that he was trying very hard to do so, which brought forth more laughter.

The Indian members sometimes objected to his sense of humour, as when addressing the Honourable Shams ud Deen, whom Grogan considered a friend, he said that his Indian friend should 'make a little elementary study of natural history. He would then find that the octopedal entomological swarms that ride upon an ox do not produce the grass nor can they eat it except in pre-digestive form.'

'On a point of order, your Excellency,' Shams ud Deen addressed himself to the Governor. 'Is the honourable member allowed to personally abuse a whole community?'

'I do not quite follow what the honourable member is driving at,' the Governor said amidst laughter.

'I am sorry, Sir, but perhaps you have not pursued the entomological studies as far as I have,' Grogan said.

'I know what he said,' Shams ud Deen replied excitedly. 'He has called a whole community ticks and parasites.'

Grogan assured his Indian friend that there was nothing racial in his statement. 'It is purely an analogy between the different factions of various groups in any community. In other words, you have your primary producers who produce direct from the land, and you have all the other factors in society who participate in this result. But unless the farmer does produce, there is nothing to digest and nothing to distribute . . .'

In October 1936 he was back in London talking to the Secretary of State about Income Tax, but Sir Francis Scott, a moderate in the Legislative Council, stated in March 1937 that when he saw Sir Philip Cunliffe-Lister in London soon after Grogan's visit, he had 'to smooth the Secretary of State's ruffled feathers' because Grogan had plainly told him that he knew nothing about economics. In the Legislative Council Grogan stated that he could not recollect being so explicit to the Secretary of State but that, of course, he did not know anything about economics. Income Tax was still a hot issue and he pursued it with all his powers of persuasion.

As he had often done before, he spoke up for the Africans. He did not think it fair that the employer should be held responsible for filling his *kodi* (employment card) with stamps. 'Why should the employer be empowered to decide how a native should spend his hard earned gains. It may be extremely inconvenient for a native at any given time to find two shillings in a month . . . Personally I am opposed to this principle because I think there is too much encroachment on the rights of the individual.'

Long before anybody in Kenya or England considered the Italians going into Ethiopia a threat, Grogan warned the Government and told them that as many as 500,000 were immigrating every year into Abyssinia (as Ethiopia was called then).

His interests were varied. Business, farming and politics were absorbing, but so were women and parties. Grogan always entertained a large number of people at Torr's for lunch and in the evening for dancing. He was generous, as his daughters and friends have attested, but not only to them. 'Kathy' and her husband were given a farm at Turi where Grogan used to visit them. 'He gave her a farm because she never had a penny,' Lilly Torr said. 'At the dances at Torr's she always wore the same velvet dress which she had sat in for years and it was all crushed.' Grogan obviously did not notice this kind of thing. He still loved his Kathy and some years later he gave her another piece of land at Taveta when she was divorced from her first husband and had married a second.

The new Governor, Sir Robert Brooke-Popham, was often a guest at Grogan's table at Torr's, but the gentleman was always falling asleep in his chair. Gertrude also attended the dances but nobody remembers her dancing with Grogan or anybody else.[2] She was by then quite heavy and matronly but she still loved Ewart as perhaps no other woman had ever loved him. She often entertained at The Gallows but Grogan was not always there as promised and when he was there and not interested in the company, he could be very difficult and silent, leaving her to entertain the guests. On the other hand, if the guests were interesting, he was the life of the party.

Grogan was a man of ideas, 'he wanted to achieve,' his daughters said. 'He was incredibly energetic, but he delegated the duller jobs and he was a poor picker of men. It wasn't that he was a very trusting man, he just thought he was too far above the small details. He used to say: " I am Grogan". Lesser people should be ruled but he was above it all. What he did was all right—somebody else behaving like that was wrong—but not for him—he was Grogan.'

Sir Michael Blundell, who was also with him in Legislative Council for some years, considered him a man with 'a magnificent financial brain. He thought on a tremendous scale—he was so constructive, but took great risks and was often in debt, which did not prevent him from going on with imaginative projects. He was very far sighted and a constructive influence in all agricultural and commercial enterprises which he set in train. His name was a byword to the settlers, and the gifts with which he was endowed far surpassed any which had been given Delamere; although his horizon was largely limited by a deep dislike of bureaucracy, an utter contempt for a Civil Service Government and a pathological distrust of the Hindu, allied with a traditional affection for the African as a whole.'

He was certainly constructive but took risks in Taveta. He was determined to turn 'the semi-desert bush country into a lush and fertile plain, planting acres of wheat, barley, maize and producing some of the best quality citrus fruit to be found anywhere in the world.'[3] That is apart from the main cultivation of sisal. The grapefruit particularly were greatly appreciated in Kenya and were known as Grogan's grapefruit.

He experimented with everything, even a creeper which produced ether and leeches trees. But to bring about this wealth to the arid land he had to irrigate and bring the waters from Kilimanjaro through miles of channels and dams, which, of course, cost the kind of money Grogan did not have in the late thirties. Even so, his farm was already a model in the area where the few farmers relied on rain alone which some years failed completely.

He was back in Legislative Council in 1939 as member for Ukamba. At the first session after his election in April 1939, he asked the Chief Secretary what the Government was going to do with the £50 they collected from every incoming immigrant. 'Are you going to put the money into some special project, such as the purchase of Torr's, or the Swamp, for the sake of argument.' Laughter was back in Legislative Council as every member knew that Grogan was not only short of money but he had been trying to sell the Swamp to the Town Council since 1929. The correspondence between Grogan and the Town Council is the subject of 4,000 entries in the Lands Department and volumes of Town Council minutes since 1929 right into the late forties. The pettiness of governmental requests was enough to make a far more patient man than Grogan lose his temper. He answered their requests for more sewerage, drainage and culverts with great patience and restraint. He would carry out the requested work, he wrote to the Town Council, but he would not reduce his price. The Council was taxing him on a value of £300,000 for the Swamp and that was the price he demanded. He had the press and the whole town on his side. How could the Council value something at £300,000 and then offer to pay £60,000, they all asked? It was a scandal, the newspapers declared, but although the negotiations went on for twenty years, Grogan never sold the Swamp to the Council but to quite a different and surprising party.

In the Legislative Council he warned about 'unrest among the natives' but he attributed this more to the financial situation than to political reasons. Income Tax had been imposed during the year he was out of Legislative Council. 'We are on the verge of another very serious economic conflict,' he said, 'yet we treat it just as we would a mushroom coming up, as if it were of no particular concern to anybody at all . . . We cannot go to London and throw bricks at the Colonial Office. Anyhow, it would not have any effect if we did, for it would not wake them up.' He considered the Government 'a kind of Punch and Judy show, the strings of which are pulled by Government officials in the Colonial Office.' He told the council of a recent meeting he had with a very important Colonial Office official who treated him 'to a two hour dissertation on tiger shooting. That was all I got from him,' he said.

He was still concerned with the role of the Italians in Ethiopia when war broke out against Germany on 3 September 1939 and, although the Italians did not join the war against the Allies until June 1940, Grogan warned the Government on several occasions that if the Italians attacked from the North, Kenya was as unprepared as it had been in the First World War against the Germans in Tanganyika. The Government took no more notice of these warnings than it did of so many other of Grogan's predictions and the Italians occupied Moyale on Kenya's Northern Frontier a few weeks after declaration of war and British Somaliland in August.

Now there was panic again in Kenya. British troops were sent for, and the King's African Rifles were rushed to the frontier. An Italian farmer claimed he had been already appointed by Mussolini to take over as Governor of Kenya once the occupation was completed. He was promptly sent to a concentration camp together with other Italian and German nationals living in the Colony, and for five years he watched the progress of the war from behind barbed wire as his dreams of becoming governor steadily disappeared.

Although by 1939 Grogan was sixty-five, he immediately offered his services to the British War Office and he was appointed Liaison Officer to Angola, French West Africa and the Belgian Congo. He travelled extensively in these countries and held talks with the respective Governments and military commanders and many years later he said:[4] 'During the war I was sent to West Africa to appraise the situation there. I knew then that if Hitler continued his sweep westward, through Spain and Portugal and down the west coast of Africa to Dakar, he would win the war. He could then have severed us from America. We have got to realise that Africa is the key position in the whole set-up of the Western world and that Kenya is a garrison, with the European, the British people in the front; for after all, when everything comes to the test, they are the lads who are always there.' Grogan realised forty years ago what the Western world is realising only now.

In the Belgian Congo he learned that the Belgians were planning to close their copper mines, a step which would inevitably lead to the collapse of the whole economy. He persuaded them to delay for a few weeks and flew to Lusaka where he pressured the Governor to appeal to the Colonial Office to place a one million pounds order for Congo copper. This was done and the mines, with their valuable cobalt and uranium sidelines, continued in operation.[5]

His attitude to the War Office was as irreverent as it was to the Colonial Office but the former took more notice of Grogan than the latter. He warned them that the resources of the Belgian Congo, now their motherland was under German occupation, would be turned over to the Germans unless some action was taken by the British and one of his signals read: 'A show of force is necessary, if only in the form of an obsolete general with red whiskers.' Perhaps the sort of language Churchill could have smiled at remembering Ewart Grogan of the flogging days. Whatever Churchill and Whitehall thought of Grogan's language, they finally sent a mission to the Congo and the danger of the Germans using the Belgian Colony's vast resources was circumvented.

In Nairobi he was a member of the War Research Council and appointed Officer Commanding No. 1, No. 3 and No. 351 Prisoners of War camps in Gilgil and Nairobi. The British had defeated the Italians in Ethiopia and handed it back to the Negus, Emperor Haile Selassie, and Kenya was the recipient of thousands of Italian prisoners of war, military as well as civilian. Grogan, of course, did not hold with too many of the rules and regulations the Government had laid down for the prisoners. To him the Italian prisoners were human beings like anybody else and on one occasion he invited an Italian general to lunch at the Rift Valley Club. This did not go down very well with the authorities, but Grogan shrugged it off as he did most governmental reproofs. 'Just because there is a war on there is no reason why I should not behave in a civilised manner,' he said.[6]

Chapter 25

TAVETA AND GERTRUDE'S GARDEN

Grogan also behaved in a civilised manner to the 900 Italian prisoners of war he had arranged to have transferred to his estate in Taveta. The settlers were again fighting at the front and somebody had to look after the farms, and the Italians arrived in Kenya just in time to save farms and businesses from going to ruin as they did in the First World War.

Taveta began to flourish during the war. Great irrigation schemes were carried out by the Italian engineers and rice cultivation started. Kenya was going through another drought period and in 1942 with the population increased by thousands of prisoners, the Colony was near starvation and Grogan suggested to the Government that his land at Taveta and Ziwani should be used for food production. This scheme was run by a committee in Nairobi with Grogan as Chairman, and being Grogan, he always saw that his schemes were passed. He gave a lease of four years to the Government and 2,000 acres were put under irrigation supervised by Italian irrigation experts, and the scheme was a great success.[1]

The Italians were also good builders and Grogan thought this was a wonderful opportunity to pursue a scheme which had been maturing in his mind for a long time. He wanted to build an agricultural college for Africans and he spent thousands building what is now known as Grogan's Castle on Girigan hill. The structure he designed with an Italian engineer was unorthodox to say the least. There was a shortage of building materials such as steel and cement during the war so he used what was available at Taveta such as sisal poles for reinforcing. He maintained that a strand of sisal was as strong as the same size steel and by using layers of sisal poles with a mixture of lime and mortar instead of reinforced concrete, he achieved what he wanted. To strengthen the upper floors of the building he added a few old lorry chassis and even aeroplane struts. The rooms, destined to become class-rooms, were huge, mostly with a central column to support his inventive ceilings and they were all different shapes. The only rectangular room was what eventually became the dining room when he went to live at Girigan. The whole building was octagonal and rooms followed the sides of the octagon. On his land he had brick and tile works and being fascinated by building he was continuously erecting workshops, labour lines, staff houses and stores. Taveta, Ziwani and Jipe housed extensive villages of labour which Grogan recruited from the Kavirondo area (around Lake Victoria).[2] The locals in the Taveta district were not very keen on the arduous labour of sisal cultivation and the sturdy Kavirondo liked Taveta especially as, being lake people and favouring a diet of fish, Grogan provided them with Telapia fish.

In the three estates Grogan often employed as many as 2,000 Africans during the sisal cutting season but a force of 1,000 was resident and apart from fish he provided shambas [gardens] for each family. He also gave them schools and clinics. Many of his old employees have said: 'He was a good employer because he provided us with everything and looked after us very well and he was not *kali* [severe, angry]'.

Besides directors such as Lord Egerton of Tatton, Sir John Ramsden and Pearce Mosdyn who only visited the estates occasionally to hunt, Grogan employed an average of twenty Europeans to supervise the many sided aspects of the three estates at Taveta. Twenty was a fluctuating figure as a lot of men considered Grogan too demanding or Grogan considered them useless, therefore, their term of employment was sometimes no more than a few months, but one man who remained loyal to Grogan and a firm friend was Tim Trafford who was general manager until 'internal feuding' forced him out in 1951.[3]

Apart from being Camp Commandant of the Italian prisoner-of-war camps for which services he was promoted to Lieutenant-

Colonel in 1941,[4] running his various business enterprises and developing Taveta, he was still representing Ukamba in the Legislative Council where he was most vociferous when economic matters were discussed.

The yearly estimates of the Kenya Uganda Railways and Harbours (as the Uganda Railway was known by then) always incensed Grogan and in December 1939 he told the Acting Governor W. Harrigan that the yearly K.U.R. & H. estimates were becoming 'a sort of annual hula-hula dance, when the honourable member [the Railways' General Manager] is decorated with flowers, usually of narcotic properties . . . but I consider myself too old to change. I remain a realist,' he said. 'I find it quite impossible to live like Alice in Wonderland [when we are] called to observe the annual beanfeast to what in all intents and purposes amounts to our national tape worm, whereas tomorrow we shall be invited to attend the funeral of obsequies of the host.' Why could not the Railway make use of local resources? he wanted to know, as in the case of Mangalore tiles. 'I am a bit of a potter myself,' he said. 'I have lived in a pottery, and I was privileged to initiate the pottery industry in this country.' He went on telling the General Manager of the Railways that the local tiles were far superior to the imported Mangalore tiles, and besides these, local timber, limes, phosphate and a dozen other assets of the colony could be utilised instead of spending Kenya's meagre reserves on expensive imports.

At a debate on estimates in January 1940 Grogan was accused by the Chief Secretary, Mr Rennie, of suffering from the effects of the budget, and he replied that, of course, he was suffering. 'I am one of the major payers, whereas you are one of the major payees.' He wanted an assurance that the Government would realise the desperate state of local agriculture and take steps instead of 'blah-blahing'. The Government should ensure the maintenance of production. 'I believe that the proper part of Government is to represent first of all our interests and to protect us from external exploitation by the Imperial Government, [then] I won't be as angry as I am today.' There was very little the Government could do right in Grogan's estimation, and it was not easy for them to avoid his anger. He was not merely the member who made the House laugh with his sardonic statements, he was no clown, he was the man who made them realise that Kenya's economic situation was no laughing matter and unless resolute steps were taken, Kenya would never be free of debt to the Imperial Government.

Gertrude, meanwhile, was still busy with the East African Women's League and was very popular with the soldiers stationed in Kenya and training for the Burmese and North African campaigns. She ran canteens and entertainment for the soldiers and as her daughter Jane said, she was 'the typical universal mother.' In 1942 she took over from Lady Baden-Powell as President of the E.A.W.L. but her term of office suddenly ended when in June 1943 she had a heart attack and three weeks later she died on 5 July. Despite his many lovers, Grogan seemed to be broken-hearted at the loss of his 'Thomasina'. Hundreds of people attended her funeral. There was not one person who had come into contact with Gertrude since her return to Kenya, who did not appreciate and love her. She was always ready to help those in need and, perhaps, people felt sorry for her considering her husband's unfaithfulness. Her funeral cortège stretched for miles and many shops closed to show respect for this loving woman who had remained loyal to the man who many people had judged disloyal to her, despite the fact that he always maintained that she was 'the love of his life'.[5]

The love of his life was no more and now he felt free to offer Kathy marriage and a legitimate life for their daughter. Kathy had divorced her husband for the second time, but refused Grogan's offer, although she still remained a good friend and often visited Taveta with him. She was not the only one. Other girl friends were guests in his primitive house at Taveta.

Whilst a huge modern structure was being built on Girigan hill he lived in a wooden hut. In fact, his European staff on the three estates lived far better than he did. Most of them occupied properly built houses with their families, but Grogan was always different. He considered the normal type of building with stone walls, tiled roof and windows unsuitable for Taveta's climate, so he built a long wooden house with a bitumen felting roof, front and rear gables on an A frame surrounded by mosquito gauze and expanded metal. The front of the house boasted a small verandah where the roof came down two feet from the ground, also surrounded by expanded metal and mosquito gauze. His theory was that the occupier was shielded from the sun, he had a high roof for air, a through draft and protection from his old enemy: the mosquito. The structure may have provided all these advantages but it was a remarkably ugly one. At one end there was a lounge and dining room combined and a kitchen. At the other end, for some unknown reason separated from the rest of the building, there were bedrooms and bathrooms separated from each other and built at different periods. His own bedroom was also separate and, as in Muthaiga, it resembled a bunker with a concrete roof.

The furnishings were not very attractive either. 'There wasn't a stick of decent furniture,' a friend said.[6] 'Sisal mats and skins on the floor, a comfortable chair for himself, but always a lot of books.'

Although Taveta was not his permanent home as he only went down to the estate to check on the work progress every few weeks, he didn't live much better in Nairobi. The beautiful homes: Chiromo, Ventors and Draycott Place, were all behind him. All he wanted now was essential comforts with the least fuss. The bombing had done great damage to Draycott Place in London which had been left in the hands of a care-taking couple. Windows were blown out, furniture, books, his precious trophies from the Walk, (including the 140 lbs. elephant tusks), were ruined, vandalised or stolen,[7] and after the war Draycott Place was sold. Not left to Jesus College as some members of the family believed.

It may sound as if Grogan was 'winding down', but although he was almost seventy he was far from retiring from any aspect of active life. No one thought of Grogan as old and the Indians in particular realised he was as aggressive as ever when he delivered a speech in December 1943 on his favourite subject: the Indian question. Although he stressed the fact that during a time of war Kenya 'must refrain from all overt activity which might cause embarrassment to the Imperial Government.'

The dislike between Grogan and the Asians was mutual. They hated him even more than he disliked them and branded him the worst of racialists. At a time when their sons were being accepted into Oxford and Cambridge, and Indians in general could stay at the best hotels in London providing they wore a collar and tie, Kenya settlers shut the doors of their hotels and clubs in their faces and Grogan to them epitomised all that was racist in British colonial rule. They fought him in the Legislative Council and they fought him in the bazaar where a story circulated that, not only had he illegitimate white children, but he had illegitimate children from African women.[8] This was hearsay, of course, and nobody has any evidence of it, but the Indians spread the story with great glee, at the same time saying that Grogan was an outstanding man and they had great admiration for him.

One Indian who did not consider Grogan anything but 'a good man' was Zia ud Deen, a Punjabi Muslim who worked for him at Taveta from 1936 until he sold the estates in 1961, and who said that he was the best employer anybody could have. According to Deen, Grogan was very considerate to his employees, be they Indian (of whom there were ten at Taveta, mostly Sikhs), African or European. Whenever Grogan visited his estates at Taveta he never failed to visit Deen and his family and at Christmas he gave presents to all the employees' children. When Deen started working for Grogan he received £22 a month (when most of the Europeans earned £40), but every year he received a bonus on the profits, and when Grogan sold out he gave Deen a year's salary, although the most precious gift the Indian mechanic received from Grogan was his .454 rifle, as in the early years Deen was very keen on hunting and Grogan no longer considered it a justified sport.

He had a provident fund for the workers, but it was the children of the estate who really loved Grogan, and when he arrived in his huge blue American car, a Lincoln Zephyr, the children surrounded him as they knew he had pockets full of sweets for them.

He allowed his grandchildren the free run of the estate and always had time for them. When his granddaughters scrambled on his knees and wanted to talk to him, he told the adults in the room to keep quiet. He had important things to listen to.[9]

Grogan was never a great driver, according to his employees. Whatever car he was driving, be it one of the two Lincolns, Jeep, or estate box body, he put the car in first gear and expected it to go. If it stopped, he walked. In fact, he mostly walked everywhere and faster than his much younger employees. 'In his cars he always had a karai, a jembe, a panga and a shovel,'[10] Deen said, 'because he hated pot-holes and if he saw one he got out of his car and filled it up.' He never accepted help from anybody right into his eighties. If he had a puncture, he mended it, but mechanical things never interested him. He often stopped the car to help the African women weed or shred the sisal on the drying lines. 'He was never like a boss,' Deen said, 'he worked with everybody and mixed with everybody.' There was never a feeling of master and servant at Taveta but they all worked a little harder when the dust of his car appeared in the distance. A very different man to the one lecturing on the Indian question.

His working clothes on the farms certainly did not distinguish him from the rest of the workers. His khaki trousers and jackets were always spotless but often worn out and mended, but he would have considered it ridiculous to dress up when he worked alongside the Africans, or built enormous bonfires of the bush he was always clearing, or engaged in his geological research. 'He always knew what the soil contained,' Deen said.

But his passion was water. The life-giving water without which his estates would have reverted to dry bush. He found underground rivers thousands of years old—at least, he said they used to be rivers, but to anybody else they looked like solid rock. Not to Grogan. He had his bulldozers build four foot high catchments at the top of all the tributaries and people asked: 'What are you doing that for? They are only dry rivers.' 'In fact they thought he was mad,' his grandson David Slater, who worked at Taveta for a while, said. 'Well,' Grogan replied to the people who could not understand what he was up to. 'I am building little dams.' 'Why? Even if you catch rain it will dry out after a fortnight.' 'It may dry out,' Grogan explained, 'but I am not going to get the water from there. I'm going to get it three miles further down the river.' Nobody understood this, but he was right. The water caught behind these dams soaked down into the lime river beds and eventually came out where he said and a spring developed there which produced 50,000 gallons of water—pure water.

The war was drawing to an end, he received the Africa Star and was promoted to full colonel, although he refused to be paid for his services, and he resigned from the Legislative Council, but a new project which he had been considering since Gertrude's death, now began to take shape.

He had always loved children, although his legitimate daughters did not seem to receive much of that love, and he wanted to leave a memorial to his 'Thomasina'. What better memorial than a home for war orphans in the Muthaiga garden Gertrude loved so much.

Mr Gerald Nevill, a Nairobi doctor, who wanted to raise money for a children's hospital heard of Grogan's proposed home for orphans and went to see him. When Nevill expressed his interest in the orphans' home, with a twinkle in his eyes Grogan said: 'Why? Are you an orphan?' It did not take Nevill long to convince Grogan that a children's hospital was needed more than an orphans' home, and Grogan immediately agreed, but when Nevill suggested that Muthaiga was not an ideal location for a children's hospital and that the other side of town where the other hospitals were, was more suitable, 'Grogan fixed me with his steely blue eyes,' Nevill remembers, 'and he said: "Young man, you are given a gift and you accept it gratefully." ' Nevill did not argue.

The architects Cobb and Archer designed the hospital and Grogan set up a trust to pay for it. The initial building, which accommodated only twenty children cost £20,000 and £10,000 for the equipment was raised by the East African Women's League, of which Gertrude had been President before her death.

Grogan watched the building grow and took great pride in it, but even after it was finished and opened in 1947, with the name of 'Gertrude's Garden Children's Hospital', he paid regular visits, played with the children, brought them gifts and organised Christmas parties. When in the early 1950s there was an outbreak of polio he immediately agreed to provide the money to build a screening ward. It is known as the Garden Wing with eight rooms and bathrooms which Grogan designed himself.

In later years when African children were admitted to Gertrude's Garden, the staff worried lest Grogan object and when he visited they covered the African children up. Grogan soon discovered the trick and every time he went to the hospital he made straight for the African children's beds and played with them as he did with the others. Although he had nothing to do with the running of the hospital, to the end of his life it was the achievement which gave him the most pleasure.

Chapter 26

GROGAN'S CASTLE, INTRIGUES AND THE SWAMP

The one achievement which was beginning to frustrate him was the great building which stood empty on Girigan Hill. When it was completed Grogan offered it to the Government for an African agricultural college and the new Governor, Sir Philip Mitchell, never even bothered to answer Grogan's offer.[1] This attitude of the Government and its top representative did not increase his love of bureaucracy. 'He had the deepest scorn of certain things like high positions, honours, and particularly pompous civil servants,' an old friend of his said.[2]

It was probably this attitude and his continuous criticism of Government policies which precluded Grogan from being honoured. This view was held by many of his friends in the Legislative Council.[3] 'Although,' as Sir Charles Markham wrote, 'knighthoods and lesser awards were given with careless abandon to many people, some of whom were only doing the job for which they were paid.' But these friends also agreed that Grogan would have probably refused a title or an honour.

Meanwhile, there stood this imposing, if somewhat strange building which had cost a great deal of money and which nobody wanted. All who knew him at that period testify to the fact that Grogan always spent more on Taveta than he made. His three factories where sisal was decorticated, washed, dried, brushed, pressed and baled, were only one example of his mania for modern equipment. Enormous bulldozers costing £12,000 each, was another. The hundreds of acres of oranges, limes, lemons, grapefruit, pineapple and avocadoes required specialised care and more money. Cattle, which died of trypanosomiasis,[4] plus thousands of miles of irrigation, transport, wages, roads and rails criss-crossing the estates, all amounted to more spending than earning.

Something had to be done about Girigan, as people in the area referred to the building on the hill, and the humorists as Grogan's Castle. Girigan was not the local name for the hill. The Taveta people knew it as Kishota Ng'onji and claimed it was a sacred place to them. There they buried their dead in pre-colonial days and offered sacrifices to the spirits of their ancestors. Grogan's building was not a popular move with the Taveta who were offended by his disregard for their sacred ground, but it is said[5] that having learned of his *faux pas*, Grogan the politician, invited the Mrigiti (medicine man) to carry out a 'cleansing' ceremony for a sum of money, as he did for every baobab tree which was felled and was also supposed to house ancestral spirits, and all went well despite the fact that the Taveta Africans believed there were ghosts at Girigan.[6]

Grogan decided that as the Government did not want his building, he would occupy it himself but the deteriorating class-rooms and a long row of lavatories were hardly suitable for a private house.

A young architect, Heini Lustman from Nairobi was introduced to Grogan by the Taveta general manager, Tim Trafford, and with Grogan Lustman re-designed Girigan to become Grogan's Castle despite its oddities of shape and materials used when it was first built. The spectacular views alone made it well worth while living in, but there is no doubt that from any angle Girigan was and is an unusual feature in that immense flat landscape.

Branching off the main Taveta road the estate road to Girigan runs through acres of sisal, silver grey and spiky, and always in view is Grogan's Castle, balancing on a small hill which at a distance does not look substantial enough to support the weight of the big white building with its octagonal tower and three storeys. At a distance it is difficult to say what it is meant to be. It could be a convent or a sultan's palace as Grogan's nephew Christopher Grogan said. Austere and lonely in the immense landscape, backed by the majestic Kilimanjaro Mountain, known simply as The Mountain at Taveta, and the Pare Mountains often shrouded in cloud. Fat baobabs are dotted among the sisal and to reach the castle a stony track winds up the steep hill. Suddenly the steps of the house appear and heavy wrought iron gates open on to a square patio with a central fountain and flower beds. Cloister-like covered passages, supported by thick columns, lead to the guest rooms.

On the opposite wall to the wrought iron entrance gates, stairs lead up to a first floor circular lounge with half moon windows and all round views of Mount Kilimanjaro, Lake Jipe and the never ending plains. At the centre of the thirty foot circular lounge a huge column holds up heavy steel girders in a wheel pattern which support the floor above and a gigantic mill wheel surrounds the columns. This is where Grogan kept newspapers, journals and magazines on all subjects from all over the world. Looking out at the bush he once said: 'Vegetable image of democracy—useless and stunted.'[7]

Grogan's own bedroom, which commands the most spectacular view of all, has a peculiar construction like a cage covered in mosquito netting where Grogan slept. Steel posts protrude from the wall to hold the bed three feet off the floor and a bath, hand basin and lavatory cabinet complete the room.

More stairs, with a G carved into the balustrade, led to another circular lounge. Steep stairs climb from this room to the top of the tower from where Grogan could see to the very limits of his territory. No wonder he felt like a God. On one occasion he is reputed to have said: 'I am God Almighty around here.' And a disrespectful bystander reminded him that it had not rained for a long time.[8]

The dining room on the ground floor is the only rectangular room in the house and even today the dining table, which could comfortably sit twenty-four guests and is made of a composition of the finest hardwood from his forests, stands there witness to the many dinners over which Grogan presided as a charming and entertaining host if the mood was right, or a difficult silent one if the company did not please him. The frequent guests never knew what to expect of Grogan. Sometimes he would receive them in his old khaki farm clothes, at other times in impeccable beige linen suits with collar and tie. His tastes in food were also very simple, and although he seemed to know a lot about food, he preferred a soup and a glass of wine of no particular vintage. After his breakfast eggs one day at Girigan, Camilla Towers said: 'A little toast and marmalade, Grogs, to take away the taste?' and Grogan replied: 'Well, wouldn't that also take away the point of eating eggs?'

He liked a little Napoleon brandy with his Churchillian cigar or cheroot after dinner, but in the day time he mostly smoked a pipe. He hated ostentation and wasting time. A guest once remarked that 'Grogan was not the kind of man one dropped in to take tea with.'

Girigan was forced upon him by the Government refusal to accept it as an agricultural college, but he would have been quite happy to end his days in the simple wooden hut.

A woman would have enjoyed Grogan's Castle far more than he did. Such a woman was Camilla Towers. In 1947 Grogan had met Mrs Towers through mutual friends, Colonel and Mrs Vair, at the Muthaiga Club. She was a small, red-haired woman known as the Marmalade Cat, approximately thirty years his junior who said she was the widow of a London architect who had died of a heart attack after two years of marriage. At the time of meeting Grogan she worked at Wardles the chemists in Nairobi and she claims that Grogan invited her to join his lonely household as a daughter,[9] although Grogan's daughters, who were in the country at the time, state that she went as his housekeeper. Whether as a daughter or a housekeeper, Camilla Towers recently wrote to Michael Grogan, Ewart Grogan's nephew, that eventually Ewart asked her to marry him, but she declined, not because of the great disparity in age, but because, although she was fond of him, she did not love him. Nevertheless, she was fond enough of him to remain with him for twenty years until his death.

When in Nairobi they lived in a house Grogan had bought from his brother-in-law, Wilfred Hunter, in Chui Road. As it had become his custom at The Gallows (now Gertrude's Garden Children's Hospital) and at Taveta, Grogan did not sleep in the main house, but in what most people considered the stables, on a camp bed covered in skins. There was a canvas wash basin standing in a corner 'as if he expected to be off on safari at any moment,' some of his friends said.[10] The main house where Camilla Towers lived was no better furnished.

In June 1947, Michael Grogan, the son of Ewart's younger

brother Philip, arrived in Taveta to work for his uncle and he described Camilla Towers as 'uncle Ewart's housekeeper. Young, red-headed and vivacious. A Rat-Catcher [Roman Catholic]' like himself, he wrote to his parents. His uncle Ewart was no Catholic but seems to have put up with visits from the local Catholic priests.

Although not interested in any religion, Grogan believed that the Catholic Holy Ghost Fathers were the only kind of missionaries who successfully educated Africans with honest dedication. He was very disappointed in the efforts of the Church Missionary Society and in 1945 Grogan promised to finance a Catholic Mission on his land at El Doro. It has been said that it was Camilla Towers who talked Grogan into giving the Catholics money and land, but in 1945 he had not even met Camilla. He gave the Holy Ghost Fathers £1,000 and 450 acres and Grogan was always satisfied with their success in educating African children, although not quite so impressed with the missionaries' success in converting the Africans. Nevertheless in October 1949 he was godfather to the first eighty-two men and sixty-four women who converted.

Apart from his daughter Joyce who had become a nun, his three other daughters, Dorothy, Cynthia and Jane had become Catholics during their school days, although later, apart from Joyce, they all lapsed, but right now he was surrounded by Catholics.

When Michael first met his uncle at the Taveta station in his huge sun helmet, Michael thought he looked like 'a human tortoise, except for the cigar,' but he was very impressed with Uncle Ewart in the beginning. 'His knowledge of everything is prodigious,' Michael wrote after he was shown around the estates. In fact, according to him, 'Uncle Ewart was the only one with real knowledge of farming.' He considered the general manager, Tim Trafford, 'a pompous old ass' who had been a civil servant all his life before he joined Grogan and was now concerned that Michael's arrival might endanger the future of his two sons whom he wanted to bring into the estate. Michael, in fact, did hope that his apprenticeship to Trafford meant his uncle intended him to take over the running of the estates eventually. His hopes and opinions of Uncle Ewart, whom he later referred to as Uncle Ego, changed with the passing of years. At the beginning he was touched by Uncle Ewart's offer to help his parents (whom he called Ming and Ding) financially, and when they refused,

Grogan explained to Michael that he didn't know what to do with his money and that 'it was false pride not to accept it within the family'.

When he first arrived Michael stayed in the wooden house (or houses, as they were all separate units) with Ewart and Camilla and he seems to have been satisfied with the comfortable accommodation, the long hours of work and the little amusement there was on the estates. Most employees had their families, but for the bachelors there was nothing except visits to each other, the occasional visit to Moshi and very little shooting 'because Uncle Ewart was against it'. But not always. On occasion the smaller type of game became a nuisance to cultivation and Grogan had them shot to feed the labour. The Game Department did not mind the shooting. The owners of the estates were allowed to shoot, but all trophies, meat etc. belonged to the Game Department. With his usual contempt for all Government regulations, Grogan shot a number of zebras, waited until they were very high, then loaded them on the train and had them consigned carriage forward to the Game Department in Nairobi.[11]

Government regulations were not the only bugbears at Taveta. Staff problems and intrigues were always simmering at the estates and although they worried Grogan, he tried to ignore them. Not so his nephew Michael whose relationship with Tim Trafford went from bad to worse. Michael felt he had been misled when his uncle wrote to his father, Philip: 'If Michael is at a loose end send him out here. I will fix him up in one of my shows and his prospects will be good as I have no male member of the family interested. I have taken care of all my dependents.' It is not surprising, therefore, that Michael expected to be treated like a Grogan and not as Trafford's 'stooge'. Although his salary was only £430 a year plus housing, the thing which most upset Michael was the fact that unless they were alone, Uncle Ewart never took the slightest notice of his nephew and never showed affection. His uncle was apparently satisfied with 'a banana and a glass of water', but other people required more—especially understanding. Even when Grogan transferred Michael to the Ziwani estate twenty miles from Taveta under Forgan, the situation did not improve much. Uncle Ewart would send him a cheque, but not a letter. 'Uncle Ewart lacked psychology in dealing with people,' apparently.

A 'controversial figure in Taveta politics' was Camilla Towers,

Michael wrote to his parents on 9 February 1948. One of the things she used to say was that Grogan could not 'separate the dross from the gold . . .' 'She was not the most detached and forgiving of people. She was rather possessive. She called the four mile road from the main road to Girigan, "my drive".'[12] Camilla Towers, according to Michael Grogan's assessment in the early days, had an 'electric temperament, [was] highly strung, [and] she either liked you or loathed you and you either liked her or loathed her. Fundamentally sincere, though full of a rather Irish type of insincerity. Her position is a difficult one really, and of course, many people accuse her of being a gold-digger . . .'

Only one month later he was writing to his parents: 'Whatever her merits or demerits she suffered very much from malicious gossip . . . originating from people who did me so much harm . . . I think Mrs Towers is a very much sincerer person than her outward appearance would suggest.'

Michael liked her and appreciated her help in getting settled. She felt sorry for him because of his difficulties with Trafford.

At seventy-three Grogan was still a very healthy and active man who had 'great knowledge and brilliance', but he began to suffer from deafness, the occasional attack of lumbago and trouble with his teeth.

In October 1947 he had a tooth removed by Dr Jimmy Guest and he developed osteomyelitis of the jaw (an infection). 'Quite a serious illness,' Mr Michael Wood, the surgeon who operated on him said. 'It meant that in the whole of one side of his jaw the bone was going bad and I spent one and a half hours chiselling away at his jaw and removing the dead bone.' The next day Grogan called Michael Wood to his bedside at the Eskatene Nursing Home and said: 'Wood, there are two things I want. One I want to have a cold bath and two I'm going home.' 'It was quite a major operation and he had been chiselled and knocked about,' but Grogan would hear no objections and Michael Wood had to let him go. His own doctors, Dr Gregory and Dr Charles McCaldin tried to talk him out of it, but Grogan listened to no one and Michael Wood had to go and remove the stitches some days later at the guest house in Muthaiga.

He liked living a rugged life. At Girigan Camilla Towers prevailed on him to put glass in the windows, an idea he was strongly opposed to and which he did not accept for his own room, with the result that his mosquito net was always being blown away. Finally he devised the wire mosquito netting stall which housed his bed. Another odd piece of furniture, and typical of Grogan, was the armchair in which he did his reading. It had a wooden canopy to stop bats' and swallows' droppings falling on his head and books. There were always bats and swallows at Girigan but now they have taken over the uninhabited building completely.

Just as during his walk when he was a strong young man, in his seventies Grogan took no notice of illnesses but he did grow a beard to hide the scar and the depression the operation had left. He was still vain enough to mind what he looked like and the white beard added to his roguish good looks.

At any rate, women still found him very attractive and he enjoyed life to the full. Torr's Hotel, which had been re-named Tarts Hotel by the young, fun-seeking army officers during the war, was still a 'swinging' place. The band played every night and cabarets were organised by Peter Colmore to the great enjoyment of Colonel Grogan. Mzee Pembe and Kipanga were Grogan's favourite entertainers as they did skits in Swahili playing the Indian duka-wallah and the policeman.

He still entertained his friends and hangers-on for lunch at the grill, and although Joseph, the Goan headwaiter with the obvious toupee, made a great fuss of him, Grogan ate very little and was not at all particular about his food. He also enjoyed watching the shows Colmore organised for the staff of the Muthaiga Club at Christmas: the only European who enjoyed this kind of entertainment because he said it was wonderful to see how the Africans laughed at the unsophisticated humour.

And that was the trouble with Grogan at that time. He liked the Africans unsophisticated. He was kind and paternalistic towards them, but like fathers and colonialists the world over, he still could not believe that the Africans could ever manage the complex affairs of their own country. For the time being nationalism was still an underground movement, the likes of Grogan had nothing to worry about, but the time was fast approaching when colonialists such as Grogan would have to change their attitude towards African aspirations.

As for his private affairs, the thorn in his side was still the Swamp Estate. He had sold a few plots to Indians at various times but the largest part, Plot 209/136R, was still being discussed by the Nairobi Municipal Council as a possible purchase. Since 1929, when he first tried to sell the Swamp, the Council had dithered and kept up an endless correspondence with Grogan regarding health measures, ditches and canals, until in 1948 he got tired of waiting for the Council's decision and he accepted an offer by Heptulla Brothers. Ahmedali Hebatullah had come to Kenya in 1929 and as he could not read or write, he asked a European to show him how to write Hebatullah. In that way his name became Heptulla. With his brother Fidaali who had come to Kenya in 1934, he bought from Grogan 130 acres of Swamp and the remaining lease, which was for another fifty years but extendable, for £180,000.

The only trouble was that Hebatullah, or Heptulla, and his brother had a capital of only £100,000 and they hesitated until they had consulted their Spiritual Leader in India who advised them to go ahead with the purchase. Grogan agreed to sell them the Swamp in instalments, so the Hebatullah brothers sold a few of the already subdivided plots and finalised the purchase in the allotted time.

Mr Husseinbhai Hebatullah, the son of the original Hebatullah remembers going to see Grogan just before Christmas 1948 after they had bought the Swamp. They first went to the Muthaiga house where Mrs Towers told them that Grogan was at the club, and there they found him sitting on the verandah reserved for male members of the club. They gave him a present 'because he had been very good to us and very fair over the sale,' Mr Husseinbhai Hebatullah said. 'Colonel Grogan appreciated the effort we had made with such a small capital and the risk we took. He was very easy to negotiate with.'

Like Grogan, the Hebatullahs had faith in the Swamp although the Council always said that it was not suitable for building because of black cotton soil, but great buildings went up and now Hebatullah Brothers are planning a huge complex with shopping arcades and flats. On each side of the Swamp, reaching the Khoja Mosque on one side and Ngara on the other, development goes on, and although Grogan Road has been renamed, the Swamp is real evidence of the vision of the man when the area was nothing more than a soggy unhealthy swamp.

Chapter 27

LEGISLATIVE COUNCIL AND MAU MAU

In the early fifties Grogan's vision of Kenya was based on economic progress. For him there was no standing still. Long before the Oceanic Hotel was built on its present site in Mombasa, on the front of the island before the entrance to Kilindini harbour and facing the ocean, he thought it was the ideal site for a hotel and when solar heating had not been heard of except by a few experts, he planned a hotel with a flat concrete roof painted black and housing two feet of water, thus insulating the hotel from the sun and providing it with hot water.

In Taveta one of his passions was minerals, and he went about with a prospector's pick most of the time. He found a great number of minerals on his estate, including mica and kyanite used for refractory bricks, and he invited his great friend, Sir Charles Markham (senior) to come and dig for it. He could have the mineral rights free, Grogan said. Unfortunately for Sir Charles, who employed 40 Europeans, 20 Asians and 800 Africans, the land was the only thing free in Taveta. Kyanite cost him all of his family's trust money.[1]

Sir Charles Markham was not the only one to lose money at Taveta. After many years of friendship and close business association, a disagreement arose between Grogan and his financial adviser and company secretary, Percy Wheelock. By

December 1951 Wheelock and Grogan were locked in a legal battle and suing each other. 'The fall of Wheelock seems to be complete,' Michael Grogan wrote. 'The whole thing arose over the commission he had taken during several years on various transactions. The sum involved was pretty big [but] the thing will probably be settled out of court.' Dunstan Adams, another friend and also an auditor, took over where Wheelock left off and continued to look after Grogan's vast interests until the latter left Kenya.

All in all Grogan's relationship with his employees was not always easy. Another nephew, Michael's younger brother Christopher, had arrived at Ziwani in February 1950. Despite the fact that Michael was not satisfied with his life as a 'mere employee', he had encouraged his brother to join him saying 'life is bigger here, there is a certain freedom and the struggle for living is not so acute as in the overcrowded factories and offices at home.' Christopher soon followed in his brother's footsteps in his displeasure with the conditions of employment, and Michael advised him never to argue with Uncle Ewart. 'One great advantage in our present set-up *is* that these difficult old men are so *old*,' Michael wrote to his brother. 'Uncle Ewart probably thinks that he can control everyone with his money . . . [but] we can be indifferent both to his money and his unpleasantness.'

In fact, Michael should have been pleased with the developments of the next few months. He received 5,000 shares from his uncle, was made manager of Ziwani when Forgan left and his old enemy Tim Trafford was told his services were no longer required.

The manner of Trafford's dismissal is not clear as in a letter to his parents of 31 January 1951, Michael stated that 'when Trafford reached Mombasa on his return from England last week, the clerk from Taveta was there waiting for him with a letter giving him his notice. He said he was going to resign, anyway!' But according to Mrs Towers it was Grogan who dismissed him after he heard that the Traffords had said some disparaging things to her. Grogan did not react immediately nor did he say anything to Camilla at lunch. He worked all afternoon on the estate and in the evening he came back to Girigan tired and dirty from making fires in the bush. They had their sundowners: Grogan beer and Camilla sherry. As usual they had their baths and changed into their evening attire. Grogan wore a light suit and mosquito boots and Camilla her customary long dress. It was only when he had lit a cigar and picked up one of his favourite Pekinese that he announced to her that he had given Trafford notice. Others have said that Trafford himself resigned. Whichever way Trafford was eliminated, Michael and Camilla Towers had won their battle.

At seventy-five Grogan was as strong and aggressive as ever. On one occasion, when Terence Gavaghan was District Commissioner at Taveta, Grogan turned up in his box-body car wearing his 'enormous topee hat, not the usual kind, but a huge one with a sloping back made of thick cork; padded jacket with long sleeves and khaki trousers,' Gavaghan said. 'Grogan had come to deliver thirty-odd spears, simis, bows and arrows. "I brought you these," Grogan said in a slow drawl. "I have just disarmed a raiding party." 'How did you do that single handed?' Gavaghan asked. 'Ah well, there was nothing much else to do but tell them to lay down their arms and when one of them argued, I kicked him in the testicles. Then I let them go on their way.' Two days later the District Commissioner received a cable from his opposite number in Tanganyika claiming that a Taveta settler had intercepted a police raiding party in hot pursuit of cattle rustlers.

Rustlers were a menace to Grogan, especially when he was experimenting with the elimination of tsetse flies. He had discovered that disinfestation took place when a certain density of cattle occurred. He studied every report on tsetse fly control and apart from the use of antrocite, he learned that by clearing a belt of bush 200 yards wide, the fly's eyesight being limited to a few yards, the cattle could be moved in and by keeping the land grazed it was progressively cleared of flies.

Rustlers, tsetse flies, economics and agriculture never completely replaced his interest in politics as became obvious during the speech he was invited to give at the Command Theatre in Nairobi on 4 July 1951. He started by saying that although he considered it a great personal compliment to be invited, he knew that the only reason for being taken out of obscurity was that Africa had always had a certain amount of respect for the *wazee* (the old). And *mzee* (old man) he was, he said. There were very few people around who remembered Stanley and Baker's widow, besides the whole gamut of historical events of the past fifty-five years, and it was those historical events which affected the present day constitutional issues of Kenya, although, he said, it was 'an infinitely wider issue' in 1951. 'In the world today the whole set-up is closing down to a desperate struggle between the East, dominated by Moscow, and the West, based on the United States of America.'

But it was the constitution of Kenya he had come to talk about and the subject could not be discussed without the Indians and the Africans being included.

'The African,' he said, 'is an entirely different matter [from the Indian]. Our approach to him should be kindly and benign. For myself I am one hundred per cent pro-African. I have had fifty-five years experience of him. I have employed him by tens of thousands. I have been involved in the most incredible messes with him at times. At the last resort the old African never let me down, but at the same time I have no illusions about him.' He spoke of some of his more harrowing experiences during his walk, but he said the African had 'come a long way from that sort of thing to people like Mr Jomo Kenyatta and Mr Mathu. They are important phenomena. They are a great and living tribute to the British rule which has wrought this change in so short a time . . .

'For all that, it is incumbent upon us to do everything we can to make use of the innate friendliness of the old African . . . Please do everything you can to adopt a friendly attitude toward the African. Give him every opportunity to participate here, there and everywhere; although his participation in Government must necessarily be a limited one . . .

'It is impossible to maintain that any African, no matter how he has been educated, can in such a short time be in a position to formulate useful opinions on important matters of central policy. The African as we know him is often very intelligent. But is he intellectual? We must encourage them and give them every opportunity in affairs, always remembering that no part in the major affairs of state can be entrusted in their hands . . .'

But it was in their hands that the Africans wanted, not only the major affairs of state, but *all* the affairs concerning *all* the people of Kenya and it was no good Grogan quoting from the Koran: 'Look not scornfully upon thy fellow man: nor walk the earth with insolence, for God loveth not the arrogant and the vainglorious: be moderate in thy pace and speak with moderate tone, for the most ungrateful of all voices is the voice of asses.'

The Africans were tired of a moderate pace and a moderate tone, the underground nationalist movement was gaining strength as Grogan, Michael Blundell and a few others well realised, and although it had not come to open combat yet, Grogan felt it was time his voice was heard again in the Legislative Council.

He stood for Nairobi West in June 1952 and during his electioneering campaign he said to the *Sunday Post* reporter: 'I have served more years on Legco [Legislative Council] than anyone else, and I can assure you that nothing of any particular use is done in Legco. It's done in committees. Little good can be achieved by throwing bricks at bureaucrats in open Council. Old age carries certain deficiencies, but it does kill ordinary petty ambitions. I have got to the stage where I can sit in the pits and spit orange pips at the dignified people in the stalls.'

When he was asked if he supported equal rights for all civilised men, he answered: 'I do not support equal rights for all civilised men unless I am given a very clear definition of what is a civilised man. If it means that sorting letters in the Post Office for twenty-five years is any qualification for giving a casting vote on a complicated issue like Company Tax, then I do not agree with it.'

He was returned to the Legislative Council with a large majority and at the swearing in he said: 'I come from the great unpaid. I want nothing but to do my last bit to serve Kenya.'

One of the first questions he tackled on 11 July 1952 was the Mau Mau rebellion which could no longer be ignored. 'I do not regard the Mau Mau people as criminals,' Grogan said. 'I think they belong to an entirely different category . . . and they should be kept quite distinct from the criminal and dealt with in some other way. Quite obviously, their movement is not going to be checked by piling all these people together and locking them up, but I believe that somewhere, tucked away at the back of my memory . . . is that there is some clause where in the case of rebellion or major subversion, the Government can recover areas of land from the Native Reserves and bring them into the category of Crown Land. Now, if the Kikuyu gentlemen knew that in the case of major subversion, in any area of their land, that a square mile of their land would be taken from them and brought into the area of Crown Land, I think we should find that all would combine to check these mischief makers. I do not regard the thing as incurable.'[2]

He was right in one thing: there was one clause in the Native Lands' Trust Ordinance. That Clause was No. 69 which said that land owned by people in rebellion reverted to Crown Land, although when Grogan suggested applying it, no one in the Government had ever heard of it. But Grogan was quite wrong in believing that the Mau Mau movement could be checked by merely depriving the Kikuyu of their land. The movement was in full swing, but when warned by Michael Blundell that it was a case of fully fledged rebellion, 'the Government belittled the facts as they tried to belittle everything,' Grogan said.[3] 'Even when trouble flared up they denied there could be a crisis. Bureaucracy's normal reaction.'

In July 1952 Grogan was elected the President of the Pioneers Society, being one of the first pioneers still remaining in Kenya. Mrs M. F. Stocker, who had arrived in 1905 and had danced at Chiromo as a young girl, was elected Vice-President, but at first Grogan protested his election. He said he was far too busy with other commitments. 'But his protests were drowned in the acclamation of the meeting and they voted him unanimously into the presidency.'[4] The Europeans of Kenya felt their colonial foundations being shaken and Grogan as President of the East Africa European Pioneers Society made them feel a little safer, also, as Robert Foran, another pioneer, wrote to him, Grogan was the only one who talked 'horse sense to the electors and I am a hundred per cent in accord with your expressed views.'

In September a new Governor was appointed. Sir Evelyn Baring arrived at the worst time for Kenya, when the Mau Mau were killing Kikuyus who had declared themselves loyal to the British Government, and Europeans in isolated farms. Within a month of his arrival, on 20 October 1952, he declared a state of Emergency. The decision by the Government to recognise that the actions of the Mau Mau constituted rebellion, as Grogan and Blundell had been insisting they had for months, did nothing to stop the killing and Grogan was at his most vociferous in the Legislative Council on methods he recommended should be adopted to stop the bloodshed.

'The only thing they [the Kikuyu] comprehend is something within visual range,' he said on 26 November.[5] 'Something positive, something definite, something immediate which they can understand, and there are only three things that touch them on the raw as a complete entity. One is land, another is cattle and another is their necks . . .' He still advocated taking their land but when it came to cattle, 'one has always got to remember that they have their women and their children,' he said. 'And the amount of stock in the Kikuyu reserve in proportion to the population is comparatively small, and, therefore, in an ordinary humanitarian sense there are limits which can be reasonably applied in taking their stock away, because we have got to think of the needs and necessities of their women and their children.

'Now, let us turn to the more immediate problem of their necks. Quite clearly if this is rebellion, and as I say, it quite obviously is, anybody who takes an active part in a rebellion, this is surely treason and the penalty for treason is to be hanged by the neck until they die. Now, having collected together an odd hundred of these alleged rascals, supposed to be agitating in this rebellion, and having popped them up to the Northern Frontier, surely the correct procedure as distinct from the highly complicated methods being adopted today, would be to charge them with treason, and having convicted some of them, hang up a reasonable proportion by their necks in the presence of the others, and the others seeing what treason meant and having learnt thoroughly that they were subject to her Majesty the Queen, I should then, if I had charge of the position—it is a great pity I have not—I should have presented the balance of that galaxy with 50 lbs of posho and a compass and told them to find their way back across the desert to their friends in the reserve to spread the joyous tidings . . . because if seventy-five gentlemen came back and said they had seen twenty-five gentlemen hanged by their neck, and that was what happened in rebellions and treason . . . I think in all probability . . . you might get the definite positive assistance of a considerable number of the Kikuyu tribe.'

He was applauded in the Legislative Council for this statement, slated in some British newspapers, which stated that he advocated hanging Kikuyus 'in bunches of twenty-five', reported correctly in *The Times* and condemned to death by the Mau Mau leaders.

The danger he was in did not change his opinions or his way of life. Unlike most Europeans he never carried a gun during the Emergency, but what did upset him was 'the suffering of the

Kikuyu people during that time and his horror at the loss of life at the hands of each other. On one occasion talking about the killing of innocent children, he had tears in his eyes,' Humphrey Slade said.

On 1 May 1953, Grogan was invited by the Kenya Empire Party to give a speech at Memorial Hall and 600 Europeans packed the hall to hear their favourite speaker once again. He spoke for forty-five minutes and when asked if he would accept the leadership of the country, he waved his cigar, pushed his glasses over his forehead and said: 'Nobody has ever led Kenya. We are much too individualistic a country. I have pushed occasionally. I have no pretentions to be leader. Mr Michael Blundell has done a first class job of the duty we entrusted to him. You should be thoroughly grateful to him.'

There were prolonged bursts of applause and he appealed for unity among the Europeans and ended by asking the audience not to harden their hearts to the African because of Mau Mau. 'That,' he said, 'would solve no problem at all. I am a humble old owl who sits on the rooftop and hoots occasionally—usefully perhaps—and acts as a book of reference to unrecorded history. I have tried to keep my eye on the political ball,' he quipped to the laughter of the crowd. He gave his appreciation of the present position and he recalled warnings given to the Government, which were brushed aside. 'They said, even after the trouble flared up, there cannot be a crisis because we have never allowed one. Michael Blundell warned the Government of a state of rebellion. The Government belittled the facts and when the balloon went up, the job of the team was to support the Government. We are the pectin which solidifies the jelly, and thrust and push the so-called Government.' The Government passed the buck to the police, he said. 'That is all very well. The Government always passed the buck somewhere. But the function of the Government is to act as a pituitary gland in the body politic to keep all parts in co-operation and in balance. The function of the police is that of the lower intestine—to get rid of the waste products of society.' He ended up by calling the Colonial Office 'a Parliamentary Whipsnade', and the people loved him.[6]

1953 was the most difficult year Kenya had ever experienced and on 14 May in Legislative Council he said: 'It is quite obvious from the oaths and whatnot in which these people are indulging today, [that] we are faced with an atavistic reversion to primaeval savagery which may go back for thousands of years. It seems almost unbelievable that the individual Kikuyu that we know can go wandering the country chopping off arms so that he can complete the ritual oath by eating putrid human flesh. That is the actual condition to which they revert . . . Even as I listen to the persistent, remorseless eloquence of my honourable friend, Mr Mathu, I have an uneasy feeling that behind his rhetoric may be his roving eye searching the front ranks opposite for a succulent morsel . . .' There were cries of 'shame' in the Legislative Council at this statement. 'Fortunately,' Grogan went on, 'despite the fact that I was informed by telephone that I was condemned to death on Saturday—I think as far as cannibalistic intentions are concerned I have some degree of immunity.'

Mr Eliud Mathu now says he was not angry at the statement —he expected it from Grogan in those days but they were good friends. Grogan admired Mathu and told him he had never heard a black man speak English so well. 'But you fight me too much,' Grogan said when he asked Mathu to have a drink with him at the bar in Parliament Building. Grogan told him he had never had a drink with a black man before and Mathu went along only on condition that Grogan would accept a drink from him. 'He was changing then,' Mathu said. 'He had respect for the educated African but he never believed that the majority were ready for independence.'

Mathu had been elected to the Legislative Council in 1944 after an education at the Alliance School in Kikuyu, in South Africa and Balliol College in Oxford. By 1952 he was one of six Africans in Parliament and in many ways he admired Grogan. He admired his stamina for walking through Africa. 'That was terrific,' he said. 'That determination made him to acquire a lot of property in the way of land from the coast to Eldama Ravine. There is nothing against that. The spirit of acquisition and determination to possess is a lesson to anybody. I don't mind acquiring something myself. Yes, he was like a Kikuyu. He loved the land, but he didn't think the black man could achieve much, he didn't have confidence to the extent that black men could govern the country. He didn't believe the Africans could become intellectually equal to Europeans. He thought me an exception.'

In a different way to Mathu, Grogan thought Jomo Kenyatta an exception. 'Grogan thought that there must be an alternative way of ending the senseless killing other than the normal force of arms,' Sir Charles Markham wrote.[7] '[Grogan] stated that in his view the Emergency had gone on far too long and he could see no end to the killing, as, even if the gangs were finally eliminated, the bitterness would remain and trouble would only break out again in the future—next time with more organisation and probably with country-wide support. He felt the Government was relying far too much on the views given them by the Chiefs and so-called loyalists, but that in the eyes of the people, the Chiefs were nothing more than servants of the Government, whilst the loyalists were really mercenaries of that same Government.

'Enlarging on this theme, he said he was in entire agreement with General Erskine [commanding British Troops fighting the gangs] about a political solution being the only answer. In [Grogan's] opinion, there was only one possible answer and that was the immedate release of Jomo Kenyatta from imprisonment on certain conditions. "Whether we like it or not," Grogan said, "there is only one man who has any authority over the Kikuyu and that is Jomo Kenyatta. We should say to him that he started it all, so he must stop it and they will listen to him. This bunch of thugs calling themselves Field Marshals, Generals, and the like, have no authority at all with the Kikuyu as a whole. They recognise only Kenyatta, Mau Mau or not, as their leader and there is nobody else." '

'He then added that he had expressed these views to his colleagues and to some members of the Government who were totally opposed to his suggestions. With that little chuckle for which he was famous, he continued: "They all think that I'm a silly old man who doesn't know what is going on. They will finish the Emergency all right, one day, but Kenyatta will still be their hero." '

Grogan wanted Markham, who was also a member of the Legislative Council, to mention his views to their colleagues, 'not that he was in any way optimistic that they would share his beliefs.'

When Markham reported back the negative response, with some sadness Grogan said: 'Pity. It might have saved many many lives, but we shall see one day whether I was right.'

Of course, he was right but at the time he was branded a crazy old man. Mervyn Hill, the Editor of the *Kenya Weekly News* wrote an 'irate letter' to Markham asking for an explanation of this 'crazy folly' of Grogan's, and he told Markham in Nakuru that he thought 'the old man had gone off his head.'

Mervyn Hill was not the only one. People stopped Camilla Towers in the street and told her they thought Grogan was becoming unbalanced in his old age.[8] He was approaching eighty, going deaf and a little blind, but his intellectual vision was as clear as ever.

Chapter 28

A HIVE OF BEES AND RETIREMENT FROM LEGISLATIVE COUNCIL

He had clear vision, but sometimes limited on certain political issues. The Lyttelton Plan was one such issue. In March 1954, the Secretary of State for the Colonies visited Kenya and put forward a proposal for the establishment of a Council of Ministers consisting of Europeans, Africans and Asians which was accepted by all members of the Legislative Council except three, and Grogan was one of the three. He did not mind so much the Africans participating in the running of the country, although he still maintained they were not ready for it, but he could not accept Asian participation. He was still of the opinion that constitutionally they had no rights. As a result of the Lyttelton Plan a new European Elected Members Association was formed and, although Grogan 'contributed to the secretarial costs' he refused to belong to it. Grogan, the maverick of Kenya politics was alone again, and he didn't care who he upset.

Even royalty. He had met quite a number of them during his years in Kenya. The Duke and Duchess of Connaught, the Prince of Wales, the Duke and Duchess of York, the Duke of Gloucester, Princess Elizabeth and her husband when she became Queen during her visit to Kenya, the Queen Mother and Princess Margaret. At a reception for the Queen Mother, when she mentioned the cannibals he had met during his walk, he explained: 'We don't have cannibals anymore, Ma'am, we have bank managers.' And to Princess Margaret who asked why he had undertaken his epic walk, he said: 'Because, Ma'am, there were no hansom cabs going my way.'

In the Legislative Council his sarcasm was always directed at the Government members. He used to refer to the Attorney General as 'the member for much law and disorder', Sir Charles Markham said. 'This was not only a perfect Grogan gem but also an admirable description of the gentleman concerned.' He still used to describe the Government as termites. 'They thrive on dead wood,' he said.

Unfortunately, because of his increasing deafness, normal conversation was becoming difficult, let alone full participation in debates. He had travelled to Johannesburg to be fitted with a hearing aid, but this, he said, drove him mad. It was the kind of aid with ear plugs, a long lead and the box of controls which he kept in his top pocket. At Torr's Hotel he often threw it across the table complaining that every time he switched it on all he could hear was the knives and forks crashing around in the kitchen.[1] 'Those infernal little machines,' he called the hearing aid.

He eventually used a trumpet but in the Legislative Council he 'was persuaded to use the hearing aid which he left near the Despatch Box by the Unofficial Front Bench and whenever somebody was speaking who Grogan thought might be interesting, he would, with great dignity, stand up, switch on the little machine and solemnly plug the lead into his ear. He adopted the reverse procedure, however, when some of the more boring members spoke, often at length. With a little smile of apology for his action, he would make the aside, which could be clearly heard: "It's not worth wasting the battery on this chap." With a sigh that was also clearly audible he would then resume his seat and go fast asleep.'[2]

His colleagues forgave him. After all he was the Grand Old Man of Kenya, as people began to refer to him then. He was the longest serving member in the Legislative Council and his experience and abilities were still greatly admired, and on his eightieth birthday he was given a demonstration of this admiration. All the members including Africans and Indians congratulated him, and some made speeches to wish him a long life. Grogan was visibly moved by this show of affection. When he stood up to reply on 14 December 1954, he said that he had difficulty in finding words to express his appreciation of 'the unexpected and exceptional compliment' the House paid him. Being Grogan, of course, he had no difficulty in finding words.[3]

The prolonged applause after the speech visibly touched Grogan and he was seen dabbing his eyes as he looked up at one of the flags he had carried on his walk and had presented to the Legislative Council. The Eminence Grise of Kenya politics was often a man of deep feelings.

When Michael Blundell's mother remarked to Grogan that he was the same age as herself and Churchill, he said: 'You know madam, obviously a vintage year.'[4] When in 1955 Churchill retired he said: 'He is the greatest living master of the Elizabethan tongue. There is always something sad about a great world figure stepping down from the dais.'[5]

On that occasion the South African *Star* and the *Rand Daily Mail*, as well as *The Times* in England and the local papers wrote long articles on Grogan's life, but when the *Rand Daily Mail*'s reporter asked him if he would seek re-election, he said: 'All I want now is to get back to the bush where I belong.'

Besides his ears, his eyes were also beginning to fail, but Grogan went on participating in all aspects of life. He did not retire into the bush. In those days he could still read and he read avidly on all subjects, but for relaxation he went to bed with an Agatha Christie.

A very welcome change from routine was the visit by an old friend, Richard Meinertzhagen, who arrived in Nairobi on 4 January 1956, and was met at the airport by the press and Grogan. They were delighted to see each other again and they sat up until late on many an evening reminiscing and exchanging news, and Meinertzhagen found Grogan's brain was still 'as clear as crystal'.

Obviously Grogan was not old enough to ignore women. Meinertzhagen wrote that Grogan remarked on Mrs Lathbury's good looks. With Grogan and others she was a guest of Meinertzhagen at dinner at the Muthaiga Club and Grogan was his usual charming self—particularly when attractive women were present.

As Meinertzhagen wrote, he had only changed physically. His interests, whether women, business, politics or being the controversial figure he always was, remained the same.

At a time when hotels and clubs were still closed to Africans and Indians, he often invited Tom Mboya to Torr's Hotel for lunch. In 1962 he said to the South African *Star*: 'I spotted him a few years back as a rising politician. I used to discuss things with him over lunch when I owned an hotel in Nairobi. He's a very remarkable young African.'

Grogan's daughters said their father thought Tom Mboya 'absolutely marvellous and a brilliant young man', but other guests at Torr's did not. Some of them would go up to Dorothy and say: 'What *is* your father doing? Upsetting everybody. Can't you stop him?' Nobody could stop Grogan and Tom Mboya had great regard for the old colonel. He did not even mind Grogan's sarcasm.

When the organisers of the Pageant at Mitchell Park (the yearly agricultural show) invited Grogan to take part in the pageant dressed as he was during his walk, Grogan replied: 'I don't mind if Tom Mboya doesn't mind wearing the sort of dress he used to wear in those days which was nothing but an elephant whisk.'

Apart from Michael Blundell and a few others, Grogan was one of the first Europeans to understand the frustrations the Africans suffered. In April 1956 he accepted an invitation by C. M. G. Argwings-Kodhek, the President of the Nairobi African Congress, to a luncheon when Kodhek said that the Africans had been 'faithfully and well served by Britain' and Grogan answered that he understood the frustrations suffered 'by the up-and-coming Africans' who had learned to live according to western standards but were not accepted socially by Europeans. In the speech he urged the Europeans to entertain 'these symbols of the new Africa in their homes'.[6]

Home, meanwhile, was not particularly peaceful for Grogan. Taveta seemed to be a hive of bees. Peter Elliot, Grogan's son-in-law married to his daughter Jane, had taken over the running of the estate and they did not communicate with Camilla, and Dorothy, who was by then a director of Taveta, was on no better terms with her father's housekeeper.

'Camilla does not come down often,' Michael Grogan wrote on 10 August 1954. 'I think she is a rather changed person nowadays. She does not take so much part in things and says very much less than she used to. I suppose she and Uncle Ewart have some mutual arrangement not to bother each other.'

The daughters felt that Mrs Towers made their father more

distant from them, but Camilla Towers maintains that it was Dorothy's dominant influence which turned the rest of the family against her.

Whichever way it was, the daughters were glad to let Camilla take care of their father, but all his friends agree that she was possessive of him. 'She looked after him very well,' Humphrey Slade said, 'but she isolated him from his family and his friends. Being an old man he was very dependent on her.' 'Grogan and Camilla Towers got out of different drawers but they got on very well in the same chest,' a Nairobi humorist said.[7] 'She rationed him to everybody. If you wanted to see him you always had to ask her permission—you had to shove her off the end of the sofa.'

Most people said she really did take care of him, although the epithets used for her were never very flattering.

The employees at Taveta, whether white, black or brown did not like Camilla Towers with the sole exception of Michael Grogan who saw her in a different light when he was being badly treated by Trafford. She certainly had no time for Trafford and it was mutual. Others, who were employees of lower status, such as the Indian Zia ud Deen, said: 'We were enemies—she was very kali. Nobody liked her. She bothered all the employees.' And the Luo Ezekel Gombe said: 'Towers was very kali with the people working for her. She never allowed anybody to get near Colonel Grogan.'

She was obviously not a great favourite with Grogan's friends and employees even though it could be understandable if the family distrusted her as they suspected her of being 'after the old man's money'. Camilla Towers, on the other hand, now says she had nothing against any members of the family and, at least in Taveta, there is evidence that she entertained his friends like 'a charming and hospitable châtelaine, and maintained a wonderful table'.[8]

At that time Grogan seems to have been pressured on all sides. His two nephews, Michael and Christopher Grogan in September 1954 threatened to leave and their uncle tried to pacify them, but they left soon after.

All in all bees were better than the people who surrounded him, but the real bees did get him at Taveta. His friend, Captain Malin Sorsbie, was asked to collect Grogan who had been badly stung by a swarm of bees, and he flew him in a Rapide aircraft to one of his doctors, Dr Guy Johnson, in Nairobi. His only remaining comfort seemed to be his Pekinese dogs whom he adored and always had a number of them around him.

Life was becoming increasingly difficult at home and in the country in general and Grogan began to think that retirement was possibly the only way to deal with the general situation.

Two years before he had already decided not to stand for re-election and in October 1956 he retired from the Legislative Council and members of all races joined in paying tribute to the Grand Old Man. Up until the end Grogan was heard on the economic and political issues which were closest to his heart and one of the issues was votes for the Africans. He remarked that in 'civic qualities and social status' the African was 'in tune with the Western cultural thesis,' therefore 'I see no justification whatsoever for not applying the principle of adult suffrage to the African,' he said. 'That is a matter of principle.' But, he said, how was the Government going to assess how much each African earned. For example the Kikuyu who communally own land, the Masai, the prostitutes etc. 'I must adhere to my belief that selective franchise is the only possible method of voting for a community in the stage of development such as the African people,' he concluded. 'After all, universal franchise was only introduced into Great Britain in 1928.'

Always controversial, at a time when most Europeans had the lowest possible opinion of Jomo Kenyatta, he wrote:[9] 'Of the Africans of my time only one will live in history—Jomo Kenyatta. Anyone who can view these matters objectively and has read Jomo's writings must have . . . a measure of sympathy for one who undoubtedly is a great African patriot as seen from the African angle . . .'

His pronouncements were always far advanced of anybody else but with the resignation from the Legislative Council an important part of his life was over although there was still much to do before he could retire to the bush.

Chapter 29

THE WINDING DOWN OF THE MORTAL COIL

As he said about Churchill: 'There is always something sad about a great world figure stepping down from the dais.' Grogan was no longer a world figure. It was a long time since his famous walk, but he was still a great figure in Kenya and in England, and to see him stepping down was sad.

Whether the Grand Old Man of Kenya, with his striking looks, long flowing white hair and white goatee beard, realised he was stepping down, it is hard to say, because at eighty-one he was in full possession of his mental faculties and he still had the physical strength to take part in the work at Taveta and outwalk anybody there, but the fact remains that, apart from resigning from the Legislative Council, by 1957 he had reduced many of his commitments. He had slowly sold properties which he had held since his arrival in 1904, such as the Equator Saw Mills' yard and offices which occupied a great part of today's Koinange Street and which later (in 1967) became Timsales, the largest dealers in timber in Kenya. His lease on the forest concession had expired and he had sold for £140,000 the land adjoining the Swamp which now forms part of the University's playing fields and the Boulevard Hotel. He had also sold the plots which made up Groganville. Most of the 'stands' which he owned in Nairobi had gone and the only one remaining was Torr's Hotel, which, after Joe Torr's resignation became very profitable during the war and since 1947 when 'Ben' (Arthur) Benbow took over the management, no longer worried Grogan who left the running of it in Ben's capable hands. Like most other employees, Benbow found Grogan easy to work for and liked him immensely.

Grogan still enjoyed entertaining for lunch at the grill and the best brandy and cigars were always available at his table. Despite the profits Grogan decided it was time to let this valuable property go. It was in the very centre of the town, opposite the New Stanley Hotel, by the roundabout where the statue of his old friend Lord Delamere stood. 'Never known him look like that,' Grogan used to say about the statue. 'Wonder what cellar he will occupy when the time comes for all white men to step down from their pedestal.'[1] He sold his beloved Torr's Hotel to the Ottoman Bank for £250,000,[2] and retired to the bush, a little deafer and a little blinder.

In his life time he had cleared and farmed some half a million acres and was now left with 120,000 at Taveta and seven acres in Muthaiga, but even those were beginning to weigh on him. His employees did not realise that Grogan had considered selling the three estates for many years, but as his nephew Christopher Grogan said: 'While the Royal Standard didn't exactly flutter at his palace on the hill, his presence was [still] felt as soon as he arrived. Everyone worked just a little bit harder and the European supervisors kept one eye on the horizon, watching for the tell-tale column of dust which heralded the approach of his jeep.'

According to Camilla Towers, who wrote to Michael Grogan recently, the reason for Grogan's decision to sell the estates at Taveta were none other than the difficulties with his family which reached such a pitch that Grogan finally announced that he had broken all connections with his family. He sold his estates and provided generously for his daughters and grandchildren. Then he left Girigan with Camilla Towers leaving everything behind.

In 1958 Grogan sold the Taveta estate, including Girigan (not Ziwani and Jipe) to a Greek consortium led by Mr Criticos, who resold it to another group 'the Patels' in 1959. These in turn sold it in 1963 to the Lancia/Shirley group who went bankrupt. Criticos was at the receiving end. By 1972 he had acquired all the three estates from the receiver. But, meanwhile, in 1958 what Camilla Towers said about leaving Girigan without removing a single item, was perfectly true. Gordon Hunter who managed the estate for the Italian group, after it had passed through

Greek and Indian hands, found the house fully furnished. The sheets were still on the beds and the toothpaste and brushes in the bathrooms, and a great deal of private correspondence was left behind.

Only Camilla Towers can know why they left Girigan in such a hurry, and she has not revealed the reasons. Was it disgust at the complications or more likely such heart-rending regrets at leaving what was so important to him that he could not bear to see it go and merely shut the door on it all? It certainly was not because of his health which by 1959 was still so good that at eighty-five he looked a healthy sixty. Asked by a newspaper reporter what the secret of his longevity was, he said: 'To smoke very heavily, drink and eat very little and not take anything too seriously.'

There were still things he took very seriously and although he was delighted when on 12 January 1960, the end of the Emergency was declared, he wrote a series of letters to the *East African Standard* fulminating against the Secretary of State for the Colonies, Mr Macleod, for having decided at the Lancaster House Conference on 'common roll'. 'Mr Macleod has proclaimed,' he wrote, 'that folk ranging from the near Stone Age to the highest products of modern science which constitute Kenya, can only be fused into a "nation" on the principle of common roll . . . What has provoked this perplexing *volte face* in constitutional mongering?' he asked.[3] He may have remained well informed and interested in Kenya politics, but he was certainly too late in his remonstrations.

On 31 October 1960 Grogan suffered a mild heart attack and was taken to the Maia Carberry Nursing Home in Nairobi and, as usual, was well cared for by Camilla Towers who was under the impression that he was a Catholic and therefore sent for a priest to hear his Confession. This did not go down well with Grogan who spoke politely to the priest but 'I was not disposed to shock the poor fellow with eighty-four years of interesting sins,' he told one of his doctors and an old friend.[4]

By March 1961 he had finalised the sale of Ziwani and Jipe to a syndicate of Asians by the name of Patel. It is said that together with Taveta the three estates sold in the region of one million pounds and Grogan claimed that that was what it had cost him to develop it. Nobody was surprised at this claim. 'Taveta was a marvel of development,' as Sir Wilfred Havelock said.

At the Muthaiga Club, which was now his headquarters and where he held court either on the verandah or in his special chair by the fireplace in the men's bar, which nobody else dared occupy, he was interviewed by a number of reporters from local, English and South African newspapers.[5] He stated that he had sent the money from the sale of Taveta to England because of tax reasons. He also said that he had provided for his descendants, including four daughters, nine grandchildren and three great-grandchildren, whom he believed had no future in Kenya, but that he himself intended to stay and watch the catastrophe. He also said he had made up his mind to sell out after a two minute talk with Macleod. Grogan could never accept Macleod's common roll policy. When asked if he would consider going back to England, he chuckled: 'The only thing I'd go back to England for, is the daffodils.'

The Muthaiga Club became his home-away-from-home since he had sold Torr's and Taveta. He always had the same table in the dining room and the same Kikuyu servant: Wachanga who had worked at his house before going to the Muthaiga Club. He was the only member allowed to bring dogs into the club. His Pekinese followed him everywhere. Grogan took most of his meals at the club and he never hestitated to fill a bag with the left-overs for his dogs. He ate so little there was always plenty over, but he favoured chicken for his pets.

When East African Ventures, which was the umbrella company for his various enterprises, was finally wound up on 24 March 1962, Grogan made trusts for his legitimate and illegitimate families.

Grogan's hearing and eyesight were getting worse and one of the things which gave his life meaning—the ability to read for hours—was being taken away from him and he had to rely on a few kind friends who went to the Muthaiga house to read to him, which was not very easy as it meant shouting down an ear trumpet. But he could still talk and he talked a great deal to the stream of people who stopped by his chair at the Muthaiga Club or had dinner with him. He was always generous with his hospitality.

He was almost completely deaf and blind but he still perceived clearly what the political situation would be like for the Europeans in Kenya after Independence. On 11 February, 1962 to a reporter from the *Sunday Post*, he said: 'There is no future for the European on the land, but in business, in commerce, and in many of the professions, there will be room (in Kenya) for him awhile'. A prophetic statement.

He was advised to see a specialist about his eyes and in October 1962 he was admitted to a Johannesburg nursing home for ophthalmic observation and treatment which only gave him temporary relief, his blindness would only progress with age which was not surprising at eighty-eight.

In November the Muthaiga Club was celebrating its fiftieth anniversary and Grogan was photographed with the servants, some of whom had known and liked him for as long as they could remember. The staff were given a party and a show, but although Grogan sat there and strained to hear and see, his wan smile showed that he understood and saw very little.

He celebrated his eighty-eighth birthday on 12 December at the Muthaiga Club 'with seventeen friends and relatives and a huge cake,' the *East African Standard* reported. Grogan could not miss one more opportunity to make scathing remarks on the British Government. 'It was a complete pantomime,' he said. 'A façade. The real Government was the Colonial Office . . . Today the country is completely bankrupt and only money from home keeps it afloat.'[6]

Edward Rodwell, the Kenya journalist, asked him what he thought of the present day situation, and he answered: 'The Lord is very good to me, he has made me almost blind and very deaf.'

The Muthaiga Club Committee honoured him by electing him Vice President in 1964 but by then he was a pathetic figure. 'I went up to him one day at the club and I touched him on the shoulder,' Sir Michael Blundell said. 'He was deaf and blind and as he turned around, he said: "I can't see you, but the voice, the voice is the voice of Michael." I asked him how he was and he answered: "Michael, just waiting to die. Just waiting to die." That was so sad for a man who had done so much. To think of all he had achieved and how he was still respected.'

Perhaps the saddest thing of all was that at ninety his mind was still clear and he knew he was finished. There was champagne at his Muthaiga house on his ninetieth birthday, then lunch and dinner as usual at the club, but he was 'just waiting to die'.

One of the last pleasures for him was seeing his daughter Joyce, the nun, in 1966 after so many years. 'He was enthralled with her as they got to know each other again,' his daughter Dorothy said. 'He said: "She radiates goodness just like her mother." Daddy had always been an atheist, but he was received into the Roman Catholic church before he died. I always felt it was due to Joyce—not that she ever tried to convert him.'

By February 1967 Grogan and Mrs Towers were gone. 'We knew nothing until they had left,' Humphrey Slade said. 'Grogan's friends were very upset when he vanished completely. We didn't even know the address. We were very sad because he wouldn't have liked to be anywhere else.'

His old friend C.B., Cavendish-Bentinck, now the Duke of Portland, agreed with Humphrey Slade. Grogan loved Kenya and he would have never chosen to leave it. 'He would have been pleased to see things turn out as well as they have. He loved the Africans,' C.B. said.

'When Camilla took father to South Africa Dorothy and I were at my house in Watamu,' his daughter Jane said. 'When Dorothy came back she rang the Muthaiga house to find out about father, but there was no answer so she rang Miss Wilmer, the matron at Gertrude's Garden, and asked if there was anything wrong.' Miss Wilmer was surprised the daughters did not know their father had gone. 'So that was that,' Jane added. 'No address. Not another word.'

Jenny, his illegitimate daughter drove them to the airport not realising she was the only one who knew her father and Camilla were going to South Africa for good. By that time he was a bit senile, deaf and blind. The last time Zia ud Deen, his Indian mechanic from Taveta, saw him at Muthaiga he cried to see the man he had always considered indestructible in the pitiful condition he was in at the end. Rose Cartwright, a very old friend, who had visited him shortly before he left, said, 'Ewart was perfectly miserable because his Pekinese had been put down.'

After they left Nairobi nobody knew anything until Jean Crawford, Grogan's granddaughter by Cynthia, who was working as a nurse in Cape Town, discovered where her grandfather and Camilla were through an old Kenya friend, Walter Shapley at the Settlers' Club. They were living in a service flat at Grosvenor Square at Rondebosch near Cape Town. 'I could only see grandfather in the hall because Camilla was being difficult,' Jean said.

Soon after, Jean was informed by a friend staying in the same block of flats that her grandfather had been taken to a Catholic hospital, near Cape Town. By then he had converted to Catholicism. He had two strokes and prostate trouble.

On 16 August 1967, Ewart Scott Grogan died and his granddaughter only learned the news through a small newspaper notice saying that he had passed away peacefully 'fortified by rites of Holy Church. Requiem Mass at St Michael's Church, Rouwkoop Road, Rondebosch, today (Thursday), at 9.30 a.m. Funeral immediately thereafter at Maitland Cemetery, 1st Gate.'

Jean barely made it to the grave and no other member of the family or friend was present at the burial. He was buried in a simple grave, but much later, when his daughter Dorothy heard of this from a friend in Cape Town, she asked the friend to have a stone placed on her father's grave.

There were articles in the South African press which announced that Grogan had left only 'an adopted daughter in Cape Town, Mrs Camilla Towers', with no mention of the real daughters or grandchildren. Both Kenyan and South African newspapers carried long stories on his life; his old college at Cambridge, Jesus College, wrote a long obituary and he was written up in various biographical dictionaries in Britain, East Africa and South Africa, but the newspaper which had published so many of his writings and commented on so many aspects of his life, *The Times*, never printed a word on his death.

'Grogan died unnoticed,' Sir Charles Markham wrote, 'depriving us of the opportunity to pay our last respects to one of Kenya's most remarkable pioneers who had contributed so much to Kenya's history.'

NOTES AND SOURCES

Chapter 1: pages 1-9

1. 'Through Africa from The Cape to Cairo'. Speech by E. S. Grogan to the Royal Geographical Society 30 April 1900.
2. Norman Wymer, author of *The Man from the Cape*, after writing his book traced the origins of his family (he is one of E. S. Grogan's nephews) and has kindly allowed me to use his discoveries. Letter of 17 February 1979.
3. Christopher Grogan. E. S. Grogan's nephew. Son of Philip, and Dorothy Slater, daughter of E. S. Grogan.
4. Harold Grogan. E. S. Grogan's nephew. Son of Walter. Letter of 13 November 1978.
5. Michael Wood.
6. Winchester referred to 'books' not 'standards'.
7. Winchester College.
8. Sir Charles Markham.
9. Mrs Brittain, Assistant Keeper of Records, Jesus College.
10. Dr Gregory.
11. Harold Grogan.
12. J.C.C.S. Report.
13. H. A. Morgan's letter of 28 July 1900.

Chapter 2: pages 10-17

1. Dorothy Slater and Dr Gregory.
2. *Sixty Years in East and Central Africa* by E. S. Grogan, 1957.
3. *Ibid.*
4. Letter by E. S. Grogan to Manley 12 October 1929.
5. When he met Rhodes in London after his walk.

6. *Sixty Years in East and Central Africa.*
7. *Ibid.*
8. Dr Gregory.
9. Information on E. S. Grogan's part in the Matabele war came from his daughters, Harold Grogan, Christopher Grogan and a number of other sources to whom he had told parts of the story.

Chapter 3: pages 18-28

1. Jane Elliot and Dorothy Slater (daughters)
2. Jane Elliot.
3. From E. S. Grogan's personal diary not used when writing *From the Cape to Cairo* through the kindness of Michael Grogan.
4. All quotes and sources in this chapter are from E. S. Grogan's book *From the Cape to Cairo.*

Chapter 4: pages 29-36

1. Heini Lustman.
2. Mirambo, known to European travellers as the Napoleon of Africa, had commanded thousands of Ruga-Ruga warriors in Tippu Tip's time (the 1880s) and helped by that powerful African the Arab slaver could cross the greater part of Tanganyika undisturbed.
3. Beer made from sugar cane or bananas or even maize.
4. All other references and quotes in this chapter are from *From the Cape to Cairo.*

Chapter 5: pages 37-44

All information and quotations from *From the Cape to Cairo.*

Chapter 6: pages 45-54

All information and references from *From the Cape to Cairo.*

Chapter 7: pages 55-62

1. *Tippu Tip and the East African Slave Trade* by Leda Farrant.
2. *Sixty Years in East and Central Africa* by E. S. Grogan.
3. All other references and quotes from *From the Cape to Cairo.*

Chapter 8: pages 63-70

1. Jane Elliot.
2. Referred to in Chapter I.
3. Royal Geographical Society.
4. Dr Gregory.
5. Ministry of Defence.

6. *Sixty Years in East and Central Africa* by E. S. Grogan.
7. Original letter and photo with Dorothy Slater.
8. Marian Szlapack.
9. *Sixty Years in East and Central Africa.*
10. Christopher Grogan.
11. Grogan had already been sent down from Cambridge.
12. Original letter with Dorothy Slater.
13. *The Times*, 1 May 1900.
14. Gordon Phillips, *The Times*' Archivist.
15. *Sixty Years in East and Central Africa.*
16. Harold Grogan.
17. Daughters.
18. *Sixty Years in East and Central Africa.*
19. Lord Cranworth's *Kenya Chronicles.*
20. Christopher Grogan.
21. Jane Elliot.

Chapter 9: pages 71-81

1. Daughters, Dr Gregory, Sir Michael Blundell and Harold Grogan.
2. *Financial Times.*
3. Letter to *The Times*, 3 April 1902.
4. A. Wykes, Hon Secretary Savage Club.
5. Dorothy Slater.
6. Terence Gavaghan.
7. *Sixty Years in East and Central Africa* by E. S. Grogan.
8. Brian Yonge.

Chapter 10: pages 82-88

1. Dorothy Slater.
2. Lord Cranworth's *Kenya Chronicles.*
3. Dr Gerald Anderson.
4. Sonny Bumpus.
5. East African (British) Directory of 1908-9.
6. Heini Lustman.
7. These coaches can still be seen at the Railway Museum.
8. Dak Bungalow : Indian word for rest house.
9. In Kamba language Tsavo means 'place of slaughter'.
10. From a report by Major Robert Foran, now in pamphlet form.
11. E. S. Grogan's Foreword to Newland and Tarlton's magazine *Farming & Planting in B.E.A.* of 1917.
12. Sonny Bumpus.
13. Eddie Ruben.
14. The Indian rupee was in use as currency and it was worth 1s 4d.

15. Eddie Ruben.

Chapter 11: pages 89-96

1. *Sixty Years in East and Central Africa* by E. S. Grogan.
2. *The Africa Protectorate* by Sir Charles Eliot.
3. Eliot to Lansdowne 9 and 10 April 1904. Correspondence relating to Sir Charles Eliot's resignation.
4. Eliot to Lansdowne 5 April 1904 F.O. 2/835.
5. Correspondence relating to resignation of Sir Charles Eliot F.O.2099 (1904) pp 6, 7.
6. Evidence to the Kenya Land Commission of 20 February 1933.
7. Dorothy Slater.
8. Robert Foran's *A Cuckoo in Kenya*, 1936.
9. *Sixty Years in East and Central Africa* by E. S. Grogan.

Chapter 12: 97-105

1. Brian Yonge.
2. Graham Boswell.
3. Lady Erskine.
4. Dr Gregory and Terence Gavaghan who were both told the story by Grogan.
5. *East Africa (British) Its History, People, Commerce, Industries & Resources*, 1908-1909.
6. From C. W. Hobley's *From Chartered Company to Crown Colony*, Christopher Grogan, Sir Charles Markham, Elspeth Huxley's *White Man's Country* and Edward Rodwell.
7. F.O. Correspondence 2/911.
8. *Sixty Years in East and Central Africa* by E. S. Grogan.
9. Correspondence relating to Sir Charles Eliot's resignation F.O. 2099.
10. Mervyn Hill's *The Permanent Way* and Heini Lustman who was told the story by Grogan.
11. Jane Elliot.

Chapter 13: pages 106-114

1. The rupee was 1s 4d.
2. C.O. 533/1 Stewart to Lansdowne 16 March 1905.
3. Speech by E. S. Grogan at the Command Theatre, Nairobi, 4.7.1951.
4. Letters to *The Times* of Jan. 1905, 14 April 1905 and 25 April 1905.
5. 28.4.1905—5.5.1905—16.5.1905.
6. *The Nile As I Saw It* from the Library of the Royal Commonwealth Society.

7. Eldoret was known as '64' until 1912 because when Mr Gosling, the Post Master General, went to establish a post office in the area in 1907 he chose Farm 64 as the most central place.
8. Mrs Ullman.
9. Karai = round metal container.
10. Baden-Powell visited Kenya many times and in his old age it became a home to him. When he died he was buried in a simple grave with the 'Gone Home' Scouts' sign in a small cemetery at Nyeri.
11. Alan Hunter.
12. *Sixty Years in East and Central Africa* by E. S. Grogan.
13. *East African Standard*, February 1906.
14. C.O.5193 'Report on Emigration from India to Crown Colonies'.
15. Since the Colonial Office had taken over the Administration of the Protectorate the title of Commissioner was changed to Governor.
16. Land Department Ref. LR.206/136.
17. Dr Gregory and Dr Anderson.

Chapter 14: pages 115-127

1. Syce = Indian word for groom.
2. Dorothy Slater.
3. Dr Gregory.
4. All information in this chapter is from the newspapers' reports on the trial and the transcript of the trial.
5. All the official correspondence regarding the Defence Committee and the flogging was issued as a Command Paper with the title: 'Correspondence relating to the flogging of the natives by certain Europeans in Nairobi'. CO.533/28 & Cd. 3562 (1907).
6. Document in the possession of Dorothy Slater.
7. The letter appeared on 10 May 1907.
8. Appeal documents kindly supplied by M. Aronson.
9. Command Papers 4117, Sadler to Elgin 16 July 1907.
10. C.O. 533/54.

Chapter 15: pages 128-133

1. Material from *The Times, The Daily Mail, The Evening Standard* and the *East African Standard.*
2. Debate in Kenya's Legislative Council of April 1908.
3. Author's italics.
4. Dorothy Slater, Cynthia Crawford and Jane Elliot (daughters).
5. On 8 March 1956 in Legislative Council.
6. Dorothy Slater.

7. Dorothy Slater.

Chapter 16: pages 134-139

1. C.O. 5183 (1910).
2. Letter from Harold Grogan, 28 January 1979.
3. Muthaiga Club history with kind permission of L. O. Oates.
4. Dr Gerald Anderson.

Chapter 17: pages 140-147

1. Dorothy Slater.
2. From *The Story of the East African Mounted Rifles* by C. J. Wilson, *The Permanent Way* by M. Hill, *Army Diary* by R. Meinertzhagen and Meinertzhagen's unpublished diaries, *The King's African Rifles* by H. Moyse-Bartlett and *Marching on Tanga* by F. Brett-Young.
3. Eddie Ruben.
4. L. O. Oates.
5. All Grogan's Intelligence reports from the Intelligence Files of the Records' Office in London.
6. *Sixty Years in East and Central Africa* by E. S. Grogan.
7. Grogan was right. Many areas were reclaimed and developed as sugar plantations.

Chapter 18: pages 148-156

1. All Meinertzhagen quotes are from his unpublished diaries held at Rhodes House, Oxford and quoted with Mrs Searight's permission.
2. The original is with Meinertzhagen's papers at Rhodes House.
3. From Meinertzhagen's *Army Diary.*
4. Dr Gregory.
5. *Sixty Years in East and Central Africa* by E. S. Grogan.
6. Their Depot in Nairobi is still known as Karioko.
7. *London Gazette*, 7 October 1918.
8. *London Gazette,* 1 January 1918.
9. *London Gazette*, 28 November 1918.
10. *East African Standard.*
11. Published by the *Leader* 29 December 1917.
12. *East African Standard.*

Chapter 19: pages 157-164

1. *Sixty Years in East and Central Africa* by E. S. Grogan.
2. *Profit and Sport in British East Africa* by Lord Cranworth.
3. *Kenya from Within* by MacGregor Ross.
4. Hansard Ser. 41, 142.
5. Kenya National Archives.

6. House of Lords' Debate 14 July 1920, Col. 161.
7. L. O. Oates.
8. Peter Colmore.
9. *East Africa Standard*, 26 February 1920.
10. In fact he was 46 having been born 12 December 1874.

Chapter 20: pages 165-171

1. *Kenya Chronicles* by Lord Cranworth.
2. *Kenya from Within* by MacGregor Ross.
3. Official Gazette, 26 April 1922, p 290.

Chapter 21: 172-177

1. 'The Fairyland of Africa' in Vol I of *The Story of the Cape to Cairo Railway and River Routes*, Pioneer Publishing Co Ltd, 1923.
2. *The Times*, June 1923 and 16 November 1923.
3. *The Times*, 4 December 1923.
4. Correspondence between Grogan and Coryndon in Coryndon files MSS.AFRS.633 at Rhodes House, Oxford.
5. Commons Debate of 2 August 1922, CO. 1451.
6. Michael Grogan.
7. *Kenya's Opportunity* by Lord Altrincham, 1955.
8. Letter to *The Times*, 22 March 1925.
9. *East African Standard*, 4 August 1926 and *The Times*, 7 August 1926.

Chapter 22: pages 178-185

1. Happy Valley material from Bumpus, Lord Delamere, Marchesa di Bugnano and Peter Colmore.
2. Dorothy Slater and Lilly Torr.
3. Titus Oates.
4. Kilindini Harbour, Wharfs & Estate Co Ltd; Equator Saw Mills; Laikipia; Kenya Creosoting Co Ltd; Torr's Hotel; Kingatori Ltd; Warazi Estate Ltd; E. A. Society for the Protection of Trade; B.H.T. Syndicate; Scottish Insurance Co; Edzawa Ridge Mining Co Ltd; Pakanesni Prospecting Co Ltd; E.A. Rice Mills Ltd.; Ziwani Sisan Estate; Girigan; Sainte Irrigation Ltd.

   E. S. Grogan held 5,000 Founder Member shares, Gertrude 1,000 ordinary shares, Mr Tannahill and Mr Tidy 10 shares each at £1 each with a registered capital of £100,000 increased to £200,000 in April 1953.
5. 'East Africa & Rhodesia' (Directory) 1930.
6. Heini Lustman.
7. 'Mugs' Muggeridge.

8. Micki Migdoll who came to Torr's as a 16-year-old drummer in the band in 1932 and by 1947 was leader of the band.
9. Peter Colmore.
10. Lilly Torr died in August 1979 at the age of 95.
11. Micki Migdoll.
12. Speech in Legislative Council on 10 June 1944.
13. W. E. Croskill.
14. 'The Fairyland of Africa' in Vol I of *The Story of the Cape to Cairo Railway & River Routes*, 1923.
15. Command Papers Correspondence on Game 1906.10.11 through Tom Ofcansky.

Chapter 23: pages 186-191

1. Dr Gregory.
2. *The Times*, 8 September 1931 and 21 December 1931.
3. *The Times* 8 January 1932.
4. Mugs Muggeridge.
5. In her book *The Land of Illusion.*
6. *The Times*, 10 January 1933.
7. *The Times*, 13 December 1934.
8. Jane Elliot.
9. Lord Delamere.
10. *The Round Table* Vol XXVI 1935-36 pp 82-97.

Chapter 24: pages 192-198

1. Eddie Ruben who was at the meeting.
2. Mrs A. M. Lewis.
3. Christopher Grogan—nephew—who worked for E. S. Grogan at Taveta.
4. Speech by E. S. Grogan at Command Theatre on 4 July 1951.
5. Record Office, Kew (London).
6. Sir Charles Markham.

Chapter 25: pages 199-206

1. Titus Oates.
2. Heini Lustman.
3. Michael Grogan.
4. Ministry of Defence.
5. Marian Szlapack (granddaughter).
6. Descriptions of house from Heini Lustman.
7. Daughters and David Slater (grandson).
8. Taj Ahmed who was told the story by his father Mohamed Ahmed.
9. Marian Szlapack.
10. Karai = container, Jembe = hoe, Panga = machete.

Chapter 26: pages 207-215

1. Sir Charles Markham.
2. Sir Humphrey Slade.
3. Sir Ernest Vasey, Sir Wilfred Havelock, Sir Humphrey Slade and Sir Charles Markham.
4. Cattle disease carried by tsetse fly and sleeping sickness in man.
5. Dr Gregory.
6. The claim by another writer that Girigan means a pride of lions in Masai cannot be confirmed as 'Girigan' or 'Grigan' is not a Masai word for a pride of lions. On the other hand the Taveta people claim that Girigan is their pronunciation for Grogan.
7. Terence Gavaghan.
8. According to Terence Gavaghan it was an Israeli visitor who said: 'Colonel Grogan you seem to be some kind of God Almighty around here.' And Michael Grogan whispered: 'Bloody dry, isn't it.' But according to Michael Grogan it was his uncle who said: 'I'm God Almighty around here,' and Camilla Towers who answered: 'It hasn't rained for a long time, has it.'
9. Mrs Camilla Towers through Michael Grogan.
10. Mr Michael Wood, Dr Gregory, Sir Malin Sorsbie and Sir Humphrey Slade. Heini Lustman remembers it as a small guest house with a living room full of books and very little furniture, a small bedroom and a bathroom.
11. J. L. Sim.
12. Letter from Michael Grogan, 21 December 1979.

Chapter 27: pages 216-226

1. Sir Charles Markham.
2. Hansard Vol XLIX—1st Session—7-11 July 1952.
3. *East African Standard*, 1 May 1953.
4. *East African Standard*, 24 July 1952.
5. Hansard Vol LII—Session 28 October-5 December 1952.
6. *East African Standard*, 1 May 1953.
7. Sir Charles Markham's unpublished manuscript.
8. Michael Grogan (letter of 1 September 1953), and others confirm the story.

Chapter 28: pages 227-232

1. Peter Colmore.
2. From Sir Charles Markham unpublished manuscript.
3. Hansard Vol LXIII 4th Session 12 October-21 December 1954.

4. Sir Michael Blundell.
5. *East African Standard* 7 April, 1955.
6. *East African Standard* 27 April 1956.
7. Peter Colmore.
8. Terence Gavaghan.
9. *Sixty Years in East and Central Africa* by E. S. Grogan, 1957.

Chapter 29: pages 233-239

1. Lord Delamere who agreed that his father never looked like the statue in the middle of Delamere Avenue now Kenyatta Avenue.
2. His grandson, David Slater who was a director of Torr's Hotel. Humphrey Slade and Dunstan Adams were also directors. November 1957.
3. *East African Standard* 6 April 1960.
4. Dr Gregory.
5. *East African Standard, The Star, The Rand Daily Mail* and *The Times.*
6. *The Star,* 12 December 1962.

BIBLIOGRAPHY

Ainsworth, John, *Diaries 1895-1945*, Rhodes House, Unpublished MSS. A.F. 277

Altrincham, Lord, *Kenya's Opportunity*, 1955

Archer, Jules, *African Firebrand—Kenyatta of Kenya*, 1969

Bennett, G., *Kenya: A Political History*, 1963

Blundell, Sir Michael, *So Rough a Wind*, 1964

Bolton, Kenneth, *A Guide to Kenya*, 1970

Boyes, John, *King of the Wakikuyu*, 1911

Broadhurst Hill, Mrs E., *So This Is Kenya*, 1936

Buchanan, Sir G., *Water—A Policy*, 1920

Buxton, Mrs A., *Kenya Days*, 1927

Cagnolo, Father C., *The Akikuyu*, 1933

Carnegie, V. M., *A Kenyan Farm Diary*, 1930

Churchill, Winston, *My African Journey*, 1908

Cobbold, Lady E., *Kenya Land of Illusion*, 1935

Cole, Lady Eleonor, *Random Recollections of a Pioneer Kenya Settler*

Colonial Office, Documents from CO.533-101 (1912) to CO.533-200 (1918) and CO.533-28.

Cook, Sir Albert R., *Uganda Memories*, 1945

Coryndon, Sir Robert Thorne, Unpublished Correspondence, Rhodes House, MSS.AF.633

Cranworth Lord, *Profit and Sport in British East Africa*, 1919

Cranworth, Lord, *Kenya Chronicles*, 1939

Covell, Sir Gordon, *Reminiscences of Military Campaign E.A. 1914-17*, Rhodes House MSS.AFR.S. 385-387

Davis and Robertson, *Chronicles of Kenya*, 1928

Delf, George, *Jomo Kenyatta*, 1961
Diamond, Stanley and Burke, Fred G., *The Transformation of East Africa*, 1966
East Africa (British) 1908-9, Directory, McMillan Editor
East Africa and Rhodesia 1930—Directory
The East Africa Red Book 1919
The East Africa Red Book 1930-31
East African Standard 1904-1967
Evans, Peter, *Law & Disorder*, 1956
Eliot, Sir Charles, *The East Africa Protectorate*, 1905
Farson, Negley, *Behind God's Back*, 1951
Farrant, Leda, *Tippu Tip and the East African Slave Trade*, 1975
Foran, Robert, *A Cuckoo in Kenya*, 1936
Foran, Robert, *Kill or be Killed*, 1933
Frontera, Ann F., *Persistence and Change—A History of Taveta*, Thesis
Frost, Richard, *Race Against Time*, 1978
Gregory, J. W., *The Great Rift Valley*, 1896
Grogan, E. S. and Sharp, A. H., *From the Cape to Cairo*, 1900
Grogan, E. S., *The Economic Calculus*, 1909
Grogan, E. S., *The Workers' Charter*, 1910
Also a great number of articles, pamphlets, lectures and letters in a variety of publications too numerous to list here
Hake, Andrew, *African Metropolis*
Hemingway, John, *The Imminent Rains*
History of East Africa, Oxford University Press, 1965
History of East Africa, Clarendon Press, 1976
Hobley, C. W., *Kenya from Chartered Company to Crown Colony*, 1929
Hunter and Mannix, *African Bush Adventures*, 1954
Huxley, Elspeth, *White Man's Country*, 1935
Huxley, Elspeth, *The Sorcerer's Apprentice*, 1948
Huxley, Elspeth, *Red Strangers*, 1955
Huxley, Elspeth, *The Flame Trees of Thika*, 1959
Huxley, Elspeth, *The Mottled Lizard*, 1962
Huxley, Elspeth and Perham, Margery, *Race and Politics In Kenya*, 1944
Jack, Major R. E., *On the Congo Frontier*, 1914
Jackson, F., *Early Days in East Africa*, 1969
Joelson, F. S., *East Africa and Rhodesia*
Joelson, F. S., *Eastern Africa Today and Tomorrow*, 1934
Joelson, F. S., *Rhodesia and East Africa*, 1957
Joelson, F. S., *East Africa and Rhodesia*, 1958
Kenya Hansard, Official Reports of Debates in Legislative Council from 1911 to 1956.

Kenya Maps and Surveys from Survey and Map Office, Nairobi
Kenya Weekly News
Land Office, Documents from 1904.
Leys, Dr Norman, *Kenya, Colour Bar in East Africa*, 1924
Leader, The (daily and weekly) 1908-1922
Lord, John, *Duty, Honour, Empire: The Life and Times of Colonel Richard Meinertzhagen*, 1971
Lugard, Sir Frederick, *The Dual Mandate in British Tropical Africa*, 1922
Lugard, Sir Frederick, *The Rise of our East African Empire*, 1893
Mangat, J. S., *History of the Asians in East Africa*, 1969
Maxon, R. M., *John Ainsworth and the Making of Kenya*. Unpublished.
Meinertzhagen, Richard, *Diaries and Papers from Rhodes House*, Unpublished. M.17
Meinertzhagen, Richard, *Kenya Diary*, 1957
Meinertzhagen, Richard, *Army Diary*, 1960
Miller, Charles, *Battle for the Bundu*, 1974
Mungeam, G., *British Rule in Kenya*, 1966
MacGregor Ross, W., *Kenya from Within*, 1927
Murray-Brown, Jeremy, *Kenyatta*, 1972
Nairobi Municipal and City Council Minutes 1939-1956
O'Shea, T. J., *Farming and Planting in British East Africa*, 1917
Paice, Arnold, Unpublished Letters 1910-1937.
Perham, Margery, *East African Journey*, 1976
Redley, Dr M. G., *The White Community in Kenya*, Thesis 1976
Riddell, Florence, *Kenya Mist*, 1924
Riddell, Florence, *Kismet in Kenya*, 1931
Round Table, The, Review of Politics of the British Commonwealth Vol XXVI, 1935-1936
Reveille, 1917-1919
Sorrenson, M. P. D., *Origins of European Settlement in Kenya*, 1968
Stapleton, James W., *The Gate Hangs Well*, 1956
Sunday Post
Williams, Howard, *Paradise Precarious*
Wilson, C. J., *The Story of the East African Mounted Rifles*, 1938
Wolf, Richard, *Britain and Kenya 1870-1930*
Wymer, Norman, *The Man from the Cape*, 1959
Younghusband, Ethel, *Glimpses of East Africa and Zanzibar*, 1908

INDEX